Postwar Germany and the Holocaust

PERSPECTIVES ON THE HOLOCAUST

A series of books designed to help students further their understanding of key topics within the field of Holocaust studies.

PUBLISHED:

Holocaust Representations in History, Daniel H. Magilow and Lisa Silverman
Postwar Germany and the Holocaust, Caroline Sharples

FORTHCOMING:

Sites of Holocaust Memory, Janet Ward
Anti-Semitism and the Holocaust, Beth A. Griech-Polelle
The Holocaust in Eastern Europe, Waitman W. Beorn

Postwar Germany and the Holocaust

Caroline Sharples

Bloomsbury Academic
An imprint of Bloomsbury Publishing Plc

BLOOMSBURY
LONDON • OXFORD • NEW YORK • NEW DELHI • SYDNEY

Bloomsbury Academic
An imprint of Bloomsbury Publishing Plc

50 Bedford Square
London
WC1B 3DP
UK

1385 Broadway
New York
NY 10018
USA

www.bloomsbury.com

BLOOMSBURY and the Diana logo are trademarks of Bloomsbury Publishing Plc

First published 2016

British Library Cataloguing-in-Publication Data
A catalogue record for this book is available from the British Library.

ISBN: HB: 978-1-4725-1374-8
PB: 978-1-4725-0581-1
ePDF: 978-1-4725-1274-1
ePub: 978-1-4725-1053-2

Library of Congress Cataloging-in-Publication Data
Sharples, Caroline, 1979- author.
Postwar Germany and the Holocaust / Caroline Sharples.
pages cm
Includes bibliographical references and index.
1. Holocaust, Jewish (1939-1945–Influence. 2. Holocaust, Jewish (1939-1945)–Moral and ethicals aspects. 3. Memory–Social aspects–Germany. 4. Holocaust memorials–Social aspects–Germany. 5. Holocaust, Jewish (1939-1945), in motion pictures. I. Title.
D804.3.S536 2015
940.53'18–dc23
2015012096

Series: Perspectives on the Holocaust

Typeset by Integra Software Services Pvt. Ltd.
Printed and bound in India

CONTENTS

LIST OF ILLUSTRATIONS

ACKNOWLEDGEMENTS

First and foremost, I wish to thank Rhodri Mogford for the original invitation to contribute to this book series, and for all his amazing support – and patience – during the production of this volume. Likewise, I would like to thank Emma Goode and everyone else at Bloomsbury for helping turn this project into a reality. Special mention must be made of Paul Moore for kindly taking on the task of reading and commenting upon drafts of some of this work. Similarly, I would also like to thank the anonymous reviewers for their constructive feedback along the way. Finally, I am most grateful to the Bildagentur für Kunst, Kultur und Geschichte, Berlin, for granting the license to reproduce the Simplissimus cartoon in this volume.

LIST OF ABBREVIATIONS

CDU Christian Democratic Union (German Film Corporation)

DEFA Deutsche Film-Aktiengesellschaft

DPs Displaced Persons

EKD German Evangelical Church

FRG Federal Republic of Germany (West Germany)

GDR German Democratic Republic (East Germany)

HIAG Mutual Help Association of Former Waffen-SS Members (veterans' organization).

IfD Institut für Demoskopie (Institute for Public Opinion Research)

IHRA International Holocaust Remembrance Alliance

IMT International Military Tribunal

KMK Kultusministerkonferenz zu Toleranz und Solidarität (Standing Conference of the Ministers of Education and Cultural Affairs of the Länder)

KPD German Communist Party

KZ *Konzentrationslager* (Concentration Camp)

NSDAP National Socialist German Workers' Party (Nazi Party)

NWRV Nord- und Westdeustche Rundfunk (North and West German Broadcasting)

OMGUS Office of the Military Government United States

POWs Prisoners of War

RSHA Reichssicherheitshauptamt (Reich Security Main Office)

SA Sturmabteilung (Storm Detachment)

SD Sicherheitsdienst (Security Service)

SED Socialist Unity Party

SPD	Social Democratic Party
SS	Schutzstaffel ('Protection Squad', an elite Nazi paramilitary organization)
TNA	The National Archives, London
USHMM	United States Memorial Museum
VVN	Vereinigung der Verfolgten des Naziregimes (Association of Persecutees of the Nazi Regime)
WDR	Westdeutsche Rundfunk (West German Broadcasting)
ZDF	Zweites Deutsches Fernsehen (Second German Television)

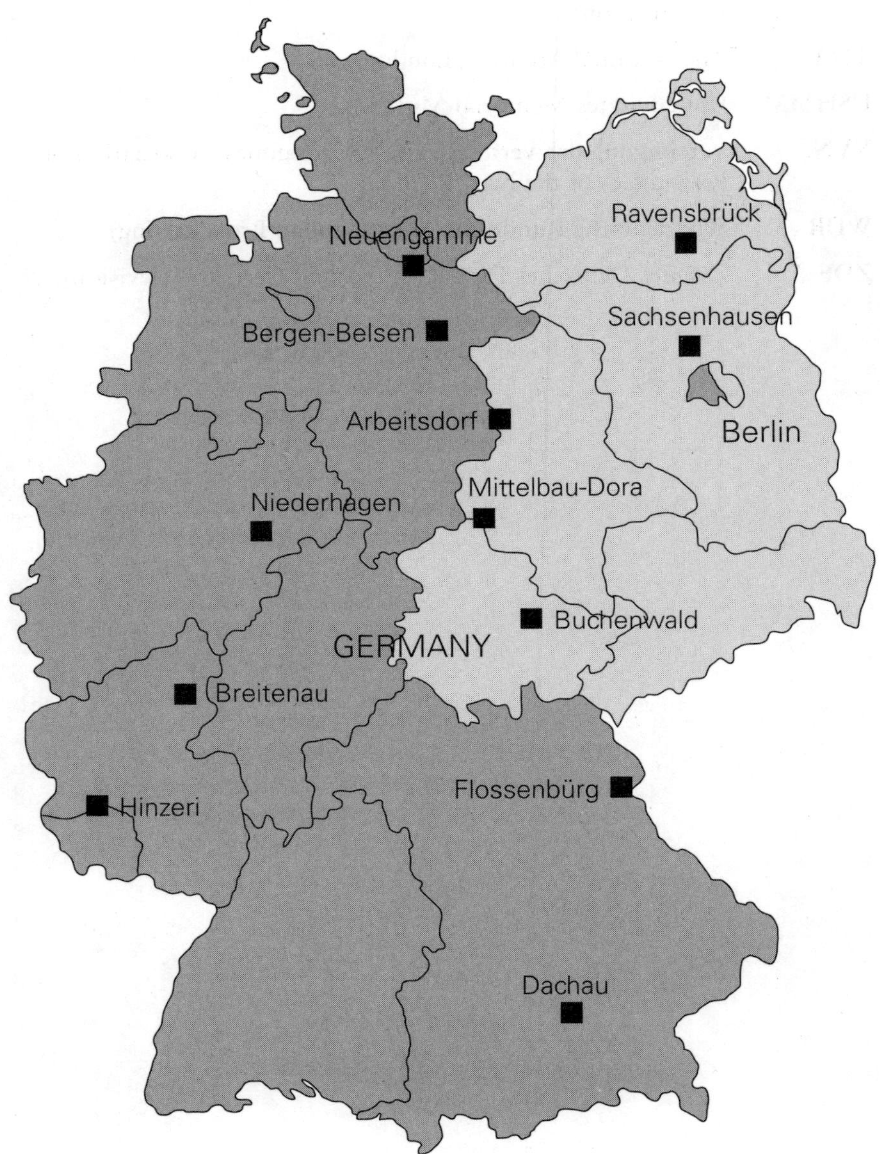

FIGURE I.1 *Map showing the division of Germany and Berlin, 1949–90.*

Introduction: Germany and the Holocaust

The beginning of the twenty-first century has witnessed a rapid growth in Holocaust consciousness. In 2000, forty-six countries from around the globe signed the Stockholm Declaration, pledging their commitment to promoting Holocaust education, remembrance and research, and emphasizing the continued, universal relevance of the Nazi genocide.[1] In the wake of this event, many nations – including the United Kingdom – began to hold an annual Memorial Day for victims of the Holocaust and, in 2005, the United Nations adopted 27 January, the anniversary of the liberation of Auschwitz, as International Holocaust Remembrance Day.[2] There are now numerous museum exhibits, memorials, films and educational initiatives, all exploring the legacy of the Third Reich.

Germany has played a leading role in this process, being specifically invited, along with Israel, to form part of the International Holocaust Remembrance Alliance in 1998 as a result of its existing educational programmes in this area. Its own annual memorial day for the victims of National Socialism (*Tag des Gedenkens an die Opfer des Nationalsozialismus*) has been observed since 1996 with a special remembrance ceremony in the Bundestag and various lectures, film screenings, theatre productions and concerts taking place throughout the country. The nation's landscape contains some 2,000 memorial sites to the Holocaust, ranging from the conservation of former concentration camps and Jewish cemeteries, to acts of memorialization at the points of deportation. An average of 450,000 people have visited the Information Centre for Berlin's imposing, nineteen square metre Memorial to the Murdered Jews of Europe each year since its inauguration in May 2005.[3] In 2008, a memorial to homosexuals persecuted during the Nazi regime was added in the nearby Tiergarten and, in October 2012, Chancellor Angela Merkel unveiled a further memorial to Sinti and Roma murdered during the Holocaust. Elsewhere, the 'Topography of Terror' exhibition on the site of the former SS and Gestapo headquarters in Berlin has proven one of the most popular historic sites, attracting over one million visitors each year.[4]

All of this points to the Holocaust occupying a prominent place within German memorial culture and a nation that has successfully confronted its past. It is a record that has frequently been contrasted to that of Japan, whose alleged failure to atone fully for atrocities committed during the Second World War has been seized upon by Chinese propagandists, not least during President Xi Jinping's visit to Berlin in spring 2014.[5] However, the process of Germany's *Vergangenheitsbewältigung* (coming to terms with the past) has been protracted, painful and highly politicized. It did not happen overnight, nor is it a linear narrative of ever-greater engagement with the crimes of the Third Reich. Instead, it is a fascinating story of silences, mythologies, generational conflict and competing memories exacerbated by forty years of division and the subsequent challenges of reunification. Focusing on this complex process, this volume explores East, West and reunified German representations of Nazism and the various ways in which the Holocaust has found political, cultural and social expression since 1945.

Divided memories

The postwar division of Germany and Berlin into four occupation zones had been agreed in principle between the Allies at the Yalta Conference of February 1945, and confirmed in the Potsdam Agreement in August that same year. Four further 'Ds' – demilitarization, decartelization, denazification and democratization – characterized Allied policy at this time and reflected their belief that Germany, now responsible for two devastating global conflicts, needed to be contained and re-educated so that it would never again threaten world peace. The division of Germany quickly came to symbolize the emerging Cold War tensions. In 1947, the British and American zones merged to form Bizonia (France would later follow suit to form Trizonia), and in 1948 a currency reform was announced for the western sectors, linked to the United States' Marshall Aid programme. In response, the Soviets instigated an eleven-month blockade of Berlin from June 1948, compelling the British and Americans to organize the Berlin air lift to keep the city in supplies. Division was formalized in 1949 with the promulgation of the Federal Republic of Germany (FRG) from the western occupation zones on 23 May and the establishment of the German Democratic Republic (GDR) from the Soviet zone of occupation on 7 October. Despite its name, the latter was governed by the Socialist Unity Party (SED) and tied to the USSR. Both fledgling German states were quickly subsumed into their respective sphere of the Cold War alliances so that by 1955, the FRG had joined NATO and the GDR had become part of the Warsaw Pact between the USSR and its satellite states. The construction of the Berlin Wall in August 1961 – an attempt to stop the 'brain drain' of East German professionals fleeing into the western sector of the city – literally cemented the division between the two states and became an iconic image of the Cold War until its fall on 9 November 1989.[6]

Both German states faced similar challenges during the immediate aftermath of the war. Much of the country lay in ruins following the devastating air war and final phase of the fighting. There was a lack of infrastructure and communications, coupled with severe food, fuel and housing shortages and a massive influx of refugees from the former occupied territories. Both sides would have to deal with former Nazi perpetrators, and make decisions over what to do with sites associated with Nazism and the Holocaust. The FRG, for instance, would have to contend with the former concentration camps of Bergen-Belsen, Dachau, Flossenbürg and Neuengamme; the GDR faced the same problems with Buchenwald, Sachsenhausen and Ravensbrück.

In addition to the physical reconstruction that would be required over the next few years, the formal establishment of two German states in 1949 meant there was also a need to construct new national identities. Each side drew upon elements of the past that would best legitimize the new socio-political order and incorporated these into powerful foundation myths. Both states were characterized by a looking back at older periods of German history with the rediscovery and adoption of heroes and traditions distinct from National Socialism. In the West, the concept of *Heimat* (translated roughly as a sense of homeland) and an emphasis on folk culture enabled people to focus on 'healthier' periods of German history, aspects in which they could still take some pride. This stress on local customs also enabled Nazism to be depicted as an external force, coming from 'elsewhere'.[7] In the East, official culture celebrated a history of class struggle, highlighting, for instance, the workers' revolts of 1848 and rejecting the Prussian militarism that was seen as leading directly to Hitler's authoritarianism.[8]

Such deliberate pointing to the continuities in German history undermines any notion of 1945 constituting a *Stunde Null* or Zero Hour for Germany, as does the number of former German politicians who returned to office after the war.[9] Arguably, though, the concept of a fresh start carried more weight in the GDR, where a complete rejection of capitalism (blamed, as it was, for the rise of fascism) enabled the state to present itself as the antithesis of National Socialism. The GDR renounced any claim to be the successor state to the Third Reich; that role was left to the FRG. Instead, with an emphasis on Communist resistance, the GDR portrayed itself as survivor, a state populated by people who had suffered and endured Nazism before being liberated by the Soviets. The USSR's victory in the Second World War was thus taken as a celebratory foundation for the whole state.

Memorial culture in both German states was generated through literature, film, television and radio broadcasts, museum exhibitions and the construction of various monuments to war and fascism. Key anniversaries such as the end of the war on 8 May 1945, or the liberation of particular concentration camps, were commemorated with the ritualized laying of wreathes and public speeches by leading politicians. However, just who was being remembered – and how – was very much affected by Cold War ideologies. While the GDR spoke of 'victims of fascism', a label that was used primarily to refer to Soviet suffering and the plight of the Communist resistance against Hitler; the FRG frequently adopted the universalism demonstrated by the Western Allies. The liberation of the camps was depicted as humankind's liberation from the yoke of Nazism; there was an emphasis on collective German suffering during – and after – the war. Soviet reprisals, including the mass rape of German women, were frequently highlighted here. Neither approach was conducive to recognizing the particular fate of the Jews during the Holocaust. Moreover, while the FRG began cultivating relations with Israel from the 1950s, signing a reparations agreement in 1952, the GDR adopted an anti-Zionist stance, allied itself with Arab states and arrested any citizens who were suspected of being in thrall to 'cosmopolitan' (i.e. American and Jewish) influences. Anti-semitic stereotypes re-emerged and those members of East German society who had been campaigning for greater recognition of Jewish wartime suffering were effectively silenced.[10]

With each German state recalling the past in different ways, reunification in 1990 was always going to pose some tricky questions. As Bill Niven notes, 'unification brought to an end both the post-Hitler period and a certain way of looking at the Third Reich … Responsibility for the National Socialist period had to be centred within one nation'.[11] A common version of the past needed to be found. During this period, narratives of German victimhood again rose to the fore, accompanied by a need to memorialize the victims of the GDR, as well as those of the Third Reich. Yet it was also a period in which the legacy of the Third Reich arguably entered public discussion more fully than ever before. Daniel Goldhagen's controversial 1996 book, *Hitler's Willing Executioners*, generated greater awareness of the role of 'ordinary people' in the Holocaust while the travelling exhibition on the Crimes of the Wehrmacht, opened in Hamburg in 1995, challenged the hitherto sanitized version of the German army's wartime behaviour.[12]

Considering memories of the Holocaust

The last twenty-five years or so have witnessed a surge of scholarly interest in the ways in which different nations have recalled the Holocaust. In part, such developments have to be seen within the wider context of a boom in memory studies, with academics exploring the relationship between history and memory, debating the merits of the term 'collective memory' and making greater use of oral testimony. At the same time, changing international circumstances, such as the end of the Cold War and the move towards greater European integration, have inspired greater reflection on experiences of totalitarianism – and helped to make new source material available to historians. Significant dates such as the fiftieth, sixtieth and seventieth anniversaries of the end of the Second World War have offered a useful framework for discussing and memorializing the past while continued examples of ethnic cleansing and mass atrocities in countries such as Rwanda, Sierra Leone, the former Yugoslavia and Sudan have also raised important questions about the extent to which we have learned the lessons of the Holocaust.[13]

As a result, we now have, for instance, a number of studies on what might be called the 'bystander' nations, countries such as Britain and the United States that were geographically distant from the Holocaust but received reports of Nazi atrocities during the war. Tony Kushner and Andy Pearce, for example, have written at length on Britain's belated engagement with the Holocaust, highlighting the initial tendency to focus postwar representations around Bergen-Belsen, a camp Britain had liberated, rather than the purpose-built extermination camps in Poland.[14] There has, necessarily, also been great interest in the postwar interpretations produced in the former fascist states. Literature on Austria, for example, has focussed on the country's reluctance to consider itself anything other than the 'first victim' of Nazi foreign policy.[15] Works on Italy have explored the remembrance of fascism, antifascism and the fate of the nation's own Jewish population during the Second World War.[16] More recently, historians have focussed on the remembrance and representation of the Holocaust in other Axis or Nazi-occupied nations, including the Netherlands, Scandinavia and the Baltic States.[17] In some cases, such as that of Hungary and Croatia, remembrance of the Holocaust has been analysed against the backdrop of contemporary efforts for these countries to join the EU.[18]

As this canon of literature demonstrates, coming to terms with a Nazi past is far from being a uniquely 'German problem' yet the majority of scholarly interest has, quite legitimately, rested with the nation where Hitler came to power in the first place. Historians have explored Germany's Vergangenheitsbewältigung from a variety of angles, considering the impact of war crimes trials, representations of the Holocaust within popular culture and the preservation of specific historic sites.[19] The majority of this historiography, however, rests with either the FRG or the post-1990 reunified German nation; research on responses to the Holocaust in the GDR remains relatively scarce. Notable exceptions here include Thomas C. Fox whose 1999 work, *Stated Memory*, examines representations of the Nazi genocide within East German historiography, landscape, literature and film; and Jeffrey Herf whose *Divided Memory* offers a detailed account of the attitudes of the SED leadership, and the struggle by returning Communist exiles to highlight the particular fate of the Jews during the Third Reich.[20] Elsewhere, references to East German responses tend to come as something of an aside, little more than a point of contrast to events taking place in its western neighbour.

This disparity between scholarly treatment of the two Germanys owes much to the fact that it is only relatively recently, with the collapse of the Soviet Union, that archival material on the GDR has become more accessible. Similarly, it can be much harder to look beyond the official, state-sponsored narrative and trace 'alternative' versions of the past in the GDR than in the democratic FRG; historians of the latter can, for example, point quite easily to the diversity of political debate and the role of pressure groups in generating public discourse about the Nazi era. At the same time, though, the availability of such sources on the FRG – and perhaps even the sheer amount of time historians have had to ponder every nuance of West German memorial culture – arguably helped to cast the FRG in the role of the 'problem state' when it came to confronting the Nazi past. Official antifascist rhetoric in the GDR contrasted its own, thorough purging of fascist elements with the fact that many former Nazis had been able to retain high-profile public positions in the FRG. While much of this was a propaganda creation – and matters were nowhere near as clear-cut in either German state – it is evident that throughout the postwar era, West Germany demonstrated reticence and unease about the past, and told it in a highly selective manner.

Conventional historical narratives, typified by Wolfgang Benz and Ralph Giordano, depicted West Germany as passing through two distinct phases. The first, during the late 1940s and 1950s, was one of silence or even 'collective amnesia' about the Nazi past; no one wanted to talk about it. The second phase, associated with the 1960s, was one of sudden, critical engagement with the National Socialist legacy when people began to discuss the past openly and acknowledge the particular suffering of the Jews.[21] In recent years, however, this model has been challenged by numerous historians who have amply shown that both periods were actually far more complex. Robert Moeller, for example, points out that the immediate postwar era saw a lively discussion about the past, albeit one that focussed primarily on non-Jewish German suffering, while the 1960s, far from constituting an era of wholesale, critical engagement with Nazism, were likewise complicated by enduring victimhood mythologies.[22]

The identification of continuing silences, evasions and distortions has been facilitated by the fact that historians have increasingly tried to look beyond official public narratives, to consider the range of voices that were trying to make themselves heard in the postwar German states. The concept of a 'German response' to the Holocaust is, of course, far too simplistic. Responses did not merely vary on either side of the FRG–GDR border, between the political Left and political Right, or between Jews and non-Jews; such dichotomies fail to take into account the sheer diversity of experience during the Third Reich and the Second World War. As Neil Gregor argues, postwar society was 'bitterly divided, full of fissures and riven with conflict – between former Nazis and non-Nazis, between indigenous inhabitants and refugees, between those who had lost their homes to bombing and those who had not, between city-dwellers and rural population and so on'.[23] Each of these groups had their own preferred version of the past and, as such, there is a distinction to be made between public and private spheres of remembrance. A rise in local case studies of particular German towns and cities, typified that of Gregor on Nuremberg, Peter Reichel on Hamburg and Harold Marcuse on Dachau, has consequently enabled historians to probe responses in far greater depth.[24] As such, we have seen scholars exploring the impact of older, local political traditions and individual community cultures, gendered experiences of war and generational influences on the retelling of the past.[25]

Within all these accounts, scholars routinely highlight several key moments as constituting important turning points in (West) Germany's relationship with the Nazi past. To take them in chronological order, these include the publication of Anne Frank's diary in 1955, the 1961 war crimes trial of SS bureaucrat Adolf Eichmann in Jerusalem – an event that was televised globally and made extensive use of emotive, survivor testimony; the 1963–5 trial of twenty-two former Auschwitz personnel in Frankfurt; the student protest movement of 1968, and the shift towards a more liberal political culture in West Germany with the election of the SPD, former resistance fighter Willy Brandt as Chancellor in 1969.[26] Brandt was the first West German leader to make an official visit to Poland and his kneeling before the memorial to the victims of the Warsaw Ghetto in 1970 has become symbolic of the nation's confrontation with, and atonement for, the Holocaust. Another crucial episode includes the popular impact of the television series *Holocaust*, screened in the FRG in 1979.[27] During the mid-1980s, however, West Germany saw two events that threatened to undermine some of the previous progress: President Reagan's controversial visit to Bitburg in 1985 (a cemetery that not only held the remains for fallen German soldiers but also members of the Waffen-SS); and the *Historikerstreit* (Historians' Quarrel) in 1985–6 in which academics publicly debated the merits of continuing to talk about the crimes of the Third Reich.[28] Indeed, it is largely in the wake of the latter two episodes that historical interest in the FRG's handling of the Holocaust truly began to emerge, exemplified by the publication of Charles Maier's *The Unmasterable Past* in 1988.[29]

These events did not occur in a vacuum, and the GDR necessarily engaged with them too, if only to enjoy a bit of point-scoring against the FRG. There were a number of high-profile political debates throughout the postwar era that kept the Nazi past alive in both states. Proposals for a general amnesty of war criminals during the 1950s were accompanied by arguments about restitution payments for victims of Nazism, pensions for former SS personnel and, in 1955, the wisdom of German rearmament. In the FRG, the 1960s and 1970s were characterized by a series of parliamentary discussions over the statute of limitations for war crimes and whether prosecutions of former Nazi personnel needed to be continued. There were also a host of political scandals as various individuals, including Cabinet members Hans Globke and Theodor Oberlander, were revealed to have been active Nazis.[30] International events also fed into this public discourse. US bombing raids during the Korean War of 1950–3 sparked comparisons in East Germany with the destruction of Dresden by 'Western imperialists' in February 1945, while West German protests against the Vietnam War during the late 1960s frequently utilized images and phrases associated with the Holocaust to reference the killing of Vietnamese civilians.[31]

Since 1990, historians such as Bill Niven, Siobhan Kattago and Klaus Neumann have necessarily turned their attention to the effects of reunification upon popular German memories of the Holocaust.[32] With the fall of the Berlin Wall representing the end of the postwar era once and for all, some scholars have spoken of a past now 'mastered'.[33] But is there truly an end point to Vergangenheitsbewältigung? Can we ever be 'done' with the past? This book explores these themes, highlighting the achievements that have been made since 1945, as well as remaining areas of contention.

Outline

The opening chapter sets out initial responses to the Holocaust in the wake of the Allied liberation of the camps and the total collapse of the Third Reich in 1945. It highlights the ways in which the Allies tried to expose Germans to the reality of the Nazi regime, with forced tours of concentration camps, the dissemination of shocking photographs of Holocaust victims and emotive newsreel footage. Particular attention is paid to German responses to Allied denazification and re-education initiatives and the resonance of the International Military Tribunal at Nuremberg, which prosecuted some of the biggest names of the Third Reich for conspiracy, crimes against peace, war crimes and crimes against humanity. In addition, this chapter addresses wider questions about German knowledge of Nazi atrocities, the scale of consensus behind the Third Reich – and the impact that the Holocaust had on Allied thinking about the 'German character' at the end of the war. The very 'Germanness' of the Holocaust can be broached here.

Chapter 2 proceeds to dissect one of the earliest and most enduring mythologies of the postwar era: that 'ordinary Germans' had also been the victims of the Nazi regime. This concept gained particular credence in the eastern zone of Germany, given the Soviet emphasis on Communist suffering during the Second World War, yet West Germany would also see a popular emphasis on misleading propaganda, the Nazi use of terror and the hardships endured amid Allied air raids. This chapter highlights the work of the Association of Victims of the Nazi Regime (VVN) and early commemorations of German suffering including the demonstrations that took place in Berlin's Lustgarten in September 1948. While many Germans undoubtedly experienced genuine war losses, this chapter underscores how a language of universal victimhood negated serious contemplation of the particular suffering of the Jews and other minorities under National Socialism.

These themes are explored further in Chapter 3, 'Acknowledging Suffering', which turns its attention directly to the treatment of the different victim groups and their campaigns for both recognition and financial compensation. The struggle to recognize the plight of Sinti and Roma is explored here, as are responses to homosexual victims of the Third Reich. Taken as a whole, this chapter underscores the multiple voices that were trying to make themselves heard in the postwar Germanys.

The issue of postwar justice is an integral theme to this volume and, with Chapter 1 having already examined the resonance of the Nuremberg trials; Chapter 4 analyses attitudes and policies towards war criminals in the separate German states after 1949. The Federal Republic was quick to discuss the possibility of a general amnesty for war criminals at the start of the 1950s, and the number of war crimes investigations being undertaken dropped sharply until the 1958 Ulm Einsatzkommando trial. Even amid a new flurry of war crimes trials in the 1960s, there continued to be a popular desire to draw a final line under the whole Nazi era and put an end to such hearings. The GDR, meanwhile, kept up the pressure on West Germany with the publication of the *Brown Book* listing the number of war criminals who now held prominent public positions in the Federal Republic. This chapter explores why the issue of war crimes trials was so controversial and the extent to which the German population engaged with notions of collective guilt and responsibility. It explores the ways in which former perpetrators could evade justice, and points to a number of high-profile political scandals that emerged as a result.

Chapter 5 focuses on the response of another particular interest group: that of the German churches. Their failure to react, as institutions, to Nazi racial policy during the Third Reich has long been the subject of controversy; this chapter explores how the churches sought to overcome this legacy after 1945. Attention is paid to the prominent role of several key individuals such as Hans Stempel and Martin Niemöller in either attacking the legitimacy of the postwar trial programme, or advocating a more critical public reflection on Nazi atrocities.

Subsequent sections of this book then proceed to explore how the Holocaust has manifested in both popular culture and the memorial landscape. Chapter 6 focuses on efforts to commemorate Holocaust victims in East and West Germany through the construction of memorials and the preservation of sensitive sites such as the former concentration camps. As well as considering how and when Holocaust memorials began to emerge in Germany, this chapter questions just who was being recalled through these designs and what this suggests about German understandings of the Holocaust since 1945. The chapter also examines the effects of reunification on the memorialization process, with particular focus on the debates surrounding the Berlin Memorial to the Murdered Jews of Europe. In the process, the chapter questions the extent to which building such memorials marks the beginning or the end of the remembrance process.

Chapter 7 looks at representations of the Holocaust in German films and television programmes. It considers how much media attention the Holocaust has received over the years, the extent to which ideological differences affected East and Western retellings of this period of history, and the impact such productions have had on audiences. More recent events, such as the use of a German-speaking actor to play Hitler in the 2004 film, *Downfall*, are also analysed.

The final section of this volume considers the development of Holocaust education in Germany. It examines the treatment of the Second World War and the Holocaust within school textbooks, and efforts to reconcile different versions of the nation's history since reunification in 1990. This chapter also considers the willingness of teachers (and parents) to discuss the past after 1945, the effects of the 1968 student movement, so often cited as a crucial turning point in the process of Vergangenheitsbewältigung, and the various scandals over youngsters' 'ignorance' of the Holocaust that have sparked calls for improved education over the years. This chapter thus enables the wider consideration of generational responses to the Holocaust, including Chancellor Helmut Kohl's famous assertion that he had the 'grace of a late birth'.

Finally, a note on the terminology. For the sake of continuity, the term 'Holocaust' is used repeatedly throughout this volume in reference to the mass murder of Jews and other minorities during the Second World War. However, it is important to keep in mind that the word itself did not gain currency until the 1960s. When using 'Holocaust' in reference to the early postwar period, then, this book is really looking at the ways in which people were talking about Nazi crimes against humanity and the extent to which there was a public understanding of the deportations, ghettoization, mass shootings, slave labour, gassings and other atrocities that took place during the war.

1

Confronting the Holocaust, 1945–9

The period of Allied occupation between 1945 and 1949 saw the German population working through their first – forced – confrontation with Nazi atrocities. Exposure to graphic images circulated by Allied photographers, together with newsreel footage from the liberated concentration camps, press reports on the subsequent war crimes trials and the first memoirs from Holocaust survivors ensured that the brutal consequences of National Socialism were becoming public knowledge. Just how closely people chose to engage with these crimes, though, varied enormously, particularly given that they were already having to contend with the realities of total defeat in the Second World War and the struggle for day-to-day survival in its aftermath. Traditionally, historians have tended to dismiss this period as one of silence in western Germany, and one of rapid purges of former Nazi personnel in the Soviet-controlled eastern sector of the country. However, as this chapter illustrates, there were competing voices trying to make themselves heard during this period, and early German responses to both Nazism in general and the Holocaust in particular merit closer attention. Indeed, it is in these initial responses, evasions and misunderstandings that we can see the foundations for persistent postwar mythologies that would have an enduring impact on Germany's relationship with the recent past. At the same time, these early responses have to be seen within the context of foreign occupation and the Allies' own difficulties in interpreting the enormity of the Holocaust.

Throughout the spring of 1945, the world was shocked and appalled by the terrible sights that greeted Allied troops liberating the Nazi concentration camps. Questions were raised immediately by politicians, intellectuals and the media alike: how could these crimes have happened within a hitherto civilized and cultured nation? Was there something uniquely 'German' about these acts of barbarism? How could a recurrence of such atrocities be prevented in the future? The Allies spent the year debating these issues, with France and the Soviet Union, raw from the recent experiences of invasion, advocating for particularly strong measures to dismantle Germany's potential to unleash another devastating war on the continent. Questions about stripping the country of its industrial capacity were accompanied by a sense that physical reparations needed to be matched by the removal of all vestiges of National Socialism, Prussian militarism, authoritarianism and aggressive nationalism; re-education was considered essential for effecting Germany's rebirth.

To this end, the Allies adopted three key measures. First and foremost, a forced public confrontation with the consequences of Nazi racial policy would shock the Germans into realizing the criminal nature of the Hitler regime and, it was hoped, spark a sense of contrition. For the majority of people, this would take the form of compulsory exposure to newsreel reports but for those living near a former concentration camp, tours of the site were frequently ordered by outraged Allied soldiers. Second, war crimes trials of major offenders would not only deliver justice on individuals but also underscore the institutional criminality of the Third Reich. The complicity of the armed forces, heavy industry, judiciary and the medical profession would be highlighted, alongside that of Nazi organizations such as the Gestapo and SS. Finally, a thorough denazification of the wider population would remove the most guilty members of society from positions of power and influence and make them pay (quite literally, in some cases, with the imposition of fines) for their past behaviour. The scheme would also eradicate traces of Nazism from the physical landscape, cleaning public buildings of Nazi insignia and destroying potential pilgrimage sites for any remaining Nazi sympathizers.

The emphasis throughout was on the thorough documentation of Nazi crimes and the need to bear witness to what had happened. The Allies, as we will see, were attuned to the pedagogic potential of these measures not only for the immediate re-education of Germany, but to offer a warning for future generations as well. A number of military surveys were undertaken during this period, particularly in the US zone of occupation, to trace popular German attitudes to the occupation, material conditions and denazification measures. The Allies were keen to monitor any lingering militaristic or fascist sentiments and, as such, these reports constitute a useful historical source for examining early German responses to the Nazi legacy. The licensed press also explored some of these issues, with particular discussion around the controversial concept of collective guilt (*Schuldfrage*). For the most part, though, 'ordinary' Germans seemed to be more concerned with venting their dissatisfaction with the Allies than reflecting on the crimes perpetrated by the now-defunct Nazi regime.

Confronting the camps

The Allies had received reports of Nazi atrocities during the Second World War, including the Riegner Telegram of August 1942, which warned of plans to exterminate European Jewry, and the Vrba-Wetzler Report of 1944, a forty-page document detailing events in Auschwitz. Their first physical encounter with a camp, however, came on 23 July 1944 when Soviet forces liberated Majdanek. Although SS personnel, hurrying to flee the advancing Red Army, had sent prisoners on a death march and attempted to destroy the camp, the Russians were still able to piece together evidence of the extermination process. The Russian war correspondent, Roman Karmen, declared:

> I have never seen a more abominable sight than Maiden, near Lublin. Hitler's notorious Vernichtungslager [extermination camp] where more than half a million European men, women and children were massacred.... This was not a concentration camp; it was a gigantic murder plant.[1]

Throughout early 1945, other concentration camps were gradually liberated, with the Russians reaching Auschwitz on 27 January and the Americans liberating Buchenwald and Dachau on 11 and 29 April, respectively. The British, meanwhile, approached camps in the north-west of Germany including Bergen-Belsen on 15 April and Neuengamme on 4 May. The need to record what the troops were seeing manifested itself very quickly. General Eisenhower, having visited Ohrdruf, a subcamp of Buchenwald, urged politicians back in the United States to come and view the horrific scenes for themselves:

> We continue to uncover German concentration camps for political prisoners in which conditions of indescribable horror prevail. I have visited one of these myself and I assure you that whatever has been printed on them to date has been understatement. If you could see any advantage in asking about a dozen leaders of Congress and a dozen prominent editors to make a short visit to this theater ..., I will arrange to have them conducted to one of these places where the evidence of bestiality and cruelty is so overpowering as to leave no doubt in their minds about the normal practices of the Germans in these camps.[2]

Politicians, religious leaders and journalists, as well as additional divisions of Allied soldiers, did, indeed, come and visit these sites for themselves and it is these first reports and footage, stemming principally from Buchenwald and Bergen-Belsen that informed the first representations and understandings of the Holocaust in the Western world. Iconic images of piles of emaciated corpses being bulldozed into a mass grave have remained with us, as have the shots of skeletal survivors peering at the camera from behind barbed wire. It is no coincidence that both Britain and the United States sent their most respected journalists to cover the liberation: Richard Dimbleby and Ed Murrow conveyed not only the necessary gravitas, but also legitimacy; it would be harder to reject the footage as atrocity propaganda with the involvement of these media heavyweights.

From encouraging members of their own side to view the camps, it was but a short step to extending this to compulsory tours for the local German population. Obviously angered by what they had encountered, there was a sense among many Allied troops that the Germans should be made to acknowledge what 'they' had done or allowed to happen. Forcing civilians to look upon the piles of bodies and even help bury the dead was seen as a just punishment, although there were also genuine health concerns too, with bodies needing to be disposed of as quickly as possible to halt the spread of disease. Mayors from nearby towns were brought in to view the scenes at Bergen-Belsen and, on 16 April 1945, around 2,000 citizens of Weimar were escorted around the nearby Buchenwald concentration camp by American troops, viewing the crematoria and the scenes of human experimentation. Film footage of this event shows how the smiling faces of smartly dressed local residents soon gave way to visible distress once they entered the camp. Some women held handkerchiefs to their face, others moved as if to faint and had to be supported by their fellow Germans.[3] Harold Marcuse records similar behaviour at other concentration camps to the extent that the order 'Hands Down' became a common utterance as visitors instinctively shielded their eyes.[4] Silent shock, however, soon gave way to unanimous protests of ignorance about the true nature of the camp. The diary entry of Buchenwald survivor Imre Kertész summarized their reaction: 'they knew nothing. No one knew anything'.[5] Likewise, Marguerite Higgins, reporting for the *New York Herald Tribune*, concluded, 'as has been the case everywhere, the German spectators in the Buchenwald tour seemed sincerely horrified, yet maintained that they had been completely ignorant of events there, and thus were free of blame'.[6]

To ensure that details of Nazi atrocities reached a wider audience, the Psychological Warfare Branch (PWB) of the US army disseminated images and vivid descriptions via the licensed press, Radio Luxembourg, newsreels and special pamphlets and posters, the latter displayed on the streets and frequently emblazoned with the accusatory slogan 'Your Fault'. A special twenty-minute documentary, *Die Todesmühlen* (The Death Mills), was compiled from the footage of camps in both Eastern and Western Europe and screened in German cinemas in early 1946, while another film entitled *KZ* was shown to German prisoners of war. How to ensure that people actually saw these films (and respond appropriately), however, would prove tricky. Susan Carruthers describes how there were initial plans to make *Die Todesmühlen* compulsory viewing, with Germans having to present their ration card for stamping as proof of their attendance. Given that the public was already having to pay to enter the cinema, though, this idea was eventually dropped.[7] Instead, all the cinemas in the western zones were compelled to show the programme at the same time but even then, viewing figures proved disappointing from an Allied point of view. In the American sector of Berlin, for example,

Carruthers notes that only 16 per cent of adults saw *Die Todesmühlen*, compared to the usual cinema-going population of 26 per cent. The West Berlin publication *Das Tagesspeigel* attributed this low turnout to 'fear of the truth', although Donald Bloxham argues that general apathy was a more likely factor here.[8] Elsewhere, there were instances of German civilians being forcibly marched into cinemas to view newsreel reports on the concentration camps. Burgsteinfurt was nicknamed 'the village of hate' by British observers when two girls laughed at the film; they were forced to watch it a second time.[9]

During this period, the Allies monitored German public opinion in an effort to assess the effectiveness of these initiatives. A survey conducted by PWB member Morris Janowitz in June 1945 concluded that 'almost every German had had direct and repeated contact with our campaign to present the facts' and that most people accepted the authenticity of the images. 'Only an isolated few', he noted, 'displayed strong scepticism or outright disbelief'.[10] Here, there was a tendency to dismiss the scenes as Allied propaganda, while one rumour insisted that Buchenwald was merely a site for burying civilians killed during air raids – a legend that not only denied any notion of systematic abuse on the part of the Nazis, but also served to depict the Allies as the villains of the piece. When the subject of Nazi atrocities was broached with members of the German public, the most common response was usually, 'Davon haben wir schon viel gehört' ('We have already heard a lot about this').[11]

The Allies tended to work on the assumption that Germans, especially those living close to concentration camps, must have known what was happening. Recent histories on the early camps produced by Nikolaus Wachsmann, Jane Caplan, Christian Goeschel and Paul Moore certainly underscore the fact that sites such as Dachau, Buchenwald and Belsen had been opened in a blaze of publicity in the Nazi press, and Janowitz himself noted in 1945 that the German public was hard-pushed to deny the existence of places that had been celebrated in Nazi propaganda.[12] What did emerge amidst the first postwar responses was an insistence that people had not known of the conditions *within* these camps. One woman, for example, told Janowitz:

> Of course, there were little rumours about the camps, but no one believed them. We thought that the prisoners might be working hard, that they might not be getting plenty of good food, and we even imagined some beatings or making the prisoners shout in chorus 'Heil Hitler'.[13]

Any acts of brutality, however, were generally assumed to be isolated incidents, or the work of a few sadistic concentration camp guards, rather than standard practice. Likewise, when a few Germans admitted hearing rumours of systematic mass murder taking place in the East, they added that they had just thought this to be enemy propaganda.

At the same time, people argued that even if they had known about conditions within the camps, there was nothing they could have done to challenge Nazi policy. One person informed Janowitz:

> You Americans can hardly understand the conditions under which we were living. It was if all of Germany were a concentration camp and we were occupied by a foreign power. We were unable to do anything to oppose them. What could one person do against that powerful organisation?[14]

Such retorts could obviously enable Germans to present themselves as victims too, a people powerless under a totalitarian state. Historians such as Robert Gellately, however, have pointed to the level of consensus that lay beneath the Third Reich and demonstrated the vital role that the 'ordinary' population played in denouncing friends, neighbours and colleagues to the Gestapo.[15]

During these early discussions, few Germans were able to provide specific information on the number of camps, or the identity of the people abused and murdered within them. Janowitz noted that 'estimates as to the number killed were usually of some tens of thousands and only a few spoke of more than one hundred thousand. One or two Social Democrats were able to conjure up the phrase "millions".'[16] As such, the claim that people had 'heard a lot' about Nazi atrocities did not necessarily equate to a critical understanding of the recent past. Instead, this oft-provided comment seems to have been a means of shutting down any further conversation on this uncomfortable topic.

It is important to note that the Western emphasis on camps liberated by the British and the Americans ensured that, from the very start, the full extent of the Holocaust was obscured. Overcrowded and disease-ridden sites such as Belsen, Dachau and Buchenwald were taken as representing the very worst of Nazi excesses; the distinction between these camps and the purpose-built extermination centres in the East went unrecognized. Likewise, the identity of the victims was never made explicit. The West spoke in universal terms about crimes against humanity, refusing to accentuate the suffering of any one group over another. The Soviets, meanwhile, were talking about 'victims of fascism' and emphasizing Soviet suffering. In neither case was the particular fate of the Jews acknowledged. The very word 'Jew' was barely mentioned in the liberation documentaries; the Allies' own representation of Nazi atrocities, therefore, could hardly be said to inspire an in-depth understanding on the part of the watching German population.

War crimes trials

The Allies had already announced their intention to punish Nazi war criminals with the Declaration of 17 December 1942. As late as the summer of 1945, though, the exact form that punishment should take remained under discussion. It was not until the London Charter of 8 August 1945 that the establishment of an International Military Tribunal (IMT) was formally decided upon as the best means for achieving justice.[17]

Between 20 November 1945 and 1 October 1946, twenty-two leading names of the Third Reich were consequently tried at Nuremberg for conspiring in crimes against peace, planning and waging aggressive war, war crimes and crimes against humanity. The latter charge encompassed the 'murder, extermination, enslavement, deportation, and other inhumane acts committed against any civilian population, before or during the war, or persecutions on political, racial or religious grounds in execution of or in connection with any crime within the jurisdiction of the Tribunal, whether or not in violation of the domestic law of the country where perpetrated'; it was, in short, an effort to take account of the Holocaust.[18]

The location of these proceedings was highly symbolic with Nuremberg having been the scene for the National Socialist German Workers' Party (NSDAP) annual rallies, as well as lending its name to the race laws promulgated in 1935. Among the accused were Rudolf Hess, Hitler's former deputy, Albert Speer, the Minister for Armaments, and Hermann Göring, head of the German Luftwaffe. In addition to these high-ranking individuals, institutions such as the German government, the NSDAP, Sturmabteilung (SA), Schutzstaffel (SS), Sicherheitsdienst (SD), and the German armed forces were also indicted. At the end of the trial, eleven defendants were sentenced to death. Göring cheated the hangman by committing suicide in his prison cell, but the others were executed on 16 October 1946. Of the remaining defendants, three men were acquitted of all charges and the rest were given lengthy prison sentences.

The IMT has dominated literature on Nazi war crimes trials, with much emphasis on the precedent it set for international law and the concept of crimes against humanity. Likewise, literature on the twelve 'subsequent Nuremberg proceedings', conducted solely before an American military tribunal between 1946 and 1949, focuses predominantly on the medical trial against Karl Brandt et al. (December 1945–August 1947) – a case that prompted the Nuremberg Code of research ethics concerning human experimentation.[19]

More recently, though, historians have begun to look beyond the high-profile Nuremberg trials to consider other war crimes proceedings that were taking place during the occupation period. Each of the Allies conducted further hearings within their respective zone of occupation and these cases necessarily fed into early conceptions of the Holocaust. John Cramer, for example, has produced an in-depth analysis of the Belsen trials conducted by the British in Lüneburg from September 1945. Indeed, it is worth remembering that the first Belsen Trial of forty-five former concentration camp personnel was actually completed before the IMT had barely begun.[20] Works by Tomaz Jardim, Joshua M. Greene and Fern Overbey Hilton, meanwhile, reflect a growing interest in the Dachau trials, a series of proceedings before US Military Tribunal that took place between November 1945 and August 1948 within that former concentration camp.[21] These hearings encompassed a range of atrocities perpetrated not only in Dachau, but also in Mauthausen, Buchenwald, Flossenbürg, Dora-Nordhausen and Mühldorf. Elsewhere, the French conducted a range of trials in Rastatt, including the prosecution of personnel from Natzweiler concentration camp, while the 1947 Sachsenhausen trial was one of the most high-profile cases to be heard before the Soviet Military Tribunal in East Berlin. Like the IMT, it included the screening of concentration camp footage as evidence for the prosecution. In total, the three Western Allies tried more than 5,000 Nazi war criminals during the occupation period, around 500 of whom were eventually executed. Unfortunately, reliable figures for the number of war crimes convictions in the Soviet zone are unavailable.[22]

In addition to trials before Allied military courts, Control Council Law No. 10, passed on 12 December 1945, also permitted reconstituted German courts to hear cases of crimes perpetrated by German nationals against their fellow citizens. This was the first time that the Germans could take responsibility for trying former Nazi personnel and, with proceedings consequently untainted by charges of 'victors' justice', these cases arguably had the potential for greater impact among the wider German population. Although war crimes and charges of aggressive war remained in the hands of the Allies, the German courts could try crimes against humanity insofar as the victims had been German or stateless individuals. As such, the courts were able to deal with political killings during the early years of the Third Reich, people who had denounced others to the Gestapo, men who had divorced their Jewish wives, facilitating their deportation to the East, *Kristallnacht* and the 'euthanasia' programme.[23]

Much of the historiography on Nazi war crimes trials has tended to focus on procedural issues and points of law, or on particular moments within a case, such as the screening of the film *Nazi Concentration Camps* during the IMT at Nuremberg.[24] More recently, though, there has been a growing canon of literature exploring the relationship between judicial process and the formation of collective memory, subjecting the popular impact of these proceedings to greater scholarly scrutiny. Donald Bloxham, for example, has challenged previous, celebratory depictions of the IMT. Whereas Michael Marrus claimed that the IMT 'presented the first comprehensive definition and documentation to a non-Jewish audience of the persecution and massacre of European Jewry during World War II', and Jürgen Wilke and Jeffrey Herf similarly praised the tribunal's (short-lived) effects on fostering public engagement with Nazi crimes; Bloxham points to significant deficiencies in the IMT's representation of the Holocaust.[25] In particular, the IMT can be criticized for depicting the Holocaust as just one in a series of Nazi transgressions, and for grouping all the various camps together in quite a simplistic manner. The Operation Reinhard camps of Belzec, Sobibor and Treblinka in the east were absent from the IMT narrative and the particular fate of the Jews remained unacknowledged. Such omissions give weight to Erich Haberer's conclusion that the IMT 'minimised the Holocaust, marginalised the victims and misrepresented the complexity of the continent-wide implementation of the Nazi genocidal policies'.[26]

Tony Kushner, meanwhile, argues that trial fatigue soon set in – and not just among the Germans: 'in Britain and the United States', he notes, 'there was relief when they finally finished nearly a year later'.[27] The sheer length of the IMT proceedings, together with the fact that it was based primarily upon the submission of official documents generated by the perpetrators themselves, created a rather sterile atmosphere. Such a format, together with frequent debates within the court over procedural matters or the accurate translation of a particular phrase, was hardly conducive to sustaining the interest of the lay public. Looking specifically at German responses to the trials, Christoph Burchard adds that the IMT engendered different reactions in the eastern and western sectors of the country, a factor shaped by the emerging Cold War tensions. He argues that while East Germans embraced the message to deal with Nazi perpetrators, their western counterparts remained suspicious and pessimistic about the precedent that had been set at Nuremberg; it was only with reunification in 1990, Burchard claims, that the legacy of the IMT was finally reappraised and Germany began to truly accept the concept of international law.[28]

Certainly, the Allies had envisaged war crimes trials as a crucial pedagogic tool. In his opening address at the IMT, Chief Prosecutor Robert Jackson stated clearly, 'the wrongs which we seek to condemn and punish have been so calculated, so malignant and so devastating that civilisation cannot tolerate their being ignored because it cannot survive their being repeated'.[29] Great care was taken to ensure that details of the trials were relayed to as wide an audience as possible, be it through the licensed press or weekly newsreel summaries. In the Soviet zone, public lectures were juxtaposed with the end of the IMT as well as the opening of the Sachsenhausen trial of 1947. Newspapers in each sector of occupied Germany also took care to report on the proceedings taking place in the other zones, thereby helping to create a fuller picture of the denazification programme. In December 1945, just one month into the IMT, the Chief of the US Information Control Division, Brigadier General Robert A. McClure, proclaimed that twelve million Germans living within the American occupation zone had access to trial information through the media.[30]

Coverage, though, was not always delivered in a measured manner. The opening of the Belsen trial in September 1945 set a precedent with sensationalist headlines and the frequent representation of the accused as demonic monsters. Chief defendant Josef Kramer, the former camp commandant, was swiftly nicknamed the 'Beast of Belsen' in the popular press. Ilse Koch, tried before the American military court at Dachau in

1947, was depicted in a similar vein as the 'Bitch of Buchenwald'.[31] Such trends enabled the defendants to be treated as oddities, a peculiar, sadistic few with little in common with the rest of the human population. This, in turn, could enable the German people to impose a comfortable sense of distance between themselves and the perpetrators of the Third Reich, reject accusations of collective guilt and evade any closer reflection on how such crimes had become possible.

However, even with the dramatic media coverage, popular German responses to war crimes trials often appeared muted. Reporting for the *New York Times*, Raymond Daniell argued that any reports on the IMT appearing within the licensed German press had been published for political reasons – the need to be seen as dealing with the past – rather than any genuine interest in the prosecution of former Nazis. Discussing the printing of the IMT indictment at the start of the proceedings, he commented, 'it is very noticeable that in restaurants newspaper readers fold their papers so that they can ignore the unpleasant reminders from Nuremberg. The trials are rarely discussed in conversation.'[32]

Just how far the 'ordinary' German people really engaged with these war crimes proceedings, then, remains questionable. Press reports from the time insist that the public galleries for the Belsen and Sachsenhausen trials were 'filled to the last space', suggesting that some were prepared to go out of their way and observe these trials firsthand.[33] Likewise, Office of the Military Government, United States (OMGUS) surveys produced over the course of the IMT concluded that public interest in the tribunal was 'very high'. Seventy-eight per cent of those questioned in the American zone in January 1946, for example, claimed to have been following the events closely in the press.[34] Reflecting at the end of the IMT, the American prosecutor, Robert M.W. Kempner, emphasized that the tribunal had received thousands of letters from members of the public across all four occupation zones expressing an opinion on the proceedings.[35] He also described how the effects of the IMT had been felt beyond the Nuremberg courtroom, with law professors at Heidelberg University using the case in their teaching, and discussion groups being set up between university and local *Gymnasium* students. Such behaviour would obviously challenge any notion of 'silence' as regards the Nazi past. A case study of popular responses to the IMT, though, illustrates the complexity of the situation and four distinct characteristics can be identified that would become typical of attitudes to war crimes trials throughout the postwar era.

In the first instance, there was an effort to put all the blame for recent events firmly on those operating at the highest levels of the Nazi state. A survey of forty towns and villages conducted in December 1945 by the US Control Division found that one-third of those questioned opposed the blanket indictment of organizations such as the SA 'for the obvious reason', the *New York Times* noted, 'that almost every family in Germany has relatives in them'. By contrast, Jackson's opening speech, in which he distinguished carefully between the Nazis and the wider population, was received favourably.[36] Second, criticisms of the Nazi leadership often focussed on the fact that they had lost the war, rather than the atrocities that had been perpetrated against the Jews and other minorities. The *Toronto Daily Star*, for example, relayed the results of an opinion poll that suggested that 'average Germans seemed interested in seeing Nazi leaders wiped out only because they blame them for their present misfortune . . . – not for moral reasons, but chiefly because they were on the losing side'.[37] Likewise, the *Milwaukee Journal* claimed that 'most Germans hope that the trial will "prove" that the regime misled the population and bear all the blame for recent events'.[38]

Third, there were also some claims of victors' justice – the notion that the trials and wider denazification process were unfair and hypocritical. The failure to have a German judge on the bench of the tribunal was criticized while the charge of *Tu quoque* (you, too) became a popular refrain, with people asking why Germans were being brought before courts while crimes committed by the Allies themselves during the war went unpunished. The bombing of Dresden, the reprisals enacted by the Red Army as they had advanced on Germany and the dropping of the atomic bombs over Japan were cited frequently in this regard.

Fourth, there was some concern over the inclusion of Wehrmacht personnel among the Nuremberg defendants. With long-standing notions of the honourable German soldier, it was felt that the blame for Nazi crimes really rested with the SS. An emphasis on doing one's duty and simply following orders – a theme echoed repeatedly by defence consul in numerous war crimes trials – saw people refusing to accept the possible complicity of the German army in war crimes and crimes against humanity.[39]

Such selective interest consequently facilitated a narrative of German suffering and a rejection of any sense of collective responsibility for the crime of the Third Reich. The amount of attention being paid to the IMT, however, waxed and waned over the course of the trial. The IMT was a long and complicated affair and, as it dragged on, *The Times* concluded that the population was becoming less concerned about their former leadership – and more embittered with the Allied occupation. Even OMGUS was forced to concede that the number of people admitting to regularly following the press coverage of the trial had fallen to 67 per cent by March 1946, and less than half of these had read the reports in their entirety.[40] Frustration at the protracted nature of the IMT was also evident as journalists took to the streets to gauge opinion. Typical comments they encountered included 'if you are going to kill them, why not kill them and have done with it' and 'I would have liked to see them all shot the minute they were captured but why take eighteen months over it?'[41]

For Kempner, there were several distinct phases in the population's attitude to the IMT. Initially, he noted, there was much interest amid the expectation of summary executions but this soon dissipated as the trial went on. In his mind, public interest only really revived when the defendants began to testify and when the proceedings began to discuss the criminality of various Nazi organizations. The number of letters being sent to the tribunal grew, 75 per cent of which praised the proceedings, offering 'messages of congratulations or ... proposals for further investigations against the defendants or against a witness who tried to cover up the activities of defendants'.[42] A minority sent unsigned messages, which drew upon Nazi rhetoric to denounce the whole affair.

Among the most striking moments of the IMT was the testimony of Hermann Göring whose stance in the witness box revived some public respect for the former First World War fighter ace.[43] Another was the announcement of the verdict in October 1946. Responses varied between the east and west occupation zones, and between different cities within those respective regions but, put very simply, the political Left attacked the resultant sentences as being too soft, while the remnants of the extreme Right, unsurprisingly, denounced the entire IMT process as being deeply flawed and unjust. In the Soviet zone, and particularly amid the heightened political atmosphere in East Berlin, the results of the IMT were greeted with public demonstrations organized by the Socialist Unity Party (SED). Particular public outcry was sparked by the fact that three of the defendants – former ambassador Franz von Papen, Hans Fritzsche, former head of the radio division in the propaganda ministry, and Hjalmar Schacht, former Minister of Economics – had been acquitted. Banners and placards were waved demanding the death sentence for all of the defendants and a ten-minute strike was held in response to the verdict. The *New York Times*, however, argued that the socialist protests were actually a relatively muted affair, attracting around 1,500 East Germans. 'Only a few people followed the poster bearers', the newspaper concluded.[44]

In the western zones, the *Tagesspiegel*, remarked how 'justified and logical the Soviet dissent against the three acquittals and the sparing of Hess's life' was, and the chief editor of a Hannover newspaper resigned his position as chair of a denazification panel upon learning of Fritzsche's acquittal.[45] There were calls for an immediate retrial, amid arguments that these men did, in fact, bear much guilt towards the German people. Here, there were references to the misleading nature of Nazi propaganda (Fritzsche) and the manner in which Hitler had been helped into power in the first place through conservative intrigue (von Papen). The latter argument accentuated the concept of National Socialism as having come from 'elsewhere' and, while the political machinations of the early 1930s cannot be denied, the emphasis on von Papen's guilt helped to downplay the level of popular consensus behind the Nazi regime and the electoral success that the NSDAP had enjoyed after September 1930. By contrast, the execution of Joachim von Ribbentrop was seen as thoroughly deserved on the grounds that he 'was a bad foreign minister', a sentiment that again suggested that the primary reason these men needed to be punished was for leading Germany into a disastrous war and consequently causing suffering to the German people.[46] Journalist Rebecca West likewise recorded an encounter with a local Nuremberg woman who was particularly eager to hear whether Sauckel had been sentenced yet: 'I shall not sleep happy till I have heard that that scoundrel pays for his crimes', the woman proclaimed, 'Never will we undo the harm he did by bringing these wretched foreign labourers into our Germany. I had a nice house, *a home*... and what did this Sauckel do but send two thousand foreign workers to the factories in the district, two thousand wretches, cannibals, scum of the earth Russians, Balks, Balts, Slavs – Slavs I tell you. What did they do when our armies were defeated but break loose? For three days they kept carnival, they looted and they ate and drank of our goods.'[47] The conditions that these forced workers had been kept in, however, went unacknowledged.

At the same time, though, the acquittal of Fritzsche, Schacht and von Papen was sufficient for some Germans to consider the IMT in a more positive light. *The Times* pointed out that 'some ... (whether they regret the acquittals or accept them) are prepared to see them as an indication that the tribunal was not after all, as most Germans thought, merely a façade for an act of vengeance and that an attempt was made to mete out justice and distinguish between degrees of guilt'.[48]

In the midst of all this, there also remained particular interest in the fate of Göring. A number of Germans took satisfaction from the fact that he had succeeded in thwarting the hangman. 'All other aspects of the trial and executions were completely overshadowed', proclaimed the *New York Times*, 'as thousands of Germans chuckled over the trick he had played on the occupying powers and once more thought of him as a hero. Göring's dramatic gesture in death appeared to have helped these Germans to forget his crimes, the millions of deaths in the concentration camps and in the war caused by the Nazi regime and the lessons of the ten month trial.'[49]

Finally, alternative versions of the past also continued to be expressed in some quarters. In November 1946, the *New York Times* noted the appearance of Nazi-style propaganda posters in Frankfurt am Main, which glorified the defendants and demanded the death sentence be administered to Jews and democrats instead.[50] Given that the Nuremberg executions had been carried out twenty-four days earlier, these reactionary protests held little more than a symbolic purpose and it is therefore interesting that they came on 9 November, a day of recurring significance in modern German history. It was on this date that the Weimar Republic was proclaimed in 1918; that Hitler made his effort to seize power with the Munich Putsch of 1923 and, of course, that the Nazis carried out the *Kristallnacht* pogrom against the Jews in 1938. Staging these protests on this particular day, then, provided an opportunity to recall some of the old ideology. The singling out of Jews and democrats for reprisals within these slogans also harked back to the legends of the November Criminals and the 'stab in the back' that had circulated at the end of the First World War. These were not isolated events. In Stuttgart too, posters appeared declaring 'Nuremberg: not justice but murder' and 'on October 16 1946 twelve Germans are being murdered by our enemies. Germans wake up' – the phrasing of the latter posters reminiscent of the 1920s Nazi election posters that had enjoined the country to arise from its slumber. A cemetery in Hersfeld saw a wreath adorned with swastikas and iron crosses promising to avenge the 'martyrs of Nuremberg', and in Angersbach a Nazi flag was found flying from a First World War memorial.[51]

Surveys conducted in the British zone by the Information Services Control Branch concluded that the population generally fell into one of two categories: those who rejected the entire tribunal as illegal and unjustified, and those who accepted the necessity of the IMT but disagreed with its results; 'hardly anyone seems to be wholly satisfied'.[52] A poll of 3,935 people in December 1946 as to whether they would like a summary of the IMT produced by a 'reliable' German source, resulted in 37.2 per cent saying they never wanted to hear another word about Nuremberg. British sources reflected that this statistic 'is not as high as might have been expected'.[53]

Denazification

While members of the Nazi hierarchy and captured concentration camp personnel stood trial for war crimes, the wider German population was subjected to the denazification process. The eradication of National Socialism had been a central feature of the postwar agreements signed at Potsdam and, in October 1946, Control Council Directive No. 38 set out the procedure by which all adult Germans would have to appear before a denazification panel and have their behaviour during the Third Reich examined. In this way, the Allies hoped to organize the population neatly into one of five categories: major offenders, offenders, lesser offenders, fellow travellers (followers) and exonerated persons. Major offenders would face trial – and potentially the death penalty; others could have their property confiscated, or face dismissal from their place of employment, pay cuts, travel restrictions or compulsory registration with the authorities. In practice, the denazification process varied between zones and over time, with the Western Allies torn between punishing or rehabilitating former Nazis; the latter notion eventually won out. As emphasized by Mary Fulbrook, 'in no zone did denazification present a simple, clear, consistent story'.[54]

Denazification, as Robert Knight points out, has rarely received a 'good press' among historians. Initial studies routinely depicted the programme as one doomed to failure, pointing to the Allies' ineptitude, as well as the questionable legality of such measures. During the 1960s and 1970s, a new wave of literature began to offer a softer perspective, emphasizing the need for the Allies to remain pragmatic. Left-liberal assessments during the

1970s and 1980s, however, attacked denazification as a lost opportunity; that much more could have been done to remove ex-Nazis and promote democracy among the German population.[55] Lutz Niethammer, who has produced one of the most detailed accounts of the scheme, claimed that denazification ultimately failed because the Allies did not cooperate with members of the German Left who were, themselves, seeking social change.[56] Early works on denazification produced by Wolfgang Friedmann, Michael Balfour and Constantine Fitzgibbon offered an overview of events in all four occupation zones, but much of the subsequent literature has been devoted to the American zone.[57] Notable exceptions here include Barbara Marshall and Ian Turner, who have offered accounts of denazification in the British zone, and, since the opening of the French archives in 1986, there has been a gradual rise in the number of studies on that particular sector of occupied Germany.[58] Likewise, the opening of the former Soviet and GDR archives since the 1990s has unleashed a wave of new studies on the eastern zone, with the effect that historians are now gaining a much more informed, overall picture of the denazification scheme. Perry Biddiscombe's 2007 monograph, *The Denazification of Germany*, offers a detailed account based on thorough archival research in all four former zones.[59] Nonetheless, the general image of denazification holds sway: it was an impractical, over-ambitious scheme that could never deliver as much as it promised. Some, such as Timothy Vogt, go so far as to describe it as a bureaucratic 'nightmare'.[60]

The Soviets are usually regarded as adopting a far more coherent – and effective – programme of denazification than the Western Allies. With Marxist theories attributing the rise of fascism to capitalism, the Soviet Military Administration (SMAD) introduced extensive land reforms that would abolish the traditional power of German landowning elites (the Junkers). There were also reforms of industry and finance and a purge of the political and administrative spheres. By 1948, an estimated 450,000 former Nazis had been ousted from public life, although policies varied between different regions of East Germany. In Thuringia, for example, there was a more measured response with 'nominal' Nazis allowed to remain in their posts if they subjected themselves to political 're-education'. Here, denazification focused primarily upon high-ranking individuals and the so-called 'old comrades' – people who had joined the NSDAP before Hitler's rise to power in 1933. In Mecklenberg–Western Pomerania, however, *all* former NSDAP members were targeted; Mike Dennis notes that by the end of 1946, between 306,000 and 390,000 people were believed to have been dismissed from their jobs in this region.[61]

Authorities in all four occupation zones, however, soon came to realize that the complete removal of former Nazis was unfeasible. Skilled and experienced individuals were required to aid the reconstruction process, so many professionals were allowed to remain in place. In the Soviet zone, around 46 per cent of doctors, dentists and chemists were former Nazis.[62]

Unsurprisingly, denazification has been routinely depicted as an unpopular process, although Barbara Marshall's analysis of the British zone suggests that there were people who critiqued the programme for not going far enough in its treatment of ex-Nazis.[63] In addition to staffing problems and a lack of resources, denazification was hampered by the fact that it appeared to be a very unfair and arbitrary process. As with the war crimes trials, it prompted accusations of victors' justice, and there was frustration at the pace of the proceedings, particularly when no account seemed to be taken of a person's 'good behaviour' in the months (and years) since the war's end. Similarly, the organization of the programme meant that people tended to be removed from their jobs, then investigated and either punished or exonerated. It was only after this process was complete that they would be allowed to return to work. This meant everyone was affected materially, regardless of their level of guilt or complicity with the Nazi regime.

Additionally, the denazification categories themselves were regarded as too rigid, failing to take sufficient account of the different levels of involvement with the regime, and the whole process was seen as favouring the 'bigger fish' at the expense of the ordinary individual. Some people sought to evade punishment by changing their names, a relatively easy means amidst the postwar chaos. Others, with good social connections, secured character references to depict them in a more favourable light; these soon became nicknamed *Persilscheine* after the famous brand of washing powder. This generated resentment among other sectors of German society, especially when known Nazis appeared to be faring so well in their postwar lives. One person in Hamburg complained to the British occupying authorities:

> We have a neighbour, an SS man, he works for the Tommy, extra food, extra rations... he has a bicycle to go to work on. An acquaintance of ours, having to go the same distance, with war wounds, heels frozen off – his bicycle was taken from him.... An SA man (since 1931!) in our street is building a house in the country. The church in Christian brotherliness, cares for these 'poor Nazis'.[64]

A man from Munich, meanwhile, having relayed in great detail the trouble he was having acquiring adequate clothing or even medical care on the basis of his previous membership to the NSDAP, criticized the fact that 'thousands of Polish Jews, who are coming into this country to idle about, promptly receive their clothing coupons'.[65] Such comments reveal lingering traces of anti-Semitism, as well as a failure to comprehend the suffering of those who had been racially persecuted by the Nazi regime. Drawing upon a sense of German victimhood, the same person added,

> It is quite right that those who have committed crimes and have made use of the Party should receive punishment but not the poor home-coming

> soldier, the idealists and ordinary citizens who have had to bear the brunt and have been exploited and duped right and left.[66]

Adding to the overall sense of unfairness was an awareness that denazification was being conducted differently in each occupation zone. The Americans, for instance, tended to be a lot harsher in their treatment of the Germans than the British. However, local politics could also create further variations *within* zones. A letter intercepted by the British in August 1946, for example, revealed an interesting discussion between two former NSDAP members:

> You in Schleswig-Holstein need not worry. The denazification there will not be carried out very thoroughly because the CDU [conservative political party] is in a leading position.... Here in Hamburg, it is more difficult because here we have a red [communist] majority. So all of us here are very anxious.[67]

Conclusion

During the immediate postwar period, there was a discussion of the past taking place across Germany. The public were exposed to graphic photographic evidence of Nazi atrocities, and the true nature of the concentration camps was being documented within the press, the newsreels and the courtrooms. These episodes had an impact at the time, producing expressions of shock and shame, but would also – as the next chapter will demonstrate – come to frame some of the narratives of *German* suffering over the next few years. Arguably, any gaps within people's understanding of the Holocaust at this point owed much to the way in which the Allies themselves were interpreting the past, focussing on the western concentration camps, rather than sites such as Auschwitz, and ignoring the particular suffering of the Jews. Emerging Cold War tensions also saw the concerns of the political present soon holding sway over any sustained interest in pursuing Nazi perpetrators. There was no second international military tribunal, and both zonal trials and the wider denazification programme were already beginning to be wound up by the end of the 1940s as the focus switched instead to fighting a new ideological enemy. This, in turn, facilitated the popular claim that the number of war criminals had always been relatively small and that all the guilt rested with the now dead, or imprisoned, Nazi leadership. Consequently, there seemed little need for the 'ordinary' population to reflect critically on their own behaviour during the Third Reich.

2

'Victims of Fascism': Narratives of German Suffering since 1945

As the previous chapter has illustrated, the public rhetoric of the immediate postwar period facilitated an emphasis on German suffering. Initial war crimes trials conducted by German courts were restricted to dealing with crimes perpetrated against German nationals, while the Western emphasis on camps such as Buchenwald, Belsen and Dachau – sites that had held substantial numbers of political prisoners – also helped to present the German people as the first victims of the Third Reich. Furthermore, denazification and the experiences of foreign occupation encouraged a sense of 'double victimhood', with the Germans suffering first at the hands of the Nazis and then at those of the Allies. Consequently, victimhood narratives became the principal means for discussing the recent past during the late 1940s and 1950s, expressed through political speeches, compensation arrangements, memorials and commemorative culture, literature and film.

While there was an element of mythmaking in all this, it is, however, important to note that the Germans had experienced genuine war losses. Around one million women were now war widows, an estimated 600,000 civilians had been killed in bombing raids, and up to 14 million people had been expelled from their homes in the East. Approximately 1.5 million German women had been raped by Red Army soldiers.[1] Clearly, the German people would have to mourn and come to terms with these losses, but this often came at the expense of any serious engagement with the fate of other victim groups. At the same time, the war had not affected the German population in equal measure. While millions were now homeless, there were others who had managed to emerge relatively unscathed. This, in turn, would ensure that the early postwar years would see Germans grumbling about other Germans, making accusations of unfair or preferential treatment. Furthermore, these narratives of German suffering would prove remarkably enduring, finding expression even into the twenty-first century. This chapter explores these themes, paying particular attention to the remembrance of the civilian air raid victims, German prisoners of war held in Soviet captivity, expellees and the 'martyrs' of the German resistance.

German victimhood in historiography

For many years, historians were reluctant to address the theme of German war losses, preferring, quite legitimately, to focus their efforts on the victims of Nazi persecution.[2] By the 1990s, though, the issue began to attract scholarly attention, with a flood of works examining the legacy of the air war and the forced migration of German civilians at the end of the conflict. This development was helped by reunification, which necessitated the reconciliation of two different postwar experiences, and encouraged new reflections on the impact of totalitarianism.[3] Several historians, including Hans-Ulrich Wehler, Eric Langenbacher and Hans Mommsen, suggested that this sudden burst of literature constituted the first, open acknowledgement of German victimhood, and claimed that the subject had been 'taboo' up until this point.[4]

Narratives of German victimhood were depicted as passing through three distinct phases that reflect wider social and political developments in both German states, as well as the impact of contemporary international conflicts. In the first phase, the immediate postwar era of the late 1940s and 1950s, an emphasis on German suffering became the principal means for discussing the recent past. In the Soviet-controlled zone and then the GDR, for example, the SED adopted the argument that the German people had been deceived and betrayed by the Nazis.[5] There was also, of course, an emphasis on the suffering of German Communists who had tried to resist National Socialism. In the West, too, there were frequent references to the Nazis' 'misleading' propaganda and the role of terror in enforcing the National Socialist state. Examples of German victimhood fed, in turn, into metaphors for the nation as a whole. Elizabeth Heineman has illustrated how the rape of German women during the final throes of the conflict became synonymous with Germany's post-1945 pillaging at the hands of the Allies.[6] Likewise, Moeller argues that the fate of the expellees became a symbol for those who had lost their homes in the bombing.[7]

The second phase, associated with the 1960s and 1970s, however, witnessed a shift from the concept of 'Germans as victims' to that of 'Germans as perpetrators'. Here, events such as the globally televised Adolf Eichmann trial in Israel in 1961, the 1963–5 Frankfurt Auschwitz trial, and the general coming-of-age of a younger, more critical generation have been routinely regarded as fostering a deeper engagement with the Nazi past. Rather than dwelling on their own losses, the Germans are seen as belatedly shifting their attention to the Holocaust. Such depictions of the process of

Vergangenheitsbewältigung are most commonly associated with the FRG, but there is evidence that in the GDR too, the 1960s saw revived public interest in the atrocities, even if it was only to critique West Germany's handling of the past.

Finally, the third phase, coming in the wake of German reunification in 1990, saw the re-emergence of the 'Germans as victims' discourse. In part, this was no doubt due to the difficulties involved in trying to carve out a new, unified national identity after forty years of division. Accounts of German suffering under the now defunct GDR created a continuous narrative of German victimhood at the hands of totalitarian regimes, and enabled a post–Cold War Western triumphalism. Other events during the 1990s, including the 'ethnic cleansing' within the former Yugoslavia, generated further reminders of the Second World War. The flight of refugees from Kosovo, for example, reignited interest in the fate of German expellees who had been forced to flee their homeland in 1945.

Broader cultural events have also encouraged the revival of German victimhood narratives. In 2001, a five-part television series, *Die grosse Flucht*, which documented the German expulsion from the East, attracted five million viewers.[8] The publication of Jörg Friedrich's controversial yet bestselling book *Der Brand* (The Fire) in 2002 also generated considerable popular interest in German victimhood. Friedrich's account of the bombing of Dresden – which was serialized in the popular tabloid *Bild*, used the language more usually associated with the Holocaust to describe the Allied air raids. Thus the war in the air became a *Vernichtungskrieg* (war of extermination) and the bombing of Dresden itself was referred to as 'barbaric' and a 'massacre'.[9] This, in turn, tapped neatly into prevailing public debates about the sending of German troops into the Iraq war, enabling critics of the invasion to compare current US behaviour with the bombing of German cities in the Second World War. Likewise, several scholars pinpoint the publication of Gunter Grass's novel, *Im Krebsgang* (Crabwalk) – also in 2002 – as further stimulating interest in German suffering; the tale is based around the torpedoing of the *Wilhelm Gustloff* in January 1945 while evacuating German civilians and military personnel from Poland.[10]

In short, Germany has been presented as going from a focus on its own suffering, to that of victims of Nazi persecution and back again. However, historians such as Robert Moeller, Bill Niven, Ruth Wittlinger and Stefan Berger argue that such interpretations are flawed. For them, victimhood was never a forbidden topic in Germany and did not simply disappear from public discussion in the 1960s. On the contrary, they see it as a remarkably enduring feature of popular responses to the Nazi past, with the fate of the expellees proving a particularly significant 'counter-discourse'.[11] The examples highlighted in this chapter would seem to confirm their findings.

Nor is it sufficient to present the German population as articulating either one view of the past or another. Hans Kundnani, for example, takes the example of the 1968ers – the generation that constituted the student protest movement at the end of the 1960s and is consequently associated with the shift towards a more critical engagement with the Nazi legacy. It was not simply a case of young, Left-wing students advocating the 'Germany as perpetrators' model versus the conservative establishment clinging to that of 'Germany as victims'. Kundnani points out that some of the key figures in the student movement, such as Rudi Dutschke, actually ignored the Nazi past and concentrated on the theme of 'Germany as victims'. Dutschke, he argues, having grown up in the GDR, had 'few of the hang-ups about the Nazi past that his Western comrades did'.[12] Similarly, Kundnani highlights the fact that Ulrike Meinhof spoke not only about German war crimes, but also about German suffering, including that at Dresden.[13] Furthermore, he notes that even when the 1968ers did talk about the struggle against fascism, there were tendencies to appropriate the Holocaust for present-day political purposes. Images and metaphors associated with Auschwitz, for instance, were invoked during the students' protests against the Vietnam War. Some youngsters even depicted themselves as 'the new Jews' in solidarity with other victims of persecution around the world.[14]

Much of the existing work on German responses to the Holocaust necessarily concentrates on public articulations of the past, examining official state-sanctioned commemorative ceremonies and civic debates over the construction of war and Holocaust memorials, or the public representation of the past through the mediums of film, museum space, literature and other forms of popular culture. However, recent attempts to break into the private sphere and explore the transmission of memories between generations have underscored the quiet persistence of alternative versions of the past. Wittlinger, for example, notes that a sense of German victimhood continued to 'outweigh' that of culpability within family memory.[15] A. Dirk Moses similarly recounts the 'considerable gap ... between the pieties of official statements and the intimate sphere of the family where stories of German suffering and survival endured a half century after the end of World War II'.[16]

A consideration of different generations' attitudes to the past also lies at the heart of Harold Marcuse's detailed exploration of the postwar history of Dachau. Focussing on the responses of those who came of age in 1933, 1943, 1948, 1968 and 1979 (in other words, people born before, during and after the Third Reich), he traces the development of three 'founding myths' of the FRG: that of German victimhood, ignorance of Nazi crimes and resistance against Nazism. Marcuse demonstrates that these myths very much intersected with one another and – most significantly – did not play out in any neat, chronological order. Instead, victimhood remained a constant theme, be it at the hands of the Nazis, the Allies or even Holocaust survivors who demanded compensation from Germany. Marcuse also notes that some people also felt victimized by anyone who dared to remind them of the Nazi past; in Dachau, for instance, there was some animosity towards tourists wishing to visit the former concentration camp, ensuring that the town's name would be indelibly associated with Nazi atrocities. Over time, criticism was increasingly directed at so-called 'professional masterers of the past' – people who assumed that all Germans, past and present, had a responsibility to atone for Nazi crimes. Such ideas were summed up in a speech by the CSU politician and Minister President of Bavaria Franz Josef Strauss who declared that the German population has 'a right not to want to hear any more about Auschwitz'.[17]

Concepts of German victimhood have thus remained a striking feature of public discourse since 1945. From the start, the development of such legends obscured the memory of the Holocaust and created, instead, a more convenient version of the recent past.[18] At the same time, though, they also held an important utilitarian value. As Hermann Lübbe argued in 1983, concentrating on German suffering eased the rehabilitation of former Nazis into public life and, by extension, the wider reconstruction process.[19]

As the German population contended with the realities of first division and then the establishment of two, separate German states from 1949, a shared concept of victimhood also helped to give people a sense of belonging. Niven sums up this sense of unification as 'all-victims-together' and Moeller likewise summarizes popular sentiments stating, 'all Germans were ultimately victims of a war that Hitler had started but everyone lost'.[20] Consequently, both the FRG and GDR presented themselves as survivors of the Nazi period and, from 1990, victimhood became the glue that would bind East and West Germans together again after reunification.[21]

War damages

After 1945, some 18 million Germans claimed to have been 'war damaged' in one form or other and there were various discussions during the late 1940s and early 1950s as to how best to compensate them for their losses.[22] Almost as soon as the war was over, numerous 'victims of fascism' committees (*Opfer des Faschismus* – OdFs) sprang up across Germany to provide urgent material aid including food, clothing and shelter for German refugees and the former political prisoners who had survived the concentration camps. These were the result of local initiatives but, by the summer of 1946, the relief effort began to become more coordinated. In July that year, regional representatives from each occupation zone gathered in Frankfurt and adopted the Charter for the Society of People Persecuted by the Nazi Regime and state organizations began to develop its wake. In February 1947, an umbrella organization, the *Vereinigung der Verfolgten des Naziregimes* (Association of Persecutees of the Nazi Regime – VVN), was established within the Soviet zone to oversee the activities of OdF committees, campaign for financial compensation for the victims and attempt to track down the perpetrators of the Third Reich to bring them to justice.[23] The VVN was also involved in organizing memorials for those who had died as a result of Nazi persecution. In March 1947, another inter-zonal conference was held in Frankfurt with the aim of establishing the VVN nationwide but by the start of the 1950s, the organization had become caught up in the political wrangling of the Cold War. In 1953, the VVN was dissolved in the GDR after accusations that its members were spying for the West. It was replaced by the *Komitee der antifaschistischen Widerstandskämpfer* (Committee of Antifascist Resistance Fighters). In the FRG, meanwhile, the VVN was seen as being dominated by Communist elements and viewed with increasing suspicion as a result; several attempts were made during the 1950s to ban it. A non-Communist version, the *Bund der Verfolgten des Naziregimes* (League of Nazi Persecuted, or BVN), was set up in 1950 and remains active to this day.[24]

While the population's need for practical assistance after the war cannot be denied, it is worth emphasizing the effects that all these efforts had upon public interpretations of the recent past. The German word used to refer to the injured party, *Opfer*, can mean both 'victim' and 'sacrifice'. The implications of this, as Alexandra Kaiser points out, is that there was consequently no distinction within public memorial discourse between someone who gave their life voluntarily (for example, a 'fallen' soldier who died fighting for his country), and someone who had endured involuntary suffering, such as a concentration camp prisoner.[25] Furthermore, the key figures behind the OdFs were the former political prisoners themselves and the red triangle, the symbol sewn onto their concentration camp uniforms to distinguish them from other prisoners, was soon adopted as the emblem of the VVN. The memory of other victim groups was thus effaced.

In December 1945, the Ministry of the Interior of Württemberg-Baden issued a decree on the assistance and 'special care' that victims of Nazism should receive. Under this law, those considered eligible for aid included

a) former concentration camp, prison, and jail inmates who were imprisoned for political, religious, or racial reasons;

b) emigrants who escaped the clutches of the Gestapo through flight and demonstrably continued their fight against the Nazi regime from abroad;

c) widows, children, and parents of those murdered and executed by Fascism on account of their struggle [against it], provided that they stood loyally by those who were murdered and executed and rejected Fascism for their part as well.[26]

The assistance in question would comprise of a cash payment, allowances for food, clothing, household goods, sickness payments and preferential allocation of housing. Yet despite the brief reference to racial persecution at the start of this document, there was no specific mention of Jews or Sinti and Roma. Instead, the aid programme was set up in such a way as to foster an image of active resistance against the Nazi regime.

In the Soviet zone (and later the GDR), reparation schemes to the 'victims of fascism' included honorary pensions, an earlier retirement age and priority access to housing and higher education. Here too, though, there was some discussion as to just who should qualify for this relief. Despite the inclusive connotations of the GDR's banner phrase 'victims of fascism', preferential treatment was given to those perceived as having fought actively against Nazism; Communists, in other words, were afforded greater status than supposedly 'passive' victims such as the Jews. This approach was evident in a July 1945 edition of the German Communist Party's (KPD) newspaper, *Deutsche Volkszeitung*, which stated,

> Millions of people are victims of fascism, including all those who have lost their homes, their apartments, their possessions. Victims of fascism are the men who had to become soldiers and were drafted into Hitler's battalions, and all those who had to give their lives for Hitler's criminal war. Victims of fascism are the Jews who were persecuted and murdered as victims of racial lunacy,...the Jehovah's Witnesses and the 'work-shy'. But we cannot interpret the term 'Victims of Fascism' so broadly. All of them persevered and suffered greatly, but they did not fight.[27]

Despite affirming publicly the need to remember all victim groups, the OdF introduced identity cards that recorded whether the holder had been a resistance fighter or not. Peter Monteath records that by May 1946, there were 15,536 active 'Fighters against Fascism' registered in East Berlin and the SBZ, compared with 42,287 'Victims of Fascism'.[28] This, he points out, was more than a matter of semantics: 'fighters of fascism' were able to claim higher levels of postwar support.

Among the non-persecuted members of the German population, meanwhile, there were further grumblings that former concentration camp prisoners were getting all the support. In February 1947, for example, the head of the Württemberg-Baden State Committee of Victims of Political Persecution by the Nazi Regime noted,

> In some ways, the officially ordered preferential treatment has proven disadvantageous to the victims of Nazi persecution themselves, since constant references to their preferential treatment have created the impression among the general population that persecutees are receiving the majority of the available goods and that not much is being left for the rest of the population. In order to cover up their own guilt, certain circles blamed the lack and shortage of goods, which was [actually] caused by the disastrous policies of the Third Reich, on the victims of political persecution.[29]

Narratives of German suffering were also embedded firmly within the foundations of the new West German state. In his first speech as Chancellor to the Bundestag in September 1949, Konrad Adenauer was, for the most part, looking firmly towards the future, setting out the new government's economic and political agenda. The past, however, was addressed in the sense that Adenauer drew attention to some of the most pressing challenges facing the FRG. Sensitive to the prevailing social distress, he spoke of the plight of the war widowed, disabled veterans, orphans and the youth whose education had been interrupted by the recent conflict – all of whom would require aid from the state. Touching upon a 'particularly serious and important topic', Adenauer also highlighted the continued absence of 'millions' of German prisoners of war who remained in Soviet captivity. Their 'fate', he argued, was 'so hard, and the grief of their dependents in Germany... so great, that all nations must help in returning these prisoners and forced labourers to their homes and their families'.[30] The Chancellor went on to praise the efforts of the Red Cross in supporting the POWS, as well as thanking the Pope for also speaking out on this issue. By invoking the Church in this manner, Adenauer suggested that this was a just cause, and that the former military personnel involved were entirely innocent figures. Finally, Adenauer also raised the issue of the ethnic Germans who had been expelled from their homes in Eastern Europe during the final phases of the war. Again, he presented himself as having right on his side, arguing that the expulsions contravened the terms of the 1945 Potsdam Treaty, and citing Winston Churchill's description of the matter as a 'tragedy'. Indeed, the case of the expellees constituted the most emotive element of Adenauer's speech, with the chancellor proclaiming, 'I find it difficult to speak with the necessary objective self-restraint when I think of the fate of the refugees who have perished by the millions'.[31]

Adenauer's speech thus placed the fate of German POWs and expellees high on the political agenda, paving the way for a series of campaigns and policy decisions to aid these groups over the next few years. The speech held an obvious appeal for the German electorate. There was no dwelling on Nazism itself, or any concept of collective responsibility. Jews were mentioned briefly insofar as Adenauer promised to eradicate anti-Semitism. The remainder of the speech, however, was focussed firmly on overcoming German war losses. In this way, the speech legitimized narratives of German victimhood and demands, among the war damaged, for recompense. As Moeller remarks, while the notion of paying reparations to Israel may have been controversial, there was no such ambivalence among West German politicians over the treatment of expellees and POWs.[32]

The sense of entitlement to some form of compensation among the 'war damaged' owed much to promises made by the Nazis themselves. In November 1940, a War Damages Decree had been issued in which the regime pledged that compensation would be extracted from the conquered territories after the war. With Germany's defeat, those affected by the conflict necessarily had to look elsewhere for restitution. Michael Hughes, however, notes that the language used to justify cases – frequently invoking notions of self-sacrifice – and the emphasis on everyone pulling together to help one another; was reminiscent of the rhetoric utilized by the Nazis when trying to establish their concept of a *Volksgemeinschaft* (People's Community).[33]

Those seeking compensation also had to prove that the damage they had suffered had not been of their own making. Some observers among the undamaged population argued that the war damaged had brought their problems on themselves because they had supported Nazism in the first place; the war damaged, however, endeavoured to play down any previous enthusiasm for the regime. Instead, as Hughes points out, 'the war damaged... passed silently over inconvenient facts and highlighted useful truths and half-truths, recasting their recent experiences as (relatively) innocent victimisation'.[34] In describing their damages, people tended to focus on their immediate cause, rather than any longer-term factors such as voting for Hitler in 1933. Similarly, there was much emphasis on war damages being wrought by 'fate', ill 'luck' or 'accident'. Within such narratives, the people themselves were rendered mere hostages of fortune, rather than actors in their own right.[35]

A recurring theme when analysing narratives of German victimhood is the appropriation of Holocaust vocabulary and imagery to depict non-Jewish suffering during and after the war. Hughes, for instance, cites a CDU politician who, while assessing the claims of the war damaged in 1948, stated, 'through their unsocial policies the Allies are driving needy Germans not into the gas chambers of the concentration camps but to the gas chamber, namely the gas tap, in their own houses'.[36] Such echoes support the notion that people were recalling the past in a very selective fashion; there was no widespread 'amnesia' or silence about the Third Reich. Hughes notes that such versions of the past worked because the rest of West German society were wary about challenging the narrative. He argues that the undamaged were no less culpable for the regime's crimes than the war damaged; 'if any of them were to initiate a widespread discussion of culpability, they would open their fellow sufferers and often themselves to attack'.[37]

Prisoners of war and the myth of the 'Clean Wehrmacht'

One aspect of the recent past that proved particularly difficult to comprehend throughout the postwar era was the role that Wehrmacht (army) personnel had played on the Eastern Front during the Second World War. Long celebrated concepts of the honourable German soldier continued to hold sway. The army, it was routinely insisted, had fought a conventional military conflict; it was Hitler's SS that had waged a war of racial extermination. These sentiments were particularly apparent during the early 1950s when West Germany saw a high-profile public campaign to try and secure the release of thousands of prisoners of war who remained in Soviet captivity. This was an extremely emotive issue for many people. In 1950, the League of Returning Veterans, POWs and Relatives of Those Missing in Action was established to coordinate the various interest groups. It attracted 160,000 members in its first year alone.[38] Various public campaigns were orchestrated to draw attention to their plight, with posters and special stamps being issued and candlelit vigils held. Some of the images used to these ends depicted skeletal figures in striped uniforms with shaved heads standing behind barbed wire – a factor that suggests that the concentration camp pictures, disseminated so widely by the Allies during 1945/6, had remained in the public consciousness. Throughout this period, there was also an emphasis on the inhumane conditions that the POWs were being subjected to by the Soviets; the SPD politician Carlo Schmid suggested that it was enough to warrant its own Nuremberg.[39] Once again, allusions to Nazi crimes against humanity were being utilized to illustrate non-Jewish German suffering.

In 1953, a travelling exhibition entitled 'We Admonish' presented the plight of the POWs to around 35 West German cities. That same year, the annual week of remembrance for the POWs included a torch relay across the FRG.[40] When Adenauer finally secured the release of the 'Ten Thousand' in 1955, it was commonly regarded as one of his finest achievements and received mass press attention. Their return was a symbolic end, at last, to the war and the POWs were portrayed as brave 'survivors of totalitarianism'. Some returned to their homes in what was now the GDR where their captivity was interpreted as having moulded them into reliable, socialist citizens. The majority, though, settled in West Germany where there was a popular refusal to regard any of these returnees as war criminals. Instead, the emphasis was on the 'ordinariness' of these soldiers, men who had simply been doing their duty.

The story of the POWs' return captured the public imagination, with numerous press reports and newsreel programmes. Writing in *Die Zeit*, Jan Molitor captured the emotional nature of the homecoming:

> On Sunday at noon, when thousands of people waiting at camp Friedland suddenly turned their eyes to the distant country road on the hillside, they saw seventeen heavy buses slowly approaching, followed by a long line of private cars. The bell began ringing in the camp. The waiting crowd did not move. Tears were rolling down some of the faces. One after another, the buses finally reached the 'welcome site' and circled around; now one could clearly see the passengers. They looked down out of the windows at us with serious expressions, young and old men, some had flowers in their hands; all waved with small, tight, helpless movements, held their lower arms stiffly and turned their hands at the wrist. One heard the scream of an old woman who recognized her son …[41]

Moeller, however, points out that not everyone in West Germany shared in the celebratory welcome being extended to these returning soldiers. Communists and members of the Jewish community 'contrasted the homecoming of the POWs with the West Germans' chilly reception of concentration camp survivors at the end of the war, the endless accounts of the suffering of the POWs with the general silence about the suffering of Jews under National Socialism, and the bounty bestowed on POWs by the West German state with the federal government's penurious response to other victims'.[42] However, these remained the voices of 'outsiders', and had little impact on the prevailing public narrative.

Victims of expulsion

Another key example of German victimhood held up after 1945 concerned the expellees. During the final phases of the war, millions of ethnic Germans who had been living in territories to the east of Germany and occupied by the Nazis, were expelled from their homes and compelled to head westwards. By 29 October 1946, there were some 9.5 million refugees and expellees living in the western occupation zones. This influx of people pushed the local authorities to their limits, struggling as they were already to cope with their own community's food and housing needs.

During the late 1940s, there was a current of opinion, particularly among members of the SPD, that expellees and refugees should be aided through the confiscation of goods from the better-off members of society. This was known as the Equalization of Burdens (Lastenausgleich) and became the subject of much heated discussion. The Berlin newspaper, *Tägliche Rundschau*, argued that such a scheme would be impractical, impossible to manage and even counterproductive as it would disrupt the repairing of both the economy and society. The newspaper pointed out that everyone in Europe was suffering, and warned that the proposal would only lead to denunciations, bribery and suspicion between members of the community. Comparing these measures with the ongoing denazification programme, the newspaper argued that 'to an impoverished grandmother, the cooking pot she hopes to get from such a law – or is afraid to lose – is much more important than the question of whether some company chief is to remain in complete or partial possession of his authority over parts of German industry.'[43] Another option under debate was to make payments to expellees based upon assessments of their future economic productivity. A critic of this model was published in *Der Leuchtturm*, with the magazine arguing that those who had caused the war should take responsibility, rather than burdening future generations with its consequences.[44]

An OMGUS poll of 1,500 people in the American zone, 250 people in West Berlin and 150 people from Bremen in November 1948 revealed that although people were wary about the means by which such a programme would be implemented, the majority approved of the basic concept of equalizing burdens. The issue of fairness arose frequently, with 50 per cent of respondents in Bremen arguing that it could not be carried out fairly. Refugees and bombed-out persons were most frequently mentioned as the ones who ought to benefit from the programme. Twenty-four per cent of the American zone respondents expected to benefit themselves. Among those who knew about the programme, 40 per cent wished that the Americans would carry it out as contrasted to only 26 per cent who wanted German authorities to implement the plan. Reasons given by the former group were almost without exception variants of the theme that the Military Government would be more just and more objective than German officials.[45] The Equalization of Burdens was eventually enacted by the Bundestag in 1952, the same year that West Germany would start paying reparations to Israel for the suffering of the Jews.

A sense of solidarity between expellees, meanwhile, was also developed through the formation of their own *Organisation der Heimatvertriebenen*. In May 1950, 60,000 expellees gathered in Hamburg and voiced their desire to return home. Journalist Marion Gräfin Dönhoff described the occasion for *Die Zeit*:

> Probably never before was the prayer…'Give us back our homeland' recited with more fervour, never before did the thoughts of so many homesick, uprooted people drift more longingly across the Iron Curtain than during these days, when so many memories were brought back to life.[46]

The Bund der Vertriebenen (Federation of Expellees, BdV) was founded in October 1957 and gained notoriety when it emerged that its first president, Hans Krüger, had himself been a former Nazi judge.

The term 'expellee' is a charged one. Not only does it serve to denote victimhood, it also suggests an experience distinct from that of 'ordinary' refugees. In other words, the history of the expellees could be depicted as more tragic and painful than that of those displaced by Nazi persecution. Some historians have suggested that the term 'forced migration' would be a better means of explaining the movement of these people, thereby placing them within the context of a much broader history of global migration.[47]

In 1993, Alfred-Maurice de Zayas published an account of the expellees, proclaiming that this English-language text would generate 'new respect for these forgotten victims', seeing their story as a means of redressing the Western world's fixation on Nazi criminality.[48] Like Friedrich's work on Dresden, de Zayas drew upon Holocaust vocabulary to describe the expellees' fate, referring to their forced flight from their ancestral homes as a 'genocide' and a crime against humanity. Indeed, this revisionist study went so far as to claim that the expellees had been worse off than Holocaust survivors because they did not receive the same levels of compassion and support after the Second World War. Brenda Melendy, meanwhile, emphasizes the way in which the expellees themselves deliberately used Holocaust metaphors during the late 1940s in an effort to strengthen their victim status.[49] There was, for instance, a widespread dread of being held under the Soviets in Moschendorf camp on the border between the American and Russian occupation zones. Descriptions of expellees being sent to this camp, notes Melendy, 'bore an unfortunate resemblance to reports of roundups of Jews in small towns in Eastern Europe by German personnel during World War II, complete with references to women and children huddling in unheated rooms, exposed to the elements, before being loaded onto trains for transport northeastward'.[50] Likewise, Daniel Levy and Natan Sznaider have highlighted how the plight of the expellees was frequently placed on a par with the victims of Nazi persecution within early postwar political discussions. In 1949, for example, one SPD politician critiqued the arrangements of the 1945 Potsdam Treaty that had redrawn European borders and prompted further mass migration, suggesting that the 'denazification of Germans' be accompanied by a 'depotsdamization of the victors'.[51] Two years later, a representative of the right-wing Party for Economic Reconstruction asked, 'were the victors obliged to match the crimes Hitler committed with new crimes?'[52]

One of the fundamental reasons behind these comparisons rests with the fact that incoming refugees were frequently held in overcrowded DP camps – some of which, like Dachau, had been former Nazi concentration camps. Consequently, it was easy to blur the boundaries between these different groups and equate the experiences of expellees and Holocaust victims. Against the background of the Cold War, focussing on the expellee experience also offered a useful reminder of Soviet aggression. For Adenauer, the expellees were a European problem, not just a German one. Such thinking enabled him to link them to the emergence of greater European integration – while also helping to present the wider Nazi past as having universal relevance. As Levy and Sznaider summarize, 'representations of expellees' fate thus served two purposes: they were aimed to assuage the moral responsibility for the Holocaust by showing that it had been part of a war in which ethnic cleansing existed on both sides; and they served as a reminder that Germany's integration into the West required continuous attention.'[53]

Indeed, despite de Zayas's assertion to the contrary, the expellees have been anything but forgotten. From the 1950s, the Ministry for Expellees, Refugees and the War-Damaged sponsored histories of the expulsion, recording as many eyewitness accounts as possible, while further expression of the expellee experience was found in the Heimatfilme of postwar West German cinema.[54] Renewed public discussion of the expellees also took place during the 1990s against the background of the collapse of the Soviet

Union and the expansion of the European Union. At the turn of the century, the matter gained added attention with a proposal to construct a museum dedicated to the expellee experience in Berlin. In 2000, Erika Steinbach, a CDU politician and head of the League of Expellees, proposed the formation of a Centre Against Expulsion to remember those Germans who had been forced to leave their homelands during the Second World War. The idea was controversial; Steinbach was accused of trying to whitewash the past and there were particularly vocal criticisms from former countries of Nazi occupation, most notably Poland and the Czech Republic. Undeterred, Steinbach continued to press her case and, in August 2006, a temporary, two-month exhibition opened in the Kronprinzenpalais in central Berlin, entitled 'Forced Paths: Flight and Expulsion in Twentieth Century Europe'. This display, which documented a history of forced migration, from the Armenian genocide through to the Yugoslavian wars of the 1990s, was generally recognized as the first step towards the establishment of a permanent museum to the expellees. 'Forced Paths' downplayed the uniqueness of the Second World War, locating the expellee experience within a century of turmoil and suffering. At the same time, it presented the Germans clearly as victims. Artefacts within the exhibition included photographs, suitcases, items of clothing and even musical instruments. The story, like that within so many Holocaust museums, was of lives cruelly disrupted. Unsurprisingly, the display attracted significant foreign criticism, with the organizers accused of rewriting history. In defence of the display, curator Wilfried Rogasch argued, 'we know that Germans committed many crimes, and that's well documented. More than 60 years after the end of the war we can start to focus on the fate of 12 million Germans who were expelled. This is an important part of our national history.'[55] Despite the criticism, the exhibition actually proved a success, attracting more than 50,000 visitors.

By 2008, the German government had agreed to the establishment of a 'visible symbol' of expulsion within the nation's capital. Plans were drawn up for a documentation centre that would trace the history of forced migration as well as the particular fate of the German expellees. However, the scheme has remained highly contentious and in 2010, two members of the League of Expellees who were helping to oversee the project generated headlines after they seemed to be encouraging a revisionist version of history. Comments made by them to the press downplayed the aggressive nature of Hitler's foreign policy and suggested a general willingness to war among other nations in 1939. Likewise, they highlighted the role of other nations in the use of forced labour and questioned why it was only Germany that had to bear the brunt of war crimes prosecutions and compensation payments to the victims. In short, the pair seemed to be relativizing Nazi atrocities and presenting all Germans as victims. Critics of the museum designs, meanwhile, have also accused the project of failing to place the expulsions within the context of Nazi crimes against humanity.[56]

Memorials and commemorations

In addition to the various campaigns for compensation, welfare and recognition of victimhood status, tales of German suffering were also evident within official, postwar commemorative culture. From September 1945, the Soviet zone had its own annual Day of Remembrance for Victims of Fascism (*Gedenktag für die Opfer des Faschismus*), which was organized by the OdF. In 1953, East Berlin saw large-scale demonstrations in the Lustgarten, organized by the VVN to recall the plight of victims of fascism. An emphasis on Communist resistance was accompanied by representations of the USSR as heroic liberators. Elsewhere in the city, the Soviets constructed an imposing memorial on the edge of the Tiergarten, marking the mass graves of the Soviet soldiers killed during the advance on Berlin, while Treptow Park also held a statue of a Soviet soldier. However, not everyone accepted this celebratory version of the recent past; the Treptow soldier was nicknamed the 'Tomb of the Unknown Rapist' by East Berliners in remembrance of Red Army acts of violence during the final throes of the war – offering an additional example of German victimhood. From 1960, the GDR also transformed the Neue Wache on Unter den Linden into a memorial for 'victims of fascism and militarism' and, since 1993, it has been re-dedicated again to all victims of war and violence. The current reference to 'totalitarianism' can be interpreted with regard to both the Third Reich and the GDR.

West Germany, meanwhile, saw the revival of the *Volkstrauertag* (Day of Remembrance), an event that had originated in the 1920s as a response to the fallen soldiers of the First World War. Having been transformed by the Nazis into a *Heldengedenktag* (Heroes' Day of Remembrance) during the Third Reich, the Volkstrauertag was restored from 1950 to commemorate both the military war dead and the German civilians who had been killed during the Second World War. Between 1951 and 1991, the West German capital, Bonn hosted an annual wreath-laying ceremony in its North Cemetery; since reunification, the focus of the event has been transferred back to Berlin. Reviving old ceremonies created a sense of continuity; familiar rituals could help people make sense of war losses – but also help to blur the differences between conventional military conflict and a war of racial extermination.

From 1958, victims of Nazi persecution were also recalled during the Volkstrauertag commemorations and, from 1973, the ceremony began to refer to 'victims of war and violence' although, as Kaiser notes, there were people who tried to resist these developments. Events away from the capital continued to focus solely on the fallen soldiers, with people gathering to pay their respects at local war memorials and soldiers' graves.[57] The 'Song of the Good Comrade', a nineteenth-century composition that had become a routine feature of German military (and Nazi state) funerals, also continued to be performed to honour the fallen. Elsewhere, Klaus Neumann shows that it was not until 1980 that Celle began to question its traditional

Volkstrauertag practice, one which centred around the war memorial of a kneeling soldier in front of the Celle palace, rather than the nearby Waldfriedhof where many non-German dead (prisoners of war and former concentration camp inmates) were buried.[58]

As well as fallen soldiers, the remembrance of air raid victims also assumed a significant place in the public memory of the two German states. In the GDR, the bombing of Dresden on 13–14 February 1945 took centre stage, with annual ceremonies of remembrance held in the city amid the ringing of church bells.[59] Commemoration of Dresden, however, was used very much for the political needs of the present. Bill Niven notes that, although the air raids had been initiated to aid the Soviet advance into eastern Germany, the GDR preferred to style it as a symbol of Western imperialism and wanton destruction – a trope that echoed much of the sentiments expressed at the time within Nazi propaganda.[60] During the early 1950s, for example, the bombing of Dresden was juxtaposed with events then taking place in Korea. Public, Western interest in Dresden also grew after 1963 with the publication of David Irving's book *The Destruction of Dresden*, which exaggerated casualty numbers and fuelled mythologies. Art historian and postwar prime minister of Saxony, Max Seydewitz, described the destruction of Dresden as a 'crime against humanity for all time'.[61] Elizabeth Corwin notes that for most of the time, historians and journalists saved their depictions of Dresden for comparisons with the dropping of the atomic bombs over Japan, using the example of Dresden to frame disarmaments campaigns. In 1959, however, a West German publication, *The Period of the World Wars*, by Karl Dietrich Erdmann, compared Dresden to the Holocaust, stating:

> Next to the names of Belzec, Treblinka and Auschwitz as symbols of horror ... stands the name of Dresden: here crowded great multitudes of homeless refugees. Into these defenseless people air squadrons ... dropped their explosive and incendiary bombs.[62]

Reflecting on a wave of Dresden literature around the twentieth anniversary of the bombing raid in 1965, and the tendency for polemical tracts against the Allies, the East German magazine *Sonntag* asked, 'How many Dresden ruins atone for the barracks of Auschwitz?' However, the article then proceeded to argue 'we have the right and the duty to criticize the causes of the destruction of Dresden', adding that the GDR had earned this right by successfully eradicating the 'Nazi spirit'.[63]

In her survey of German responses to Dresden, Corwin records a reader's letter published in *Die Zeit* in February 1953 in which the author drew comparisons between Dresden and the SS annihilation of Oradour in June 1944. The letter writer noted that those SS personnel had since been imprisoned or executed for the massacre, while the Allies had faced no repercussions for their actions.[64]

The anniversary of the war's end – 8 May 1945 – would also prove a difficult date for Germans. In 1955, Hans Rothfels, the editor of the *Vierteljahreshefte fur Zeitgeschichte*, argued that the date should be recalled in terms of both those killed by Germans and those Germans killed in the 'inferno of the people of the East'.[65] His emphasis was on the atrocities committed by the Red Army, rather than Auschwitz.

Resistance myths

Both German states wished to demonstrate that they possessed a legitimate foundation in the German past. Focussing on examples of resistance against Nazism was one obvious way of trying to achieve this but both the FRG and GDR exaggerated the extent of opposition – and critiqued each other's version of the past.

In the GDR, the emphasis was on the history of Communist resistance against the Nazi regime. The names of old KPD members were revived and celebrated, becoming the heroes of the new German state. Ernst Thälmann, for example, who had stood against Hitler during various elections at the end of the Weimar Republic, now became a key rallying figure. Thälmann had been arrested by the Nazis during their purge of the political Left in March 1933 and had eventually been murdered in Buchenwald in 1944. Now, his image was displayed on posters and recruits to the GDR youth movement, the Young Pioneers, were required to dedicate themselves to his memory. The graves of Rosa Luxembourg and Karl Liebknecht were also transformed into official memorial sites, used for regular ceremonies and demonstrations.[66] As Niven points out, though, such representations of the past omitted some salient details, including the fact that the Nazis had broken KPD resistance within the few years of the establishment of the Reich.[67]

In West Germany, reactions to the German resistance were rather more complicated. The principal focus rested on the July 1944 bomb plot against Hitler orchestrated by members of the military, including Klaus von Stauffenberg. The very timing of this act, however, remained controversial. The fact that it occurred when the nation was at war was considered an act of treason by many. David Large highlights a 1952 opinion survey in which just 20 per cent of those questioned believed that people should have resisted during wartime, 34 per cent felt that the resistors should have waited until after the conflict had been concluded and 15 per cent insisted that there should have been no resistance at all. Thirty per cent of those surveyed held negative opinions of the conspirators and 50 per cent opposed proposals to name a school after Stauffenberg.[68]

Adenauer, however, was quick to realize the potential of using the memory of the July 1944 resistors to underscore the legitimacy of the new West German state. It also helped to deflect attention from the fact that conservative politicians had helped Hitler into power in the first place. The fate of Stauffenberg and his comrades also gained further recognition from June 1953, when a popular uprising in East Germany was brutally crushed by Soviet forces. On 20 June 1953, a memorial to the bomb plotters was unveiled in the Bendler Block and, from that point onwards, the anniversary of the conspiracy was marked with the laying of wreathes and the delivering of commemorative speeches. In 1955, the street outside the Bendler Block was renamed after Stauffenberg and, in 1968, a public exhibition space was added. Now, argues Niven, the bomb plotters were celebrated as the 'harbingers of freedom, democracy and even the European idea'.[69]

The legacy of resistance was both difficult and comforting. On the one hand, being able to point to such figures enabled the German population to take some pride in their countrymen and reject accusations of collective guilt. Pointing to the fate of resistance martyrs also underscored the sheer danger of trying to oppose the Nazi regime – facilitating the argument that one had to go along with things, that it was impossible to resist without immense danger to oneself and one's family. However, certain silences remained. The fact that the military resistance really only emerged once the war was going badly tended to be glossed over, as did the extent to which figures such as Stauffenberg had previously identified with tenets of National Socialism. Letters that he sent to his wife during his time in Poland, for instance, reflect the wider racism of this period, referring to the local population as an 'unbelievable rabble'.[70] This side of him, however, was usually ignored in the postwar retelling of his heroic exploits.

Other resistance groups, meanwhile, struggled to gain any recognition in postwar West Germany. Given the Cold War climate, the role of trade unionists and KPD activists was not widely discussed in the FRG until the détente of the late 1960s. The growing popularity of regional history also facilitated this, with more research being undertaken into examples of resistance – usually that of the workers – at the grassroots of German society. The legacy of the Edelweiss Pirates, meanwhile, remains controversial to this day. This group of young Germans sabotaged infrastructure during the war, aided deserters and helped to disseminate Allied propaganda leaflets. Their legacy was not helped by the fact that many of the pirates rejected the return of party politics after the war and continued acts of violence against the Allies and fellow Germans who colluded with them; several were tried and sentenced before Allied military courts.

Conclusion

Victimhood narratives held several important functions after 1945. In both Germanys, a legacy of suffering helped to legitimize the new state and generate a morally positive national identity. In the East, there was the pride that came with focussing on courageous Communist fighters; in the FRG, the population's emphasis on 'fate' enabled them to be seen as 'victims of forces beyond their control'.[71] Creating a 'victims together' narrative also facilitated postwar integration, helping the FRG assimilate refugees and expellees as well as those who had previously supported the Nazis. As Hughes argues, 'they could scarcely establish political stability if they permanently ostracized either group'.[72]

3

Acknowledging Suffering: Recalling the Victims of Nazi Racial Persecution since 1945

On 8 May 1985, the West German president, Richard von Weizsäcker, gave a speech before the Bundestag to mark the fortieth anniversary of the end of the Second World War. This was the culmination of a series of commemorative events taking place across the FRG at that time. In his speech, Weizsäcker reflected on the turmoil that had embraced the German population in 1945, acknowledged the hardships and fears they had endured and celebrated the progress that West Germany had made over the past forty years. Most significantly, he also drew attention to the victims of Nazi persecution, stating:

> Today we mourn all the dead of the war and the tyranny. In particular, we commemorate the six million Jews who were murdered in German concentration camps. We commemorate all nations who suffered in the war, especially the countless citizens of the Soviet Union and Poland who lost their lives .... We commemorate the Sinti and Romany gypsies, the homosexuals and the mentally ill who were killed, as well as the people who had to die for their religious or political beliefs. We commemorate the hostages who were executed. We recall the victims of the resistance movements in all the countries occupied by us. As Germans, we pay homage to the victims of the German resistance and among the public, the military, the churches, the workers and trade unions, and the communists. We commemorate those who did not actively resist but preferred to die instead of violating their consciences.[1]

It was a carefully crafted political speech that reflected the diversity of the wartime experience and arguably one that contained something to appeal to most sectors of West German society. Familiar references to German suffering and resistance were tempered with a keen awareness of the atrocities that had been committed in Germany's name. The use of inclusive terminology with phrases such as 'occupied by us' showed that Weizsäcker was prepared to acknowledge the country's historic responsibility. Elsewhere in the speech, he rejected ideas that people had not understood the true character of National Socialism, noting that 'Hitler had never concealed this hatred [of the Jews] from the public' and arguing that while the actual killing might have been hidden from public gaze,

> every German was able to experience what his Jewish compatriots had to suffer.... Who could remain unsuspecting after the burning of the synagogues, the plundering, the stigmatization with the Star of David, the deprivation of rights, the ceaseless violation of human dignity? Whoever opened his eyes and ears and sought information could not fail to notice that Jews were being deported.[2]

Everyone, Weizsäcker argued, needed to think about their own behaviour during that period.

Weizsäcker's speech was widely celebrated in the press and among academics. The German philosopher Jürgen Habermas, for example, described it as one of the 'few political speeches to have done justice to the trial of the Nazi past'.[3] Saul Friedländer praised the president for not shirking from detailing the scope of the crimes and for recognizing the centrality of the persecution of the Jews to Nazi ideology.[4] Mary Fulbrook also talks of the president's 'remarkable empathy and understanding for a range of experiences and feelings', 'willingness to accept historical responsibility', 'refusal to engage in over-simplifications' and 'clear-sighted confrontation with current political realities'.[5] Other scholars have similarly pointed to Weizsäcker's speech as a transformative moment within West Germany's handling of the past; Andrew Beattie proclaims 'it was the pinnacle of an inclusive, differentiating approach to the past'.[6] Certainly, as this chapter will demonstrate, it stands in stark contrast to some of the country's earlier responses to the Holocaust. At the same time, though, there remained some silences within Weizsäcker's comments. Clearly, there were some things that, politically, the president could not say but, when juxtaposed to two other events of the mid-1980s – the Bitburg Controversy and the *Historikerstreit* – it is evident that there remained significant debate in the FRG over the very need to keep addressing this 'darkest chapter' of German history. This chapter explores some of these issues, as well as broader campaigns to provide financial compensation to Holocaust survivors and the place of the Holocaust within East and West German commemorative culture after 1945.

Historians and the Holocaust

In 2003, Nicholas Berg attacked West German historians en masse for their alleged failure to sufficiently engage with the Nazi genocide. In particular, he accused scholars of being reluctant to take seriously the works of Jewish historians and survivors; of failing to integrate victims' suffering into their accounts of the Third Reich on the grounds that it was too emotional and likely to get in the way of the facts.[7] GDR historians, meanwhile, have also tended to be dismissed for blindly following the state-approved Marxist-Leninist interpretation of the past. During the 1970s, for example, Konrad Kwiet declared that 'antisemitism, the history of German Jews and their persecution are not themes considered worthy of study for their own sake' among GDR historians.[8] Likewise, Kurt Pätzold notes that there was no dedicated research centre for the Holocaust at any point during the GDR.[9] Such declarations, however, fail to tell the full story and the historiographical treatment of the Holocaust within both Germanys merits further consideration.

First of all, we need to recognize the very real constraints that German historians were operating under after 1945. People needed time to process what had happened and to mourn their own losses before they could start to reflect critically on the legacy of the Third Reich. The documentation available for academic research was piecemeal – much had been lost, damaged or deliberately destroyed during the final phases of the conflict; or captured by the Allies to aid war crimes prosecutions. While the latter records were eventually returned, the division of Germany and Cold War politics meant it was difficult for historians to access information held in the 'other' German state. The new political climate also had an important effect on historiography that was being produced. Thomas Fox argues that, with the East German government assigning all of the blame for National Socialism onto the West, there was seemingly little need for GDR historians to reflect any further upon responsibility for the Holocaust. Instead, they were encouraged to focus their research on recent Communist experiences, the history of the German Communist Party and its efforts to resist Hitler.[10] Konrad Jarasuch describes GDR historians as the 'guardians of the moral flame' in that they promoted the Comintern definition of fascism and focussed their research efforts on underlining the relationship between state monopoly capitalism and the development of National Socialism. Consequently, Western academics in turn tended to view GDR publications as formulaic and deterministic – little more than state propaganda.[11] East German historiography on the Nazi era was further influenced by the USSR's anti-Zionist campaign, which rendered 'Jewish' topics too sensitive for extensive research during the late 1940s and early 1950s.[12] Those attempting to draw attention to the suffering of the Jews risked being branded as dangerous 'cosmopolitan' elements. In a state where censorship and purges were rife, there was little incentive for GDR historians to dwell too closely on the Holocaust.

Second, it is necessary to note that despite all of the above conditions, there were some East and West German historians who did attempt to document the Holocaust soon after the war. Fox and Pätzold, for instance, underscore the fact that as early as 1948, Siegbert Kahn and Stefan Heymann had produced books in the Soviet zone that presented anti-Semitism as an essential feature of Nazi ideology.[13] West Germany, meanwhile, saw the publication of Holocaust survivor Eugen Kogon's *Der SS-Staat: Das System der deutschen Konzentrationslager* in 1946 and Helmut Genschel's *Die Juden und wir* in 1957.[14] In 1951, the Institute for Contemporary History (IfZ) was established in Munich to conduct research into the recent past. The very notion of doing 'contemporary history' at this time was unfamiliar territory for German historians and it would take time before this field gained widespread professional recognition. The IfZ, though, fostered the first major West German studies on the Nazi state such as Hans Buchheim's *Das Dritte Reich* (1958) and reproduced key documents on the Holocaust in its own journal, including, in 1953, the publication of the Gerstein Report, an eyewitness account of the gassing of 3,000 Jews in Belzec extermination camp.[15] Once again, such features challenge any notion of the immediate postwar period being one of 'silence' towards the Nazi past.

Third, it is important to bear in mind that the development of German (particularly West German) historiography on the Holocaust bears striking similarities to that taking place in other countries, including Britain and the United States. Writing in 2004, Dan Stone commented that 'it is hard now to imagine a time when the Holocaust was not central to western consciousness or when there was a dearth of writing on the subject'.[16] Yet, during the 1950s, the first postwar accounts of the Third Reich produced by Leon Poliakov, Gerald Reitlinger and William Shirer struggled to find publishers for their works.[17] Likewise, Holocaust survivors also found it difficult to tell their stories; few people, it seemed, wanted to listen to them. After six years of fighting, most people, it seemed, just wanted to move on and focus on the future, rather than the Nazi past. Reluctance to engage with the Holocaust was not occurring only in Germany.[18]

It was the 1960s that saw some of the biggest developments in Holocaust historiography. In 1960, Siegbert Kahn published a collection of documents on KPD responses to Kristallnacht and other incidences of Nazi racism that would become a core text within GDR historiography.[19] In 1961, the American scholar Raul Hilberg published his seminal work, *The Destruction of the European Jews*, which detailed the whole industrial-style machinery of the Nazi genocide and inspired a wave of scholarly interest in the crimes of the Third Reich.

Concurrently, the sensational kidnap, arrest and trial of Adolf Eichmann sparked a new public interest in the workings of the Nazi state, the scale of the Holocaust and the experience of the victims. The fact that the Eichmann trial, held in Israel, relied extensively on witness testimony encouraged more survivors to start telling their life stories. Regular, televised reports on the proceedings also helped to generate greater public interest in the case while Eichmann's own role, as the person responsible for timetabling the deportation of European Jews, fostered a new appreciation of both the scale of the Holocaust and the role of bureaucrats in its implementation. Likewise, in West Germany, the 1963–5 Frankfurt Auschwitz trial promoted a better understanding of the extermination camps in the East. The case drew upon detailed reports on the structure of the SS, the concentration camp system and Nazi policies against the Jews that were compiled for the occasion by leading historians including Buchheim, Broszat and Hans-Adolf Jacobson. The resulting 1968 publication – *The Anatomy of the SS State* – would become a key text for understanding Nazism.

Contemporary politics also played a part in the upsurge of Holocaust literature. In the GDR, the capture of Eichmann became propaganda opportunity against the FRG. Fox points to Heinz Kuehnrich's *Judenmörder Eichmann: Kein Fall der Vergangenheit*, as an obvious example of this, a book that detailed both Eichmann's role in organizing the murder of European Jews, and the various delays that had occurred in bringing him to account. It was, in short, a means of critiquing West Germany's handling of the Nazi past, accusing the Bonn government of actively protecting notorious war criminals.[20] By the end of the decade, though, a thawing of Cold War tensions as well as improving East–West German relations through the programme of Ostpolitik, facilitated greater dialogue between historians and access to archival material.

In 1966, Helmut Eschwege finally had his book *Kennzeichen J* published, which represented the first comprehensive East German effort to document and analyse the persecution of the Jews. This was followed in 1973 by Klaus Drobisch, Rudi Goguel, Werner Mueller and Horst Dohle's work, *Juden unterm Hakenkreuz* (Jews under the swastika).[21] In 1975, the final volume of Wolfgang Bleyer's history of Germany (*Deutschland von 1939 bis 1945*) detailed the deportation and ghettoization of European Jews, as well as the role of the Einsatzgruppen and the Wannsee Conference.[22] Another key text published during this period was Victor Klemperer's work, *LTI Notizbuch eine Philogen*, which explored Nazi language. It went through multiple editions.[23]

West German historians, meanwhile, were also starting to pay much greater attention to the role of racial ideology within the Third Reich. In 1972, Andreas Hillgruber became the first scholar to locate the extermination of the Jews within the context of Hitler's expansionist foreign policy with his study of the war in the East. That same year, Karl Schleunes presented the notion of the 'twisted road to Auschwitz', rejecting the existence of any *systematic* policy for the murder of European Jewry and pointing instead to the 'trial and error' approach adopted by subordinates pursuing rival policies.[24] In 1984, the first international conference of Holocaust historians took place in Stuttgart, an event that sparked a protracted debate about the origins of the 'Final Solution' that would rumble on into the 1990s. Specifically, historians argued as to just when the decision had been taken for the systematic mass murder of European Jewry.[25] Again, Hitler's intentions came under close scrutiny here, but attention was also paid to decision-making on the ground, the impact of the invasion of the USSR in June 1941 and the different stages of the killing process, from ghettoization to mass shootings and experiments with poison gas. During this period, there also emerged a greater awareness of the fate of the different victim groups, with works published by Ulrich Herbert on forced foreign labourers in 1985, Michael Zimmerman on Sinti and Roma in 1989, Burkhard Jellonnek and Rainer Hoffschildt on homosexuals in 1990 and 1999, respectively, and Detlef Garbe on the persecution of Jehovah's Witnesses in 1994.[26] Consequently, the Holocaust was being explored in much more detail, but, as the Historikerstreit of the mid-1980s demonstrates, it was not a straightforward process of ever-greater critical engagement with the crimes of the Third Reich.

The limits of Holocaust consciousness

The Historikerstreit, or historians' quarrel, was a public debate among high-profile academics that took place between 1986 and 1987. It questioned where Nazism and the Holocaust should stand in the history of the German nation, and was played out across the pages of leading West German broadsheets such as *Frankfurter Allgemeine Zeitung, Frankfurter Rundschau, Die Zeit, Süddeutsche Zeitung* and the popular news magazine *Der Spiegel*. It occurred against the backdrop of the fortieth anniversary of the war's end and proposals to construct museums of German history in Bonn and West Berlin – plans that critics feared would only serve to exonerate the nation's past. Public discussion of the Nazi legacy had already been stirred with the 1985 Bitburg Controversy, in which the then US president Ronald Reagan visited a cemetery containing graves of the Waffen-SS, as well as those of the regular German army.[27] Discussing his upcoming trip to Germany in a White House press conference, the president declared of the soldiers, 'they were victims just as surely as the victims in the concentration camps'.[28] In response to the resultant public criticism, Reagan added a visit to Bergen-Belsen concentration camp to his itinerary, but the damage was already done.

Furthermore, the mid-1980s were also characterized by a political shift back towards conservatism; the new West German Chancellor Helmut Kohl famously talked about having the 'grace of a late birth' and it appeared that many West Germans shared in this notion of diminishing responsibility for the Nazi past. Already, Martin Broszat had warned that the history of the Third Reich was being written from a distance as if it were that of a foreign people.[29] Now, it seemed, there were other West German historians who hoped it could stop being written about altogether.

The opening shots of the Historikerstreit were fired with the publication of Michael Stürmer's article, 'A Land without History' in the *Frankfurter Allgemeine Zeitung* on 25 April 1986 in which he argued that a continual fascination with the Third Reich blocked out more positive aspects of German history that were crucial for the formation of a national identity. Stürmer, a conservative historian at University of Erlangen-Nürnberg, was close to the political establishment, serving as a speechwriter and adviser to Chancellor Kohl. A specialist in the Kaiserreich, he suggested that Hitler had corrupted older, Prussian values which, in themselves, had been perfectly healthy. Such an interpretation was linked to the wider calls for closer European integration being made at this time; by marking the Hitler period out as an aberration (reasserting traditionalist arguments), Stürmer sought to present the FRG as a stable and reliable partner in this process.[30]

On 6 June 1986, Ernst Nolte published his infamous contribution to the debate, a piece entitled 'The Past That Will Not Pass', in *FAZ*. Like Stürmer, Nolte represented the political Right and was a Professor of Modern History at the Free University of Berlin. In his article, he queried the uniqueness of the Holocaust and, by extension, the very need to continually rake over this chapter of German history. For Nolte, the Holocaust was one of several terrible events to take place during the twentieth century and he preferred to see the Russian Revolution of 1917 as having the more significant, long-term effect. He pointed to the existence of Soviet gulags and earlier examples of mass deportations and killings to question the 'originality' of Auschwitz; indeed, he argued that Nazi policies had merely been a reaction to Soviet atrocities. Nolte also highlighted the persistence of crimes against humanity in the postwar era. Reference, for instance, was made to the Vietnam War, the Cambodian genocide and the Soviet invasion of Afghanistan to relativize Nazi deeds. Given all of these other horrors, Nolte argued, there was little need for the German people to feel especially guilty about; the past should be consigned to history once and for all to enable Germany to recover its status among the international community.[31]

Unsurprisingly, such comments generated a rapid response from other scholars, led by the left-liberal philosopher, Jürgen Habermas. His article, 'A Kind of Settlement of Damages' was published in *Die Zeit* on 11 July 1986. In it, Habermas criticized those who wished to whitewash the past, attacking the apologia being employed by the likes of Stürmer, Nolte and Hillgruber, particularly the latter's comparison between the Holocaust and German soldiers' experiences on the Eastern Front against the Red Army.[32] Nazism, he stressed, was not just a response to Bolshevism and the uniqueness of the Holocaust needed to be acknowledged. Habermas was, in turn, attacked by Nolte, Hillgruber, Joachim Fest and Klaus Hildebrand. Among those leaping to his defence were Broszat, Hans-Ulrich Wehler, Jürgen Kocka and Hans and Wolfgang Mommsen.

The Historikerstreit, then, centred around two key issues: were Nazi crimes unique and could the Holocaust be compared to other genocides? Had German history followed a *Sonderweg* (Special Path) and, if so, why? The resultant debate was a highly passionate affair, complete with personal attacks on opposing historians. It generated much media attention within the FRG and abroad; Geoff Eley records that 136 separate items were published in the West German press alone between the summer of 1986 and January 1987.[33] Norbert Frei emphasizes the 'generational coherence' of the German participants, noting that most of them had been born during the Weimar Republic and had consequently experienced the Second World War as members of the Hitler Youth or as young soldiers.[34] In other words, the Historikerstreit could be seen as the emotional reaction of a group that had a personal connection to the Nazi era and that had also suffered at the end of the conflict. Although the Historikerstreit itself did little to add to our understanding of either the Third Reich or the Holocaust, it was important for increasing public discussion about the Nazi legacy – and inspiring new directions in academic research. Michael Geyer proclaims that 'it was a debate – it was *the* debate – about the past and present of the Third Reich'.[35] As such, it was a moment that underscored the complexities of West German memory culture, and the difficulties of 'coming to terms' with the past.

Against this background, the speech made by Richard Weizsäcker in 1985 may assume new significance. Michael Lane Brunner argues that rather than constituting a genuine confrontation with the past, Weizsäcker's speech was actually talking about remembering in order to forget. He sees the speech as playing into prevailing public conventions, finding a balancing point between the usual right-wing political discourse that focussed on the victims (because there were no longer any perpetrators in their eyes) and praised the German character to create a positive national identity; and the tropes of the political Left that presented its own history as one of resistance; avoided efforts to 'explain' Nazism for fear of being seen to justify it; stressed the need to give victims a greater public voice and found a way to praise the new German democracy.[36] Analysing Weizsäcker's words, Lane Brunner underlines the ways in which the president suggested there had only been a small number of perpetrators, and merged the suffering of Germans and the racially persecuted. He also points to efforts to mitigate German behaviour, with Weizsäcker making reference to the British policy of appeasement and the USSR's signing of the non-aggression pact. Overall, Lane Brunner argues, this was a speech that was much more about the prospect of German reunification than entering into a serious discussion of the past.[37] There certainly remained an emphasis on widespread German resistance and celebratory tales of courage, yet consideration must, of course, be paid to Weizsäcker's position as head of state. Performing a balancing act between left and right political narratives is, perhaps, only to be expected from a president tasked with speaking for the whole nation – and the speech should be praised for drawing public attention to the experiences of multiple groups persecuted during the Third Reich – giving Sinti and Roma and homosexuals a belated place within official memorial discourse.

Reparations and restitution

Acknowledging the victimhood of different groups during the Third Reich was about more than securing a place within official commemorative ceremonies and political speeches. There were also important practical questions to answer about the provision of financial compensation to Holocaust survivors, the restitution of property that had been looted, damaged, destroyed or 'Aryanised' by the Nazi regime, and the payment of reparations to the fledgling state of Israel to cover its costs in admitting Jewish refugees from Europe. Following the liberation of the concentration camps in 1945, Allied medical corps, the United Nations Relief and Rehabilitation Administration and representatives from non-governmental organizations such as the Jewish Committee for Relief Abroad and the American Jewish Joint Distribution Committee all worked hard to aid survivors and displaced persons.[38] Within the camps, former prisoners also formed ad hoc support groups and attempted to confiscate goods and housing from local NSDAP members.[39] However, with no existing model to work from, official Allied policy was relatively slow to respond to the needs of Holocaust survivors. Postwar peace conferences continued to focus on reparations to nation states, rather than individuals and, under the terms of the 1952–3 London Debt Conference, it was agreed that the question of compensating victims of National Socialism would be a matter for a future, reunified Germany.[40] In 1947, US Military Law No. 59 did establish a process for the restitution of Jewish property and variations on this were then adopted by the French and British in their respective occupation zones as well. However, the policy remained uneven and subject to arbitrary decision-making among local authorities. It also, of course, focussed solely on damaged or stolen property, rather than the human suffering that had been unleashed by the Nazi regime. Among the 'ordinary' German population, restitution tended to be seen as another example of unfair victors' justice. Victims, meanwhile, frequently had to endure lengthy and expensive legal proceedings in their fight to regain what had been taken from them. This in itself was hardly conducive to postwar reconciliation or encouraging other victims to stand up for their rights. Consequently, the early postwar period was characterized by a number of campaigns by Western Jewish organizations and, from 1948, the state of Israel, to extract a proper reparations and compensation agreement from the Germans.

As Jeffrey Herf has summarized, the GDR's interpretation of National Socialism was based upon four fundamental ideas: (1) Communist solidarity with the Jews only extended to those of working class backgrounds; (2)

anti-Semitism was an instrument of the ruling class and thus needed to be defeated; (3) Jews could not be regarded as a persecuted nationality as they did not constitute a nation in the sense of having a common language, shared territory or common culture; (4) Nazism was primarily focussed on the destruction of the working class, rather than anti-Semitism.[41] Consequently, there was little recognition of Jewish suffering within official GDR commemorative culture. The Appeal to the German People of 11 June 1945 presented the attack on the USSR as the most heinous of Nazi crimes and made no reference to the Jews. Similarly, although Walter Ulbricht's book, *The Legend of German Socialism*, published in 1945 made reference to death camps and gas chambers, there was no specific mention of the Jews.[42]

However, this does not mean there was complete silence on the matter. There was a minority of German Communists who did recognize the centrality of anti-Semitism to Nazi ideology and who fought hard for Jewish Holocaust survivors to receive recognition after 1945. Chief among these was Paul Merker, a high-ranking Communist who had spent the war in exile in Mexico. He was supported by the likes of historian Siegbert Kahn, and politicians Leo Zukermann – who would become Chief of Staff to GDR president Wilhelm Pieck; Julius Meyer who would become a member of the GDR parliament, and Otto Grotewohl, leader of the SPD in the Soviet zone.[43] These then, were not the voices of a lowly few, but people who had access to high government and public recognition.

Addressing Pieck in May 1948, Merker argued, 'the Jewish population was plundered and almost annihilated, for reasons of so-called racial policy. Therefore, this constituted the destruction of a national or religious minority, a destruction that the German people allowed to happen. In this instance, our zone, too, cannot avoid instituting certain measures for the partial restitution of the damage that occurred.'[44] Merker directly challenged the existing Communist framework for discussing National Socialism. He rejected the premise that the Jews were not a nation and argued that, in terms of restitution, they should have priority over resistance fighters who had at least had made willing sacrifices for their cause.[45]

However, growing anti-Zionism within the Soviet Union from the late 1940s meant that individuals such as Merker were silenced. A series of arrests were made of so-called 'cosmopolitans', people who were deemed as identifying with Jewish, i.e. American concerns. Implicated in a series of espionage trials, Merker was arrested in 1950, interrogated by the Stasi and, in 1955, sentenced to eight years in prison. While he was, in fact, released in January 1956, he remained sidelined in East German politics. Zuckermann and Meyer fled to West Berlin, thereby ensuring that the 'three leading advocates for Jewish interests in East Germany were eliminated from the political scene'.[46]

Likewise, as Israel began to align itself with the West, the GDR rejected that nation's demands for compensation. Notes sent by Israeli campaigners to both Berlin and Moscow during the 1950s frequently went unanswered and no payment was ever secured. Instead, a ruling in autumn 1951 saw property belonging to foreigners being transferred to the East German state rather than being restored to the individual.[47] This meant that Jewish survivors who had fled abroad were unable to recover their assets. Jews living within the GDR did come under the welfare scheme for 'victims of fascism', receiving medical care, pensions and priority housing although, as we saw in the previous chapter, 'active' victims, i.e. Communist resistance fighters, received the better care. The GDR argued that it saw little reason why it should have to help foreign Jews as well; the purge of Nazism from East German society was regarded as reparation enough.

As it was, in 1953, the East German Ministry of Labour called for a revision of the existing compensation provisions, arguing that 'the recognition criteria for the racially persecuted were laid down in the recognition guidelines at the behest of then-president of the Jewish Community Julius Meyer, who ... was [later] unmasked as a Zionist agent and fled the republic'.[48] The implication of this statement was that Meyer had been an unreliable source and thus the whole policy towards Jewish victims merited a rethink. The Ministry, seeking to equate Communist resistance fighters and those who had been forced into political exile with the fate of the racially persecuted, also took issue with the fact that,

> in contrast to resistance fighters, political émigrés, and other groups of victims of Nazi persecution, those persecuted on racial grounds, including Jewish émigrés among others, are not required to present evidence of their organized struggle against the Nazi regime abroad or of their unblemished anti-Fascist-democratic stance during the Nazi period and after 1945.[49]

Elsewhere, other victims of Nazi persecution continued to face discrimination and, in the case of homosexuals, denunciation to the authorities. Between 1946 and 1948, 22 East Berliners had their victim status and accompanying welfare revoked when it emerged that they had been prosecuted for homosexuality during the 1930s.[50] Similarly, Gerald Hacke notes that, when Jehovah's Witnesses refused to participate in the 1948 plebiscite that was supposed to legitimize the future GDR, they went from being acknowledged 'victims of fascism' to 'enemies of the state'.[51] Their subsequent history in the GDR is one of discrimination and persecution. In the FRG, too, remembrance of the suffering of homosexuals was constrained by the fact that homosexuality remained a criminal offence until 1969. At that point, *Der Spiegel* ran a cover story on the treatment of homosexuals during the Third Reich, belatedly seeking to bring their fate to public attention.[52] It was only in 2002 that the German parliament issued pardons to the thousands of homosexuals who had been imprisoned by the Nazis.[53]

GDR responses to the compensation issue were also affected very much by prevailing Cold War politics and ideological interpretations of the recent past, as well as Stalin's anti-Zionist campaign. According to the GDR, it was the FRG that was the true 'successor state' to the Third Reich and so it was West Germany that bore legal and moral responsibility for any reparations arising from the Nazi era. At the same time, the USSR's efforts to extract reparations for the suffering of the Soviet people assumed greater priority than other victim groups. Furthermore, Tovy argues that Cold War divisions meant that Israel was being discouraged from pursuing its demands from the GDR for fear that the signing of any reparations treaty could be seen as legitimizing the East German state.

The FRG, however, began to enter into reparations negotiations from the end of 1951. In September that year, Adenauer informed the Bundestag:

> The government of the Federal Republic of Germany, and with it the great majority of the German people, are aware of the immeasurable suffering brought to the Jews in Germany and in the occupied territories in the era of National Socialism. In an overwhelming majority, the German people abhorred the crimes committed against the Jews and did not participate in them. During the period of National Socialism, there were many Germans, acting on the basis of religious belief, the call of conscience, and shame at the disgrace of Germany's name, who at their own risk were willing to assist their Jewish fellow citizens. In the name of the German people, however, unspeakable crimes were committed which require moral and material restitution. These crimes concern damage to individuals as well as to Jewish property whose owners are no longer alive. The first steps have been taken on this level. A great deal remains to be done. The government of the Federal Republic will support the rapid conclusion of a law regarding restitution and its just implementation. A portion of identifiable Jewish property is to be returned. Further restitution will follow.[54]

This was a historic occasion, paving the way for the signing of the Luxembourg Agreement on 10 September 1952, which pledged DM3b to Israel, and DM450m to the Conference on Jewish Material Claims against Germany, an organization that represented Jews living outside of Israel. This reparations treaty recognized Jews' fundamental right to compensation and secured the FRG's responsibility for providing this. The move also contrasted sharply with the responses of the GDR, yet, at the same time, Adenauer's depiction of the Nazi period remained somewhat problematic. As Jeffrey Herf notes, in the speech actually more time was spent praising German responses than discussing the fate of the Jews. Again, narratives of resistance were at the fore, and the circle of perpetrators responsible for Nazi crimes was being rendered as small as possible.[55]

Adenauer, of course, was speaking to a German audience – and one that had already expressed reservations over the treaty. Within his own political party there were those who doubted the nation's ability to pay and who continued to press the cause of non-Jewish Germans who had been rendered 'war damaged'. Viewed in this light, Adenauer's comments can be seen as an effort to reassure his critics that he had not forgotten the needs of his fellow countrymen. Greater support for the treaty was forthcoming from the SPD, with their leader, Kurt Schumacher, stressing the moral imperative to offer restitution and remember those killed by the Nazis. When the Luxembourg Agreement was finally ratified by the Bundestag in March 1953, the SPD was the only political party to prove unanimous in its support for the treaty.[56]

The 1952 treaty with Israel opened the door for similar petitions from other nations that had either been directly affected by Nazi occupation, or was now receiving a number of Holocaust survivors. In 1956, France, Belgium, the Netherlands, Luxembourg, Greece, Denmark, Norway and Britain submitted requests for compensation to be extended to their people too. Italy, Sweden, Austria and Switzerland then added their demands with the result that between 1959 and 1964, eleven separate bilateral agreements were signed with the FRG, known collectively as *Globalabkommen* (Global Agreements). These measures helped to underscore the geographical scale of the Holocaust. More cynically, Susanna Schrafstetter argues that they also reflect the political realities of the time amid early initiatives for European integration and the FRG needing Western support for its rehabilitation on the international stage.[57]

However, as Andrew Woolford and Stefan Wolejszo argue, 'for all of the success of Jewish Holocaust survivors and their supporters ... other groups victimised by the Nazis have been less able to achieve similar acknowledgement of their victimization'.[58] While West Germany's compensation arrangements began to be reviewed in 1956, there remained significant flaws in its procedures. First, compensation was only available to those who had lived within German borders after 1 December 1937 or had moved to the FRG after 1945, a ruling that favoured people who had been German nationals at the time of their persecution. Second, it was limited to people who now lived within states that had diplomatic relations with the FRG. This, therefore, excluded people in the GDR, USSR and other parts of the Soviet bloc – areas of Eastern Europe that had borne the brunt of the killing process. Third, compensation was also only offered to those people who had endured racial, religious and political persecution. While this phrasing might seem to encompass most Holocaust victims, in reality it continued to sideline the experiences of Sinti and Roma. 'Gypsies' could only apply under the category of 'racial persecution' if their claim related to the period after December 1942, the point at which Heinrich Himmler had issued his order for the deportation of Sinti and Roma to Auschwitz. This regulation meant that there was no recognition of the violence and mass arrests that had occurred during the earlier years of the Third Reich.

Instead, acts perpetrated against Sinti and Roma during the 1930s, such as the mass roundup and internment in Marzahn concentration camp prior to the 1936 Berlin Olympics, were depicted as state security measures against 'criminal' elements. In this way, older prejudices continued to hold sway and Nazi policy initiatives appeared justified. In May 1948, the head of the compensation programme in North Rhine-Westphalia had to issue a reminder to his staff that 'Gypsies and Gypsies of mixed blood fall under the category of racially persecuted and are to be treated according to those guidelines. The same rules apply to them as apply to Jews and half-Jews and I request that you process all the applications currently pending accordingly.'[59]

Julia Knesebeck, however, demonstrates that such pleas had limited impact during the postwar era. In 1950, authorities handling the compensation arrangements in Düsseldorf wrote to the State Minister of the Interior, arguing:

> If one were to compensate these Gypsies, who are *an inherently asocial* section of society, which has *never added anything* to the well-being of the Volksgemeinschaft for *their self-inflicted incarceration*... one would have to expect, in my opinion, the animosity of broad sections of society. Expellees and victims of bombing, the unemployed and pensioners on benefits, as well as all tax payers, will have no sympathy for taxes paid through great sacrifice to be spent in such an economically irresponsible manner.[60]

The language of this source is significant, very much echoing the ideological rhetoric of the Third Reich as it distinguishes between those members of the population who contribute something of value to the community, and those who remain a 'burden'. In 1952, the mayor of Gräfenhausen similarly betrayed a continued prejudice against the Sinti and Roma, insisting,

> I'm strictly opposed to allowing the Gypsies to resettle anywhere near the village limits; it would lead to the same circumstances that prevailed before 1939. The citizens of this community must fight hard for their daily bread and those Gypsies just want to feed themselves at the expense of others.... In conclusion, allow me to stress once more that I will not tolerate the settlement of Gypsies... and will seek to prevent it with every means at my disposal.[61]

The efforts of Sinti and Roma, as well as homosexuals and petty criminals, to receive compensation during this period were hampered by the fact that they basically had to prove that they were 'no longer' a threat to society. An Allied conference in December 1946 had already established a ruling that the so-called 'asocials' had to have a clean record for both the period of their internment within the concentration camps and the postwar era if they were to receive compensation.[62] This emphasis on supporting only the most 'deserving' members of society continued throughout the 1950s and into the 1960s. Cold War politics, meanwhile, meant that the FRG was also reluctant to acknowledge the suffering of Communists, viewing them as suspicious elements. In 1949, the Stuttgart *Oberregierungsrat*, Ernst Heller, declared:

> not everyone who calls himself a victim of political persecution is justified in doing so. The term 'victim of political persecution' has been much abused. The concentration camps included, alongside victims of political or racial persecution, many professional criminals and other asocial elements as well. The latter inmates, in particular, were much better at coping with camp life and its hardships and privations than politicians and journalists. Thus, proportionally speaking, more asocials survived than victims of political persecution.[63]

Knesebeck, meanwhile, argues that other former concentration camp victims were often wary of being associated with these 'criminal elements', fearing that it could affect their own victim status within postwar Germany. Consequently, groups such as the Sinti and Roma were unable to call upon the support of other survivors' organizations to help them press their case.[64]

The very term used in West Germany to describe compensation policies – *Wiedergutmachung* – was also controversial. The literal translation, to 'make good again', supposed that everything could be made better; critics thus accused the FRG authorities of trivializing the Holocaust.[65] The term also implied that people could just pay up to make the past go away, rather than working through it in any critical manner.

In 1965, in response to continued lobbying from the Claims Conference, the FRG passed amendments to the existing compensation legislation that enabled previously excluded groups to apply. However, the law itself was not reopened for discussion and thus the legitimacy of these victims' claims was still not properly recognized.[66] This revised compensation agreement was known as the Final Law (*Schlussgesetz*) – the very title betraying the hope that this would constitute an end, once and for all, to this matter. Technically, Sinti and Roma could now seek recompense more easily, yet the immense bureaucracy involved in making a claim continued to work against them. Woolford and Wolejszo explain that the compensation process required claimants to present several forms of identification and other documentation, failing to recognize that the Nazis had already seized these from their victims. In addition, not all victims had the benefit of a lobbying body or political representation to help them be heard.[67]

By the start of the 1980s, however, Sinti and Roma had started to gain more recognition. In 1978, West German officials met with representatives of the World Romani Congress to hear their demands, and in 1982, the

Central Council of German Sinti and Roma was established. Some, however, had been driven to drastic measures to achieve this; in 1980, Sinti and Roma had gone on hunger strike to draw attention to their cause.[68] Arguably, greater public awareness of the Nazi genocide, thanks in part to the 1979 screening of the American television series, *Holocaust*, also created a climate in which existing compensation measures came under scrutiny. Debates over financial restitution to Holocaust survivors continued and in 2000, Germany established the Remembrance, Responsibility and Future Foundation to seek a 'legal peace' (or end) to such claims.

Public commemorations

We have already seen how public remembrance of the war, typified in West Germany's *Volkstrauertag* and East Germany's Day for the Victims of Fascism, focussed on fallen German (or Soviet) soldiers, murdered resistance fighters and the civilian victims of the air war. However, as an analysis of the anniversaries of Kristallnacht demonstrates, there were sporadic attempts to acknowledge the suffering of other victim groups in as well. As early as 1946, the Soviet zone of occupation marked the eighth anniversary of Kristallnacht with the waving of Zionist flags and the singing of Hebrew songs.[69] In the FRG, the twentieth anniversary of the pogrom in 1958 saw representatives of the Protestant and Catholic churches attending a commemorative ceremony within a Jewish cemetery in Bielefeld, and young trade unionists holding ceremonies at the former Dachau and Flossenbürg concentration camps. Willy Brandt, the then mayor of West Berlin, urged West Germans not to forget about the persecution of the Jews, while the FRG president, Theodor Heuss, gave a speech to the Jewish Central Council in which he stated:

> The memory of the 9th of November awakens terrible actions that we all had to experience as brutality, lies and deep lack of respect were manifested in the destructive anger against the Jewish places of worship. To remember this day is of exceptional duty in this time because the number of those grows who would like to flee into the convenience of wanting to forget or have already fled. The infamy of this time has created a burning memorial. The flames would like to sink slowly into themselves but their dark embers react during these decades as a burning shame.[70]

For the most part, though, early commemorations of the pogrom were confined to the surviving Jewish communities in each German state. Reflections on the Nazi violence appeared within the Jewish press, yet were largely absent from the mainstream media throughout the 1950s and 1960s. In his survey of leading West German newspapers, Y. Michal Bodemann notes that, instead, the primary interest in 9 November as a historical date rested with the anniversary of the Kaiser's abdication in 1918.[71] Likewise, coverage in the SED-controlled newspaper, *Neues Deutschland* in the GDR focussed on 9 November 1918 as a moment of working class 'revolution'. Kattago notes that in 1948, the former resistance fighter and GDR historian Walter Bartel explicitly linked Kristallnacht to the events of 1918, arguing that the pogrom of 1938 was the result of the failure to break the monopoly of capitalist power at the end of the First World War.[72] By 1968, Kristallnacht received two articles in *Neues Deutschland*, but this contrasted with the fourteen pages that continued to be devoted to the formation of the Weimar Republic. When the fate of the Jews was mentioned, it was usually as a means of celebrating the eradication of fascism and anti-Semitism from East Germany.[73]

Historians such as Harold Marcuse and Janet Jacobs agree that it was only during the late 1970s, that Kristallnacht began to enter national memory culture.[74] In 1978, Helmut Schmidt became the first West German chancellor to attend a Jewish commemorative ceremony for Kristallnacht, marking the fortieth anniversary of the pogrom with a speech at Cologne synagogue. While declaring that 'the night of 9 November 1938 marked one of the stages along the path leading to hell', Schmidt also took a moment to perpetuate older narratives of German ignorance and condemnation of Nazi racial policy, stating: 'the truth is ... that many Germans disapproved of the crimes and the misdemeanours; also that very many others at the time knew nothing or almost nothing. The truth is that, nevertheless, all this took place before the eyes of a large number of German fellow citizens.'[75]

Ten years later, Kristallnacht's place within the national historical consciousness was 'solidified' amidst the widespread commemorations for the fiftieth anniversary of the pogrom.[76] In the FRG, a special postage stamp was issued depicting the destruction of a synagogue in Baden-Baden.[77] In Dachau, an exhibition on the life of local Jews was displayed within the city hall, and a memorial plaque, dedicated to those who had been forced to flee after the Nazi violence, was unveiled by the city's mayor.[78] Special ceremonies were held within both East and West German parliaments although, as Elisabeth Domansky notes, the CDU had been somewhat reticent towards the prospect of devoting an entire Bundestag session to this occasion.[79] In the East German Volkskammer, there were speeches by the parliamentary chair, Horst Sindermann, who had himself been a victim of Nazism, and a representative of the GDR's Jewish community. GDR politicians, however, used the occasion to emphasize the support that German Communists had given to Jews during the Third Reich, thereby retaining the traditional narrative of heroic resistance.[80] West German politicians, meanwhile, refused to invite the leader of the Central Council of Jews in Germany to address the Bundestag. Instead, the speech-making was left to Philipp Jenninger (CDU). Effectively, this decision reduced German Jews to passive objects, denying them a voice in an event purporting to commemorating their own suffering. As it was, the style and content of

Jenninger's speech completely overshadowed anything else. Rejecting the conventional framework for public discussions of the Nazi past, Jenninger presented himself as speaking for and to the non-Jewish community. He began by declaring,

> Today we have come together in the Bundestag…because not the victims but we in whose midst the crimes took place have to remember and account for what we did; because we Germans want to come to an understanding of our past and of its lessons for our present and future politics.[81]

There were several areas of contention in this speech. First, the 'us' and 'them' language utilized by Jenninger reinforced the separation of non-Jewish and Jewish Germans, a theme that the ceremony was, of course, supposed to critique. Second, most of his speech proceeded to concentrate on the perpetrators rather than the victims. Third, in attempting to explain the roots of anti-Semitism, Jenninger seemed to come dangerously close to explaining, rather than rejecting, Nazism. Fourth, as he made this effort to document what had happened, Jenninger quoted from Nazi sources, without making it immediately clear where his voice ended and theirs began.[82] The speech was not well received within the Bundestag with several members of the Green Party, FDP and SPD walking out in protest. Jenninger was forced to resign shortly afterwards.

Since reunification, memorials to the Kristallnacht pogrom have flourished across Germany, with particular efforts to mark the sites of former synagogues and Jewish cemeteries. The 9 November, however, remains contested. While the early postwar period witnessed an emphasis on the anniversary of the end of the First World War and German monarchy; matters have become further complicated since 1989 with the date also representing the anniversary of the fall of the Berlin Wall. There has thus been a tension between using the day to celebrate German liberation from totalitarianism, and mourning the destruction of the European Jews. In November 2013, the seventy-fifth anniversary of Kristallnacht was marked with a variety of initiatives. The German Foreign Ministry and the Berlin Centrum Judaicum organized a public exhibition within the New Synagogue entitled 'From the Inside to the Outside'. This event, which ran for six months, was based around reports compiled by foreign diplomats and served to demonstrate the wider world's failure to mount an adequate response to the persecution of the Jews.[83] At the same time, around 100 Berlin businesses – including KaDeWe, the largest department store in Europe – put stickers on their windows that gave the illusion of them having been smashed. Younger Germans were targeted through social media, with history students 'live-tweeting' the events of the pogrom.[84]

Historians have advanced several different interpretations of the meaning of modern German Kristallnacht commemorations. Bodemann sees the proliferation of memorials to the pogrom as just another extension of the nation's 'theatre of collective memory'.[85] Others such as Jeffrey Olick and Daniel Levy argue that the memorialization of Kristallnacht has become another means of depicting anti-Semitism and the Holocaust as the work of a criminal few. Domansky, meanwhile, sees the rhetoric surrounding Kristallnacht as enabling Germans to both 'remember' and 'forget'.[86] Jacobs agrees that an increase in memorials has actually enabled the memory of the Holocaust to be more distant. By focussing on the destruction of synagogues and transforming burned pieces of the Torah into commemorative 'relics', she argues that it has become easy for Kristallnacht (and, by extension, wider Nazi policy towards the Jews), to be seen as an attack on religion rather than people.[87]

Conclusion

Today, the Holocaust occupies a central position within German remembrance culture, and, since the mid-1980s, there has been growing recognition of the crimes committed against a range of different victim groups. The process for acknowledging the suffering of other minorities, though, including the Sinti and Roma, has been slow. As mentioned previously, it was only in 2000 that the Federal German government issued an official apology for the homosexuals that had been persecuted under National Socialism. Similarly, it took until 1997 for the German president Roman Herzog to declare: 'the genocide against the Sinti and Roma was motivated by the same racist hysteria, with the same malicious resolve, and executed with the same wilful intent for systematic and total annihilation as the genocide against the Jews'.[88] Since 2012, both of these groups have been commemorated in memorial form within central Berlin. However, as the discussions over the Kristallnacht commemorations reveal, there is still some potential for evasions and distortions within the public retelling of the Holocaust, and battles for restitution continue to be waged.

4

The Pursuit of Justice

Arguably, one of the clearest yardsticks of Germany's response to the Nazi past since 1945 is its attitude towards the prosecution of war criminals. As we have seen in Chapter 1, the Allies conducted their own judicial programme in the immediate aftermath of the Second World War, and this had frequently been regarded with suspicion by the ordinary German population. Accusations of victors' justice were rife, and opinion polls revealed some hesitancy in accepting that guilt for Nazi atrocities extended beyond a handful of radical perpetrators operating at the highest levels of the regime. When the Allies departed and sovereignty was bestowed upon the new West German state, the number of war crimes investigations declined sharply. It was not until the late 1950s that a new wave of legal proceedings emerged and the Holocaust began to be documented as never before. This chapter explores these developments, taking into account the levels of public engagement with war crimes trials, amnesty campaigns and the debates, up until 1979, over the statute of limitations for Nazi atrocities. The primary focus is on the FRG, where the available source material gives us a better insight into both popular reaction and the very number of war crimes cases being heard. The GDR, however, was never silent on this matter and thus some attention will also be paid to examples of East German trials, and the state's persistent criticism of the West's judicial record.

War crimes trials, history and memory

Historians have been relatively slow to analyse the post-1949 war crimes trials, preferring to focus their attention on the more high-profile, Allied-led proceedings of the late 1940s. An abundant secondary literature on the IMT has, for example, been steadily joined by studies of the Belsen trial conducted in the British zone in 1945 and the subsequent Nuremberg proceedings led by the Americans, 1946–9 – the latter encompassing the prosecution of German industrialists, medical personnel, members of the Einsatzgruppen and the judiciary.[1] Here, the primary interest has rested with the Allies' own understandings (or misconceptions) of Nazi crimes, points of international law and the effects of Cold War politics, rather than the responses of the watching German population. Likewise, such attention as has been paid to later war crimes trials has generally rested with the 'bigger' cases: the prosecution, in Israel, of Adolf Eichmann in 1961, or the trial of twenty former Auschwitz personnel in Frankfurt between 1963 and 1965.[2] There has also been a growing interest in the Majdanek trial, which has the distinction of being the longest war crimes procedure in West German history, running from 1975 until 1981 in Düsseldorf.[3] Accounts of East German trials, meanwhile, were hampered for many years by the inability to access the necessary archives; the literature on GDR war crimes prosecutions is thus still emerging.[4] While accounts have paid some attention to the pedagogic impact of war crimes proceedings, the trials' effect on Vergangenheitsbewältigung has often been assumed, rather than probed in any great depth. Recently, however, there has been growing interest in the relationship between justice and the formation of historical memory, with a number of scholars exploring the extent to which war crimes trials were able to effect a more critical public understanding of the Holocaust.[5] We have already seen that events such as the Eichmann or Auschwitz trials of the 1960s have often been advanced as key turning points in effecting greater West German discussion of the past – but it is important to remember that many more 'smaller' war crimes proceedings were taking place right across the FRG during that period as well. These afforded opportunities for schools to observe trials first-hand as part of their history lessons, and often stimulated local interest into the history of their own community under National Socialism. Some trials saw members of the public haranguing the defendants and demanding the most severe forms of justice be administered upon them. Other cases had the opposite effect, revealing the persistence of local loyalties to the accused and the refusal to contemplate that people they knew personally could ever have been involved in wartime atrocities. Consequently, an examination of the public resonance of war crimes trials underscores the complexities of postwar memory cultures.

Prosecuting Nazis in East and West Germany

There are three main phases in the history of Nazi war crimes trials within West Germany: the 'denazification' period of 1945–52 in which the Allies assumed the leading role in administering justice; 1952–7 in which the West German authorities wound down trials and questions of a general amnesty for war criminals came to the fore; and the period from 1958 when the establishment of the *Zentralstelle der Landesjustizverwaltungen zur Aufklärung nationalsozialistischer Verbrechen* (Central Office of the State Justice Administration for the Investigation of National Socialist Crimes; referred to hereafter as 'Zentralstelle') enabled the coordination of war crimes investigations and a new wave of trials dealing explicitly with crimes against humanity.

Between 1949 and 1992, the FRG conducted more than 100,000 investigations and convicted around 6,500 individuals. The majority of these cases (85 per cent), however, related to 'lesser crimes' or acts committed between 1933 and 1939.[6] The figures also obscure the nation's initial reluctance to take any action with regard to Nazi perpetrators. Between 1947 and 1950, the Allies had rendered 5,006 convictions, of which 794 had resulted in death penalty. By contrast, there were 123 convictions for war crimes before West German courts in 1953. A year later, this figure had fallen to just forty-four.[7] The trials that were conducted during the 1950s also tended to be relatively small affairs. Just 8 per cent of these cases involved five or more defendants at any one time. While capital punishment had been abolished under the new West German state, in the trials held between 1950 and 1957 just 7 per cent resulted in the maximum punishment – life prison sentence for the accused.[8] Those that did receive such punishments tended to be the last 'big names' of the Third Reich, including Ilse Koch who stood trial in 1951. In fact, the majority of cases heard in West German courts before 1957 ended in the acquittal of all concerned.[9]

From the very beginnings of the FRG, there was a vocal section of the West German population that insisted all of the 'really guilty' parties had been dealt with and that war crimes proceedings should therefore be brought to an end. Those who had already been tried and convicted by the Allies began to have their sentences reduced or commuted altogether, and there were popular calls for a general amnesty of suspected Nazi war criminals. Veterans' organizations, members of the clergy and prisoners' charities were among those piling on the political pressure, alongside, of course, the relatives of the war criminals.[10] The inclusion of the amnesty issue within Adenauer's opening speech to the Bundestag on 20 September 1949 indicates its central place within West German politics at this time. Adenauer stated:

> The war and the confused postwar period have brought such great problems and such temptations for many people that human understanding for certain offenses is called for. The question of an amnesty will therefore be examined by the Federal Government and the possibility will also be examined of approaching the High Commissioners in an effort to secure an amnesty for sentences pronounced by Allied Military Courts. In the conviction that many people have already been stoned for guilt which, regarded subjectively, is not heavy, the Federal Republic is determined wherever possible to let bygones be bygones.[11]

This was clearly a useful platform for German reconstruction but by the 1950s, even the term 'war criminal' had become contested. If used, within the press or between amnesty campaigners, the phrase was placed firmly between quotation marks to demonstrate people's scepticism of Allied justice. There was a growing preference to use the term 'Nazi criminal' instead, the distinction between the two helping to impose a sense of distance between perpetrators of atrocities and the majority of the population. The term *Kriegsverurteilten* – war condemned – was also used when speaking of those already sentenced for their crimes, a phrase distinct from *Kriegsschuldig* – the 'war guilty', again underscoring the implicit innocence of those who had the misfortune to become embroiled in war crimes proceedings.[12] Such language added to the sense that the number of genuine war criminals was very small, and precluded any wider soul-searching regarding the recent past. Norbert Frei similarly notes the use of euphemisms such as 'actions connected with the war events' and 'Germans domiciled with the Western powers' to describe those now in custody.[13] This was a language that, again, served to create a sense of distance from the crimes of the Third Reich. Here, the reasons why German nationals are now sitting in a prison cell are conveniently glossed over; instead it appears as a matter of chance or bad luck. With an emphasis on 'war events' and the actions of the Allies, responsibility is thus taken out of the Germans' hands.

Similarly, disbelief in the legitimacy of the trials was evident in a 1952 opinion poll conducted by Elizabeth Noelle-Neumann when people were invited to comment on the *sogenannten*, or 'so-called' war criminals sentenced at Nuremberg.[14]

Rather than being ostracized from society, many convicted war criminals were able to enjoy considerable sympathy and solidarity from their compatriots during this period. Candlelight vigils would be staged outside the prisons and a 1952 campaign by the Frankfurt-based newspaper, *Abendpost*, resulted in over 200 offers from members of the public to swap places with prisoners on Christmas Eve so that the latter might spend time with their families.[15] Frei also recounts the case of two prisoners who escaped from Werl and were able to elude the authorities through the support of members of the public; the fishmonger who denounced their temporary hideout in Aurich, on the other hand, was labelled a 'traitor' and had his house targeted by an angry mob.[16] Katharina von Kellenbach, meanwhile, has shown how a number of wives of convicted war criminals remained loyal to their husbands, stressed their essential goodness and cast doubt on the validity of their convictions. She cites the example of a woman married to a deputy commander of an Einsatzgruppe who stated, 'my husband is so young and devoted to his son and to me with such love and tenderness… that I cannot believe that he could have committed a crime of such magnitude deserving such a harsh penalty'.[17]

Official state figures for the Soviet occupation zone and the GDR show that 12,890 people were prosecuted for Nazi war crimes and crimes against humanity in eastern Germany between 1945 and 1989. Of these, 90 per cent were tried before 1955; the greatest majority before 1951.[18] To emphasize this further, Rüter records that amid the Waldheim trials in 1949, 3,224 former Nazis were convicted in just two and a half months in trials that lasted, on average, just twenty minutes.[19] The contrast with the FRG is striking. The rapid pace of the war crimes hearings reflected the SED's determination to enact a thorough purge of East German society and establish the new state firmly on antifascist credentials. Arguably, the sheer number of cases before the 1950s enabled the GDR to soon leave the Nazi past behind and look firmly to future instead. This, then, was the basis for the GDR's superior attitude over the FRG, and the persistent attacks on the West's judicial failings over the subsequent decades. Critics in the West, meanwhile, could use the rapidity of GDR proceedings as evidence that they were little more than show trials. In 1965, a report by the West German Minister of Justice emphasized the harsh conditions that awaited those affected by 'indiscriminate' arrests in the Soviet zone after 1945:

> Tens of thousands were sent to penitentiaries, prisons and concentration camps including, for example, Buchenwald [and] Sachsenhausen.... Starvation and in some cases torture were used there to extract 'confessions' as the basis for trials by Soviet military tribunals.... Even ordinary German soldiers who had been taken prisoner appeared in their thousands before military tribunals, which usually sentenced them to uniform terms of 25 years imprisonment or in many cases to death.[20]

Conditions within the Soviets' 'special camps' were, indeed, extremely harsh and, from 1946, a significant proportion of those interned were people accused of hindering the construction of a Stalinist state, rather than atrocities committed during the Third Reich. At the same time, though, the Justice Minister's comments betray some of the popular myths of the postwar period, dismissing the notion that there had been large numbers of Nazi perpetrators and vehemently rejecting the bracketing of honourable German soldiers with such criminals. Talk of concentration camps being used to house these prisoners further served to underscore the 'innocence' of these characters, victims of totalitarian injustice. Finally, the timing of this report is significant, coming in the wake of the notorious *Brown Book* – an East German publication that had listed the number of former Nazis still holding public office in the FRG, and critiqued the West German judiciary's record on war crimes prosecutions.[21] This, then, was the West hitting back with an attack on the GDR's own concepts of justice.

East German trials focussed predominantly on crimes that had been committed against members of the political Left. Up until 1952, 53 per cent of the trials dealt with people who had denounced friends, relatives or colleagues to the Gestapo.[22] As a result, the proceedings underscored notions of German victimhood. The persecution of the Jews barely figured in war crimes proceedings at this point; the first Sachsenhausen trial, conducted before a Soviet Military Tribunal in October 1947, for example, concentrated on the gassing of 18,000 Russian prisoners of war.

There were also significant legal differences between war crimes trials conducted in East and West Germany. Most defendants in the GDR were prosecuted as principals, rather than accessories, in the crimes – and the charges themselves spoke of 'crimes against humanity', rather than 'murder' or 'manslaughter' as was standard in the FRG.[23] As such, the GDR could be seen as giving more credit to the enormity of Nazi atrocities and it is notable that, while the FRG spent the 1960s and 1970s wrestling with the issue as to whether Nazi crimes should be subject to the statute of limitations like any other acts of murder; East Germany signed the 1968 UN Convention on the Non-Applicability of the Statutory Limitations to War Crimes and Crimes Against Humanity. Unlike the FRG, the GDR retained the death penalty after 1949, and the acquittal rate for war crimes trials was also much lower. Friedman notes that not a single person was exonerated after 1952.[24]

Jonathan Friedman argues that where West Germany did stand out was in the fact that it did more to tackle the problem of senior Nazis involved in the Holocaust. One hundred and ten members of the Einsatzgruppen (mobile killing squads) and ninety-three guards from Auschwitz, Treblinka, Sobibor and Majdanek were prosecuted over the course of the Federal Republic. These cases were heard, by and large, from the mid-1960s onwards. In the GDR, by contrast, only seven senior concentration camp personnel were tried for their role in mass murder.[25] In addition, Wendy Lower's work on the East German trials of the 1950s and 1960s suggests that when the Holocaust was invoked by prosecutors, it said more about the politics of the present than a genuine engagement with the past. The highly publicized 1953 trial of Erna Dorn, for example, forged a connection between her past role as a guard at Ravensbrück concentration camp and her alleged instigation of the workers' uprising in East Berlin in June that same year.[26]

From September 1955, the East German legal system was freed from direct Soviet oversight at district and regional level. Prosecutors now had the space to establish their own procedures and decide what, if any, action should be taken against suspected Nazi war criminals. Like the FRG, there was a widespread desire for amnesty and, during the mid-1950s, many of those serving prison sentences of less than twenty-five years were released. Lower argues that these amnesties became an important means for both establishing the GDR as an independent state, and eliciting loyalty from the East German citizens.[27] Former Nazis may have been 'forgiven' but they were not forgotten; those who did not conform to the prescribed social and political norms could find their cases reopened. Likewise, when suspects were arrested in relation to Nazi atrocities, interrogators were often more concerned with establishing their postwar record of behaviour than the events of the Second World War, with attention being paid, among other things, to whether an individual was a member of the SED or had ties to the West. Lower comments, 'one is tempted to conclude that the actual [Nazi] crimes were taken seriously only when their prosecution could be instrumentalized for other political aims'.[28]

In 1967, the GDR established a special centre, Department 11, to compile documentation on Nazi war crimes. Stasi Chief Erich Mielke declared that, 'for international and national reasons the German Democratic Republic is obligated to expose and prosecute Nazi crimes, war crimes, and crimes against humanity as well as the increasing development of neo-Nazism in West Germany and West Berlin. This obligation necessitates a determined uncovering of ruling Nazis and war criminals, active fascists, and fascist agents who are operating [in West Germany] in key positions of the state, political parties, economy, and military.'[29] Although this did mean that East Germany was becoming more and more informed about the Holocaust, Lower points out that the Stasi remained more concerned with identifying potential domestic threats than bringing Nazi perpetrators to account for crimes against humanity. She also suggests that the very establishment of the documentation centre stemmed from a need to demonstrate the robustness of East German judicial investigations to the rest of the world, occurring at a time when the GDR was increasing its own, damning attacks on the FRG's record for war crimes prosecutions.[30]

The collection of documentary evidence on the Holocaust, however, did not necessarily equate to a wider, East German public understanding of the genocide. Lower notes that the trials of 'lesser criminals' that did take place during the 1960s tended to be a quiet affair. In contrast to the events in the FRG during the same period, there was no real effort to publicize details of the atrocities under discussion, or to transform the trials into occasions for pedagogy.[31]

'The murderers among us'

The turning point in the FRG's pursuit of war criminals is generally regarded as the 1958 Ulm trial of ten former Einsatzkommando members, the first major prosecution of former Nazi personnel to take place under West German jurisdiction.[32] The case itself came about through the chance discovery of former *SS-Oberführer* Bernhard Fischer-Schweder, head of an Einsatzkommando unit responsible for the mass murder of hundreds of thousands of Jews and Communists along the Lithuanian border in 1941. Subsequent investigations unearthed nine more members of his unit, all of whom had been living quietly in West Germany, holding respectable jobs as lawyers, salesmen, policemen or, in one case, an optician.[33]

The resultant trial was reported faithfully in the West German press, enabling people to learn more about the crimes committed along the Eastern Front, and the vast scale of the Nazi machinery for mass murder. Indeed, in relaying details from the trial, many newspapers behaved as if this was the first occasion that they had heard of the killing squads, despite the fact that the Americans had conducted their own proceedings against twenty-four Einsatzgruppen personnel between 1947 and 1948. The Coburg-based *Neue Presse* endeavoured to explain this discrepancy:

> when most of us were first acquainted with the terrible atrocities ... they seemed incredible to us. Unfortunately, it was enemy soldiers and offices that had to show us the crimes which were committed by our government in our name. Today, no one can say anymore: 'I don't believe all that!' Today the executioners and murders ... are judged before German courts. German judges attempt to judge crimes of a satanic regime with the standards of democracy.... [34]

This, then, was something that could no longer be dismissed as 'victors' justice'. Observers within the British embassy agreed that 'the fact that the trials are carried out by German courts in a fair and impartial manner undoubtedly gives the verdicts more validity in German eyes than those of the Allied war crimes trials', yet noted that the reaction of most members of the public continued to be one of 'personal dissociation'.[35]

There was, however, considerable emotion as it emerged that the victims of the mass shootings had included the elderly as well as women and children, and bewilderment when the defendants appeared as 'more of less harmless-looking men'.[36] The *Süddeutsche Zeitung*, comparing the charges listed in the indictment to the sight of the grey-haired or balding middle-aged figures in the dock, declared, 'their faces do not fit their crimes'.[37] The fact that such 'monsters' had been able to live undetected for so long generated a widespread sense of shock, anger and dismay. References to 'the murderers among us' were quickly taken up by the West German press, with one publication stating firmly, 'one can only draw a line under the past if one can say, with confidence, that all or at least the predominant part of the concentration camp criminals are punished'.[38] Dick de Mildt argues that it is in this connection that the real impact of the 1958 Einsatzkommando trial can be seen, for, 'at one stroke, the Ulm trial painfully brought to light the poor quality of Germany's dealing with its past crimes, particularly with regard to their prosecution'.[39] Peter Steinbach agrees, seeing the Ulm case as convincing politicians and civilians alike of the need for an urgent, systematic examination of all Nazi crimes.[40] Consequently, the Zentralstelle was established in Ludwigsburg to coordinate investigations into suspected war criminals, and a new wave of war crimes trials began. However, although contemporary opinion polls revealed a 54 per cent approval rating for renewed proceedings, the popular enthusiasm fostered by the Ulm case proved unsustainable.[41] Critics of the Zentralstelle dismissed it as a second, unnecessary denazification process, and older mythologies continued to hold sway.[42]

Popular responses to war crimes trials

The two most high profile war crimes cases of the 1960s were the prosecution of Adolf Eichmann in Jerusalem in 1961, and that of former Auschwitz staff in Frankfurt between 1963 and 1965. Both have been routinely credited with effecting a shift in popular West German attitudes to the past and for increasing public awareness about the Holocaust. The Eichmann trial, detailing the deportations to the extermination camps, was the first time that the specific plight of the Jews had been at the centre of a war crimes trial. The fact that it was held in Israel obviously helped to underscore this further, while the extensive use of survivor testimony enabled the story of the Holocaust to be described in a vivid and dramatic manner. The Frankfurt Auschwitz trial, meanwhile, was significant for being staged within West Germany itself. It covered a range of crimes perpetrated within the camp, with particular emphasis on the behaviour of medical personnel and the various forms of torture that some of the defendants had devised for their victims.

On the surface, both cases seemed to have a significant public impact, generating intense media coverage. Yet neither trial managed to make the front page headline within the West German press; even the local Frankfurt newspapers tended to relegate the Auschwitz hearings to the inside pages.[43] The style of the coverage can also be seen as working against any critical self-reflection on the past. During the Auschwitz trial, for example, the *Frankfurter Allgemeine Zeitung* ran a series of sensationalist and macabre headlines declaring 'A Mountain of Children's Bodies' or '25,000 Murdered in 24 Hours'.[44] Rebecca Wittmann suggests that such headlines constituted 'a pornography of the Holocaust, that both sold papers and distanced the general public from the monsters on the stand whose actions were reported in graphic detail'.[45] As a result, she argues, 'the public felt a lack of interest in the trial and its possible lessons' as it didn't seem to apply to them.

The Eichmann trial, meanwhile, had been greeted with a certain amount of introspection in 1961. In the run up to the proceedings, Chancellor Adenauer expressed 'a certain amount of concern as to the effect…on opinion about us Germans as a whole' and, drawing upon the standard narratives of German victimhood, urged the world to remember that Nazism had 'committed just the same crimes against Germans as Eichmann did against the Jews'.[46] Keen to present a favourable impression of the FRG to international community, Adenauer was also quick to emphasize examples of philo-Semitism and the signing of the Reparations Treaty with Israel in 1952. In West Berlin, Mayor Willy Brandt also took care to distinguish between the FRG and the Germany of old, declaring, 'the people of the world must know and be told that Adolf Eichmann does not reflect the thinking of the German people. The crimes he committed do not reflect the basic tenets of the German Federal Republic.... A new Germany desiring to live in a democratic community has been born and lives in the hearts of the greatest majority of my people.'[47] Anticipating the uncomfortable months ahead, the liberal newspaper *Die Zeit* informed its readership that 'Eichmann is an inescapable fact. He stands for our past, which we will have to accept with as much decency, honesty and dignity as we can muster'.[48]

Opinion poll data and readers' letters to the West German newspapers offer some insight into the responses of the 'ordinary' population to these war crimes trials. These ranged from a genuine engagement with the proceedings and a demand to learn more about the Holocaust, to continued attempts to relativize Nazi atrocities. Some wrote to express their sorrow for what happened, or to advocate the harshest possible punishments for the defendants. Others, particularly during the Eichmann case, questioned the validity of such proceedings. In each case, a sense of trial fatigue soon set in. In 1961, the sheer scale of the media attention actually appeared to work against public interest. During the very first month of proceedings, an observer for the *New York Times* noted, 'there is only one emotion that practically all Germans share about the trial, the wish that it was done and finished with'.[49] The Frankfurt Auschwitz trial, lasting for two years, produced similar results. Despite having room for sixty observers, the public gallery within the courtroom remained relatively empty, with local school trips being its chief visitors.

In August 1961, a survey of 2,000 West Germans conducted by the Allensbach Institut für Demoskopie found 72 per cent of those questioned agreed that 'people like Eichmann' had to be punished. Fifty-one per cent of respondents, though, remained concerned as to the effect renewed war crimes proceedings would have upon the FRG's reputation abroad. Against the backdrop of the construction of the Berlin Wall, 61 per cent also argued that 'what the communists do today is just as bad as, or even worse than, what Eichmann is accused of'. German victimhood was invoked further when 59 per cent agreed with the statement that 'one has to consider that many people suffered and died during this time, and not just in the concentration camps'.[50] More than half of those questioned expressed their hope that the trials could soon come to an end so that people might finally be able to move on from the past.

Both trials, however, did enjoy a wider, cultural resonance in the FRG. In 1961 in Munich, for example, a public exhibition was organized with documents and photographs explaining Eichmann's role within the Nazi hierarchy.[51] During the course of the Auschwitz trial, Frankfurt similarly played host to two exhibitions on the Holocaust: between November 1963 and January 1964 there was a documentation of the history of the Warsaw Ghetto, and between November and December 1964 there was a display on Auschwitz itself. The latter even included photographs taken from the ongoing trial. Both proved a tremendous success with some 61,000 visitors attending the Warsaw Ghetto exhibition, and 88,000 people flocking to that on Auschwitz.[52] Elsewhere, the city of Cologne produced its extensive *Monumenta Judaica: 2000 Years of Jewish History and Culture along the Rhine*, an exhibition that examined the political, social and economic history of the Jews in Germany, Jewish contributions to art, science and literature, and Jewish religious practices in the Rhineland.[53] *Monumenta Judaica* attracted 67,000 visitors within its first five months of opening alone – an average of 4,200 people a week. Some days saw a total of twenty-five guided tours around the display and the accompanying guidebook had to be reprinted to meet the unprecedented demand.[54]

The end of the Auschwitz trial in 1965 also saw the launch of Peter Weiss's play, *The Investigation*. The author had personally attended the daily courtroom sessions in Frankfurt and the resultant script was based upon actual dialogue spoken by the defendants and witnesses. On 19 October 1965, the play was performed simultaneously on twelve stages across the country free of charge and broadcast on the radio, enabling its message to reach a much wider audience.[55] One year after the Auschwitz case, Frankfurt returned to the topic of the Holocaust with a series of school and public lectures given by survivor and trial commentator Hermann Langbein. These events were part of a wider state programme for political and cultural education and appeared to demonstrate a generational divide within West German society. It was observed that older people who attended the sessions frequently drew upon the popular apologia of the early postwar period in their responses to Langbein, while younger West Germans repeatedly questioned how such crimes could ever have been possible, and what could be done to prevent their recurrence in the future.[56]

By contrast, other war crimes trials conducted during this period saw locals rallying around the accused. During the Cologne Sachsenhausen trial between October 1964 and May 1965, for instance, the chief defendant Otto Kaiser enjoyed a public display of support from his friends, neighbours and colleagues. This loyal band even presented a petition to the court in which they insisted Kaiser was a 'highly respectable, brave, hardworking and reliable man'.[57] Although this was not enough to prevent Kaiser from eventually receiving a fifteen-year prison sentence, it was an action curiously reminiscent of the support shown for war criminals amid the amnesty campaigns of the 1950s.

The prosecution of former Buchenwald guard Martin Sommer in Bayreuth in 1958, meanwhile, offers an intriguing counterbalance to the more usual accounts of trial fatigue. Sommer's case attracted immense public interest, with crowds gathering daily outside the court to heckle the accused. Inside, the public gallery was routinely filled to the last space. In part, this reaction stemmed from the fact that the majority of his victims had been political opponents interned in the concentration camp. This, then, was a trial that could enable people to reflect upon both German suffering, and the courage of those who dared to resist Nazism. But there was also an additional source of fascination in the form of Sommer's wife, a woman who had married him after the war and now proceeded to 'stand by her man'. Her detached demeanour within the court as witnesses described the systematic abuse they had endured at her husband's hands attracted an array of public criticism, especially within the tabloid press. Indeed, the public backlash against Frau Sommer was so intense that she was dismissed from her job as a hospital nurse, despite the fact that she was not the one under indictment.[58]

The war crimes problem

Those seeking to bring former Nazi war criminals to account faced a number of challenges. First of all, simply finding suspects could be a tricky matter. Some had fled abroad, some had changed their names and some were now deceased. Extradition processes from other countries could be protracted. Evidence was not always complete or accessible and, where there were documents, their significance was not always understood. As time went on, there was the added problem of ageing defendants and witnesses. Health problems could enable a suspect to evade justice, while failing memories sometimes made it difficult to confirm an individual's identity.

An additional problem for the FRG during the 1960s and 1970s was posed by the statute of limitations. Under the West German penal code, there was a period of fifteen years to initiate investigations into cases of manslaughter, and a twenty-year deadline for murder cases. The start date for the statute of limitations was deemed to count down from the end of the war in May 1945. Thus, the limit for manslaughter cases would run out in May 1960, and that for murder in May 1965. Prosecutors had to launch their investigations before the limitation period ran out but, once these were under way, the clock would stop and the case could be heard for as long as necessary. This tight timeframe, then, also helps to explain the resurgence of war crimes investigations at the turn of the decade.

During the 1960s, the West German government faced three choices regarding the prosecution of Nazi perpetrators. It could uphold the Basic Law and allow the Statute to come into effect, thereby bringing an end to war crimes investigations; or it could vote to extend it, granting prosecutors additional time to gather evidence and initiate proceedings against remaining suspects. Alternatively, the Statute could be abolished altogether, enabling war crimes trials to continue unimpeded for as long as necessary. It would become an issue of intense parliamentary debate in West Germany. Members of the Bundestag were allowed a free vote on the

Statute in the spring of 1965. Opinion was split between and within political parties. Broadly speaking, though, the conservative CDU tended to argue that prosecutors had now had sufficient time to bring suspects to account and the Statute should therefore be allowed to come into effect. The FDP also wanted to uphold the Statute, maintaining that any other move would undermine public faith in the rule of law. The SPD, though, generally agreed with survivors' groups that the magnitude of Nazi crimes must override other concerns, that the original criminal code had been drawn up to deal with crimes committed in 'everyday' circumstances rather than a racial war of extermination, and that investigations into those responsible should thus continue.[59]

In October 1963, the IfD found that just 34 per cent of people questioned approved of continued trials.[60] In May 1965, as parliamentary debates over the Statute reached fever pitch, pollsters again took to the streets to gauge public feeling on the matter. Three hundred and forty-four people over the age of twenty-one were interviewed across the Federal Republic, with the results showing 32 per cent in favour of further trials and 57 per cent preferring to draw a final line (*Schlußstrich*) under the whole Nazi era.[61]

The apparent reluctance to challenge the Statute of Limitations stemmed from a variety of concerns. There were legitimate questions over the possibility of securing a successful conviction so long after the event, given the fragility of witness memories. It could also be argued that continued trials served no social purpose; the perpetrators of Nazi crimes had long since been reintegrated into the fabric of West German society.[62] Furthermore, there were genuine concerns about the legality of making any alterations to the Statute. Recalling the subversion of the legal system during the Third Reich, many critics were wary about any further potential threat to civil liberties and the rule of law. Leading representatives of the FRG also downplayed the number of Nazi war criminals that remained at large, arguing that the statute would only benefit a minority of people. In 1965, as the deadline for war crimes investigations loomed ever closer, the Justice Minister, Ewald Bucher, similarly refuted the need to make any adjustments to West Germany's legal framework, arguing, 'we must be prepared if necessary to live with a few murderers'.[63]

Debates over the statute also revealed the persistence of apologetic narratives of the past. In the IfD's 1965 survey, two-thirds of those opposed to further trials based their conviction on the simple refrain that other war crimes had been committed and gone unpunished. Even when people did voice support for changing the Statute, their reasoning was based primarily on the potential damage that could be done to the nation's reputation if war crimes trials were to be wrapped up.

In March 1965, after prolonged parliamentary discussions, the Bundestag agreed on a compromise, voting 344 to 96 to extend the Statute of Limitations to 31 December 1969. This meant the clock would effectively be reset to start its twenty-year countdown from the moment of the Federal Republic's formation in 1949, rather than the war's end in 1945, thereby giving prosecutors an additional four years to launch their investigations. The justification for this move was that the courts had been in no position to operate properly amid the upheaval of the immediate postwar era.

Over the next four years, the West German courts continued to document the Holocaust in increasing detail. Over 120 cases were heard between May 1965 and May 1969, encompassing a range of Nazi atrocities from the mass shootings committed by police battalions and Einsatzgruppen along the Eastern Front, to crimes perpetrated within specific camps such as Flossenbürg, Mauthausen and Auschwitz.[64] At the same time, though, debates over the statute of limitations had led to legal discussions as to just what, exactly, constituted an act of murder. According to Article 50, Paragraph 2 of the West German Penal Code, the maximum penalty facing those convicted of being an accessory to murder was likely to be the same as that for the main offender. In autumn 1968, however, amid large-scale investigations into the administrative personnel of the RSHA, this article was amended. Now, if the court could only punish murderers if it was satisfied he or she had acted out of 'base motives' such as greed, revenge or blood lust. Without this motivation, the highest penalty that the defendant could receive would be equal to the fifteen-year prison sentence awarded in manslaughter cases – and the statute of limitations for investigations into these sets of crimes had already come into effect back in May 1960. With prosecutors out of time to begin investigations into these perpetrators, many 'desk murderers', together with those who simply claimed to have been following orders, could thus evade justice. As a result of this ruling, the emphasis remained on a radical few, the so-called 'excess perpetrators' who killed out of a lust for blood – characters that could be rendered quite distinct from the ordinary population. In the process, the vital role of middle-class professionals in the development of the Holocaust continued to be obscured.[65]

On 26 June 1969, the Bundestag again voted to extend the Statute, this time for an additional ten years. Two hundred and seventy-nine members supported the bill, 126 opposed it and there were four abstentions. A decade later, the vote was much closer, yet finally, on 3 July 1979, the application to remove the Statute for all cases of murder was passed after a ten-hour parliamentary debate, 255 votes to 222.[66] The path was now free for West German prosecutors to continue their work in relation to the crimes of National Socialism. Why the change of heart? Clearly, the increased opposition vote between 1969 and 1979 demonstrates that the problem of Nazi war criminals remained highly contentious; public opinion too was shown as increasingly opposed to further legal proceedings.[67] To some extent, the answer has to rest with broader cultural developments taking place at this time, particularly the screening of the American television miniseries, *Holocaust*, in the spring of 1979. That broadcast, as we will see in Chapter 7, provoked a tremendous emotional response from the West German population, helping them identify with the victims of Nazi persecution as never before.[68]

Conclusion

The problem of what to do with Nazi war criminals remained a contentious issue throughout the postwar period. When prompted, most West Germans readily agreed with the need for judicial proceedings to bring those responsible for the Holocaust to account. There was a keen awareness that the rest of the world was keeping an eye on the FRG and that any apparent attempt to sweep the past under the carpet could harm the country's fragile reputation. It would also play all too easily into the hands of Communist agitators in the GDR.

The trials themselves had the potential to generate intense emotion, excitement and moments of high drama. They could become talking points within the German media and in the Bundestag, and prompt a range of commemorative activities at the grassroots level of society. The greatest interest was, perhaps, reserved for those cases where the public could easily identify with the victims, with the Sommer case attracting far more public attention with its depiction of Buchenwald than trials dealing with faraway killing centres and non-German victims. At times, though, the sheer length of the proceedings (and, indeed, the number of trials taking place) could work against any sustained public engagement. It is also notable that war crimes trials were almost always accompanied by a sense of shock at the 'revelations' that emerged over the course of trial testimony. There was thus a seemingly endless cycle of horror and outrage being expressed in response to Nazi crimes, followed by a period of flagging interest until the next incident came along to jolt people out of their indifference.

Thanks to the abolition of the statute for limitations in 1979, war crimes investigations can, and do, persist in Germany to this day. In May 2011, following a lengthy extradition process and various medical examinations, John Demjanjuk was convicted of being an accessory to the murder of 28,060 Jews at Sobibor extermination camp. Heralded at the time as the 'last Nazi war crimes trial in Germany, if not the world', the case highlighted the difficulties in bringing remaining perpetrators to account and set a new precedent in terms of the reduced burden of proof required for convictions.[69] Demjanjuk was sentenced to five years' imprisonment but the judge released him into the care of a nursing home in the spa town of Bad Feilnbach. At the time, many local residents expressed their unhappiness that this popular tourist location should come to be associated with such a notorious figure, a number of would-be guests changed their holiday plans while others protested, perhaps a little too much, that his presence did not bother them.[70]

In spring 2013, meanwhile, it was announced that fifty former Auschwitz guards would stand trial in Germany for their role in the Holocaust.[71] In July that same year, the Simon Wiesenthal Institute launched a poster campaign in Berlin, Hamburg and Cologne with the slogan, 'late, but not too late', appealing for the public's help in identifying and tracing any remaining Nazi war criminals, especially former extermination camp personnel and remaining members of the Einsatzgruppen.[72] In each case the message was the same: the passage of time has not diminished the guilt of these perpetrators, and that old age should not be a barrier to their prosecution.

5

The German Churches and the Holocaust

In recent years, numerous German institutions have been subjected to scholarly scrutiny over their relationship with the Nazi regime. We now have a significant canon of literature on the Wehrmacht's complicity in mass shootings along the Eastern Front during the Second World War, and the role of big business in funding NSDAP campaigns and exploiting slave labour during the Holocaust.[1] However, the behaviour of the Catholic and Protestant churches – the only institutions to emerge intact after the Third Reich – is perhaps even more intriguing. While remaining remote from the actual killing process, the churches nonetheless played a facilitating role in the Nazi persecution of the Jews. Centuries of anti-Judaism within Christian teachings fed into anti-Semitism and helped the Nazis to find theological justification for their actions. Members of the clergy could also provide solace to individual perpetrators, helping them to ease their conscience over their violent deeds. Significantly, the churches also retained an institutional silence on Nazi racial policy, despite receiving numerous wartime reports on the atrocities and despite having what one might see as a special moral responsibility – or Christian duty – to condemn acts of hatred, discrimination and murder. As a result, the leadership of both denominations has received much criticism. Scholars such as Michael Phayer, Hannah Holtschneider and Matthew Hockenos have analysed the ways in which the church sought to rebuild relations with the Jewish community after the war, revise Christian interpretations of Judaism and make some effort to atone for the past.[2] The slow pace of these developments has, in itself, offered some valuable insights into Germany's Vergangenheitsbewältigung and, as this chapter will illustrate, the churches' responses to the recent past echoed the victimhood and resistance myths circulating within wider German society at this time. Focussing particularly on the period 1945–50, this chapter looks at early protestations of guilt, Christian aid to Holocaust survivors and the ways in which church leaders intervened within wider public discussions on denazification and war crimes investigations.

The churches during the Third Reich

In 1933, the vast majority of Germans were Christian; Jews accounted for less than 1 per cent of the population. The largest Protestant Church was the German Evangelical Church (EKD) with around 40 million members and twenty-seven regional churches. At this point, religious affiliation corresponded broadly to regional divides, with Protestants concentrated in northern states such as East Prussia and Schleswig-Holstein, and Catholics in areas such as the Rhineland, Bavaria and Upper Silesia. After the war, division, coupled with the influx of refugees from Eastern Europe, would create a greater mix of religious communities. The core of NSDAP electoral support at the start of the 1930s came from the Protestant areas of the country. German Catholics, who had already endured Bismarck's attempts to curb their influence in the *Kulturkampf* (cultural struggle) of the 1870s, were traditionally represented by the *Zentrum* or Catholic Centre Party. However, many leaders within both denominations welcomed the rise of Hitler, sharing in the popular nationalism of the period as well as the frustration with the prevailing political and economic situation. Point 24 of the NSDAP's 1920 programme also served to reassure voters that the Nazis would protect traditional Christian values. Pledging to respect the 'freedom of all religious confessions', the Nazis spoke of a 'positive Christianity' that would help restore Germany to greatness.[3]

During the Third Reich, the Nazis routinely borrowed elements from Christian and Pagan traditions in an effort to forge National Socialism into the new religion for the masses. Fete days were appropriated for the celebration of the Volksgemeinschaft (People's Community) and Hitler himself was frequently depicted as a Messianic figure within Party propaganda.[4] Although postwar church representations of this period would accentuate a history of repression by the Nazi state, it is clear that many church figures were keen to align themselves to the Nazi movement. Kevin Spicer, for example, has explored the attitudes of the so-called 'brown priests' among the Catholic clergy in Freiburg, noting that some willingly joined the NSDAP or even the SS.[5]

Elsewhere, the German Christian movement was a Protestant faction that supported the notion of a national 'Reich Church' and embraced much of the regime's ideological rhetoric.[6] Christopher Probst, for instance, has explored the ways in which some Protestants looked back to sixteenth-century texts on Judaism to try and justify anti-Semitic measures under Nazism.[7] In 1936, there was even an outcry when the regime tried to prevent Protestants from using the swastika on altars and church newspapers.[8] Admittedly, not everyone shared this approach and there were individual leaders in both the Catholic and Protestant churches who did oppose Nazism at great personal risk to themselves, whether it be denouncing government policy through their sermons or helping to hide Jews and other persecuted minorities. In 1934, for example, a group of Protestant church leaders broke away to form the Confessing Church in opposition to the German Christian movement. In its founding document, the Barmen Confession of Faith, this group rejected the idea that Hitler, as Führer, could supplant God in their allegiance.[9] Two key members of the Confessing Church were Dietrich Bonhoeffer and Martin Niemöller; both would be arrested and imprisoned by the regime and could thus be held up as powerful resistance symbols after the war. Bonhoeffer, who was executed in Flossenbürg concentration camp in April 1945, would be much-mythologized as a heroic martyr, inspiring several films and plays on his life story and the naming of numerous streets and public buildings in his honour. Examples of Catholic opposition, meanwhile, can be seen in the efforts of Berlin bishops to coordinate a protest against Nazi violence in the wake of the 1938 Kristallnacht pogrom, and the establishment of a welfare office in the German capital to provide food and clothing for victims of Nazi persecution – including Jews. One of those involved in this programme was social worker Margarete Sommer, who also attempted to document the deportations and conditions in the concentration camps. During the war, she produced several reports on Nazi atrocities and urged the Catholic Church to take action.[10]

Neither of the German churches, however, made any official, institutional censure of the Nazi state. Instead, the Church's priority seemed to be on trying to preserve the status quo, defending themselves against state incursions and avoiding action that might provoke reprisals against members of their congregation. As such, when Pope Pius XI issued his circular, *Mit brennender Sorge* ('With burning anxiety') in March 1937, it was focussed primarily on the harsh treatment currently being meted out to German Catholics, accusing the Nazis of violating the 1933 Concordat with Rome in which they had promised to respect the rights of Catholics.[11] Contemporary reports compiled by the district police and the Nazi security service, the SD, reveal the regime's own anxiety about the churches' hold over the masses and their potential to become powerful beacons of resistance activity. In June 1939, for example, police in northern Bavaria noted, 'the more attempts are made to keep a watch on the [Catholic] Church ... the more the peasantry support their priests .... For the time being, the Party's propaganda is helpless in trying to resist this.'[12] Certainly, there were examples where the population was galvanized into successful acts of protest during the Third Reich. In Oldenburg in 1936, there was a popular backlash against the regime's plans to remove crucifixes from schools.[13] In 1941, Bishop von Galen made a fiery speech against the 'euthanasia' programme, copies of which were circulated among the population.[14] In both cases the regime publically backed down (although 'euthanasia' continued to be practiced in secret within the concentration camps). Fearful of upsetting public morale during wartime, the regime was also wary of taking serious action against von Galen personally for his sermon. Officials within the Party Chancellery noted: 'Dr. Goebbels ... was ... afraid that if any action was taken against the bishop, the population of Münster could be written off for the duration of the war, and for that matter the whole of Westphalia'.[15] Such moments of opposition, though, were confined to incidences where the rights of ordinary German Christians were being directly impinged.

Statements of responsibility

In the aftermath of the Second World War, German church leaders had to contend with their own silence as well as the fact that ordinary Christians had been complicit in the crimes of the Third Reich; the perpetrators of the Holocaust were not ungodly monsters but people who, for the most part, had been educated in the Christian faith. Early postwar statements drew upon Biblical parables and the conventional Christian vocabulary of sin as clergy retreated into familiar texts to try and make sense of what had happened. During this period, there was a lot of pressure on the churches to do and say the right things. The Allies were looking to them for evidence of a 'better Germany', a group that could offer moral guidance to the people and ease the nation's 're-civilization' after Nazism. Expressions of sorrow, contrition and collective responsibility would aid postwar recovery and help the churches reclaim their positions of influence. Ordinary Germans, meanwhile, were also turning to the churches for both emotional support and material assistance as they tried to rebuild their shattered lives. They wanted to hear messages of hope, not another lecture in wholesale German guilt. The church leadership therefore had to maintain a tricky balancing act between appeasing foreign opinion and reassuring the domestic population that they had their best interests at heart. A series of public statements between 1945 and 1949 thus wavered between a frank discussion of the Nazi past, and efforts to exculpate the church's own difficult legacy.

In the summer of 1945, individual churchmen did utter critical indictments of the levels of popular consensus behind the Third Reich. In June 1945, for instance, the Catholic Bishop of Mainz, Albert Stohr, attacked the German people for not rejecting extremism. In Rottenburg, Bishop Sproll likewise criticized those members of the population who now protested their ignorance of Nazi crimes. These same people, he argued, would have been only too keen to boast of these deeds if Germany had won the war.[16] In August 1945, German Protestant leaders gathered for a conference in Treysa. The resultant 'Message to the Congregations' offered the following 'confession':

> Long before God spoke in anger, He sought us with the Word of His love and we did not listen. Long before our churches became piles of rubble, our pulpits were restricted and our prayers were silenced. Shepherds allowed their flocks to languish, and congregations deserted their pastors. Long before the sham government of our land collapsed, justice had been thwarted. Long before men were murdered, human beings had become mere numbers and human life trivialized. When a man's life becomes worthless, he thinks nothing of taking human life.[17]

In this statement, the EKD interpreted the horrors of the Third Reich as the consequences of people elevating a political figure above God. Christianity itself is not criticized; instead it is modern secularization and the people's failure to adhere to the central tenets of their faith that has brought destruction. The church leadership is critiqued only insofar as they allowed their congregation to be led astray. Even here, though, the blame is actually being placed elsewhere. A later passage in this document comments, 'our people were separated from the church. The public was no longer allowed to hear its words; no one heard what it preached.'[18] Here, then, is an emphasis on Nazi terror and repression; the church was left almost powerless to intervene and save the population. Hockenos further underscores the limits of the EKD's message by drawing attention to the fact that the inclusive terminology at the start of this statement – 'our churches', 'our pulpits' – quickly disappears, leaving the identity of those doing the murdering anonymous.[19] Thus, it is implied that those responsible for reducing the country to this terrible state came from somewhere else, outside of the church. Similarly, the use of the word 'sham' in the above extract conjures up the idea of National Socialism as being just a big illusion. References to misleading propaganda and false promises were a typical trope of postwar explanations for previous levels of support for the NSDAP. The population, it was routinely argued, had been 'duped'; the EKD's statement is part of this apologetic rhetoric.

At the same time, the EKD also sought to highlight the existence of Protestant resistance against the Nazi regime, noting that 'when the church took its responsibility seriously, it reminded the population of God's commandments and minced no words when it condemned concentration camps, mistreatment and murder of Jews and the sick, and sought to protect youth from the seduction of National Socialist propaganda'.[20] Unfortunately, the aforementioned isolation of the Church meant that these enjoinders failed to reach people. The statement made no mention of the internal divisions between the German Christians, the Confessing Church and all those in between who hoped to save the church from self-destruction. Instead, the Confessing Church was held up in the Treysa Message and other postwar statements as the alibi for all Protestants, exaggerating the scale of church resistance, ignoring institutional silences and enabling former members of the German Christians to retain their posts without too many awkward questions. Consequently, the Treysa document was more about celebrating the church's liberation from Nazism than an effort to confront the recent past. References to the church as having now 'lost its fetters' were accompanied by calls to renew church life and look to the future.

That same month, the first postwar gathering of German Catholic bishops led to the publication of the so-called Fulda Letter. As with the EKD's Message to the Congregations, the latter part of this document focussed on the need for a fresh start and the restoration of Christian values in Germany, but it began by thanking the congregation for its loyalty through 'difficult times', stating:

> We know that for many of you it had not been without danger to listen again and again to our episcopal pronouncements, which spoke out against the errors and crimes of our times. With deep interest and inner sympathy, millions and millions have followed our remarks, when we upheld the rights of the person, when we rejected the interference of the State with Church life, when we spoke of the unheard-of oppression by State and party in all spheres of spiritual and religious life, when we raised our voice against racial arrogance and hatred of other nations. We know well that informers were ready everywhere to hinder you in your progress and in your career once it had been discovered that you had listened to such sermons.[21]

Here was a narrative of Catholic loyalty, adherence to Christian values at great personal risk to oneself and, once again, that of widespread church resistance to National Socialism. The Fulda Letter depicted the Catholic Church as an institution that had regularly spoken out against Nazism, quietly omitting the fact that such pronouncements had usually been the preserve of a few individuals like von Galen, or else concerned much more with the Nazi oppression of Christians than the victims of racial policy. Elsewhere, the bishops expressed their gratitude to Christian parents for helping to protect Catholic schools, young people for standing up for ideals and priests and laity for defending Church law; the repetition of the word 'thank' throughout this statement equating to a message of deliverance from evil. The overall tone of the letter is one of self-congratulation, giving German Catholics a positive and comforting narrative of the recent past. When an implicit reference to the persecution of the Jews was made in a subsequent passage of the document, the emphasis again rested with the brave Christians who had tried to save them, rather than the Jewish victims themselves:

> how it warms our hearts to remember that time and again Catholics of all walks of life and of all ages were not afraid to protect fellow Germans of another race, to defend them and to show them Christian charity. Many perished in concentration camps because of such charity.[22]

For all of these criticisms, though, the Fulda Letter was notable in that the bishops did admit a widespread responsibility for the crimes of the Third Reich – and that people 'even of our own ranks' aided and abetted these deeds. Coming close to admitting the failings of the Church leadership, the bishops conceded that

> a grave responsibility rests upon those who, because of their position, could have known what was going on in our midst; who because of their influence could have prevented such crimes and have not done so and even made them possible, thereby manifesting their solidarity with the criminals.[23]

The failure to define, precisely, who these people were, though, still enabled some sense of distance to be maintained between these characters and the Church itself. The document also took care to consider why such people may have failed to act, stressing their lack of freedom to manoeuvre and their ignorance of the regime's actions. As with the EKD message from Treysa, there also remained an emphasis on state terror with references to the imprisonment and mistreatment of those priests who did dare to speak out. References to people being 'misled' by Nazi propaganda appeared again too, along with the excuse that people had been forced to join the NSDAP. Ultimately, both the Tresya statement and the Fulda Letter were characterized by apologia and self-justification. The Catholic bishops concluded that guilt rests with individuals rather than institutions and should be measured accordingly. This was, effectively, an attempt to shut down the question of collective guilt.

For both Catholics and Protestants, the very notion of expressing 'guilt' or 'repentance' for the past was bound up in theological traditions. However, earlier tensions and splits within the EKD did not magically heal themselves after 1945. As Matthew Hockenos has detailed, the EKD remained broadly divided between conservative Protestants such as Otto Dibelius, Theophil Wurm and Hans Meiser – nationalists who wanted to restore the Church to its pre-1933 position – and reformers, many of whom had been members of the Confessing Church, who wanted a thorough restructuring of the Church and its teachings.[24] The conservative Protestants rejected the premise of collective guilt, arguing that confession was a private matter between an individual and God. In their eyes, any 'confession' made by the Church as an institution would therefore be inappropriate. Reformers such as Martin Niemöller, however, insisted that the Church as a whole had been guilty of inaction during the Third Reich and should admit this publicly. Indeed, the Tresya Message to the Congregations needs to be seen as an initial compromise between these two factions. Behind that public image of church unity, the EKD conference had heard other, reforming members urging a far more critical confrontation with the recent past. Their Message to the Pastors in August 1945 stated, 'we confess our guilt and bow under the burden of its consequences'.[25] It emphasized collective responsibility as well as the sheer difficulty of articulating an adequate response to Nazi atrocities. Using terms such as 'demonic' and 'apocalyptic', the Message to the Pastors insisted that 'moral standards are inadequate to measure the greatness of the guilt that our people have assumed'.[26]

The question of German guilt was contentious, dividing church leaders and the general population. Many German Catholics, for example, took issue with the Fulda Letter, arguing that the bishops needed to do *more* to acknowledge the widespread guilt and responsibility that the community bore for the crimes of the Third Reich. The Austrian writer, Ida Friedrich Gorres, published an open letter in which she critiqued both the Church's failure to respond to wartime atrocities, and its apparent postwar triumphalism at having survived Hitler.[27] Michael Phayer argues that it was really only after 1959, though, that German Catholic bishops began to speak more openly – a shift prompted by the death of Pope Pius XII, the new wave of West German war crimes trials, political scandals concerning former Nazis, and a new generation of postwar appointees to the bishopric.[28]

German Protestants, meanwhile, were enraged by the EKD's Declaration of Guilt in October 1945. European church leaders had travelled to meet with the EKD leadership in Stuttgart in an effort to promote international reconciliation after the Second World War. Their presence, arguably combined with an awareness that the Tresya Message had not gone far enough, prompted a fresh statement from the Protestant leaders:

> Through us, infinite wrong was brought over many peoples and countries.... We did fight for long years in the name of Jesus Christ against the mentality that found its awful expression in the National Socialist regime of violence; but we accuse ourselves for not standing to our beliefs more courageously, for not praying more faithfully, for not believing more joyously, and for not loving more ardently.[29]

In this statement, the churches were clearly keen to reassure their European brethren – and the Allied occupation authorities – that they did not pose a threat to the postwar order. In particular, the church leadership was anxious to protect itself from any further external interference. Consequently, the role of resistance against the Third Reich was accentuated and the rhetoric of a thorough soul-searching was adopted. Yet while these words may have played well to a foreign audience, the Stuttgart Declaration was not universally popular in Germany. Instead, the EKD's apparent confession provoked memories of the hated War Guilt Clause of the Treaty of Versailles at the end of the First World War. There was concern that any admission of 'collective guilt' would only legitimize Allied reprisals and the demanding of heavy reparations. Drawing upon a series of letters penned by members of the public, Hockenos notes that there was a greater preference among the general population to focus on the guilt of 'others'. Several writers drew attention to Allied atrocities during the war, and he quotes one man from Frankfurt am Main who argued 'certainly repentance must be urged but we are not the only ones guilty [and] we should not be the only ones to roast on a spit'.[30] A woman from Hann-Münden commented, 'you have in the name of the EKD recognized a guilt, which in no case the German people bear alone'.[31] One Protestant pastor, Hans Asmussen, hit back at such critics, insisting, 'we are not traitors to the Fatherland'. Noting the popular grumbling about victors' justice and German suffering, he added, 'what does the injustice being done to our people today mean for the confession of our guilt? Firstly, it means nothing. It doesn't change in the least the evil that we Germans did in Poland, in Greece, in Holland. It in no way covers up our guilt toward the "non-Aryans". It in no way justifies our silence and cooperation in the evil 12 years.'[32] Niemöller, who had played an integral role in drafting this declaration, received hate mail for his pains. Hockenos notes that part of the problem here was that Niemöller refused to play the role of victim, despite having spent seven years in a concentration camp. Niemöller argued that he was only interned from 1937; even if that experience excused him from having to confront the Nazi legacy, he still had to face up to his actions during the first four years of the Third Reich.[33] Other members of the congregation, however, responded sympathetically to the Declaration. One war widow, who had been a Nazi and then the wife of a pastor within the Confessing Church, commented,

> The Stuttgart Declaration of Guilt impressed me deeply, and I passed it on, even to people who didn't want to accept that guilt. I had been in this conflict since 1933, and that has always made it hard for me. I was simultaneously a party member and a victim of fascism. I think it was much easier to be one or the other. We learned much too late that certain combinations simply aren't possible.[34]

Church reflections on Judaism and the Holocaust

The Stuttgart Declaration consequently sparked some significant public discussion on the recent past, yet the extent of its own engagement with Nazism remained limited and the history of the Church's early support for National Socialism was glossed over. It spoke about National Socialism in very abstract terms; there was no specific mention of the persecution of the Jews or even an effort to define the Nazis' crimes. Explicit discussion of the Holocaust was also missing from Catholic public discourse. Michael Phayer has identified just two examples of German Catholic leaders expressing sorrow during the late 1940s specifically for Jewish suffering: the 1948 statement during the Mainz Katholikentag (Catholics' Day), which referred to crimes against 'the people of Jewish stock', and the on-going efforts of

Cardinal Konrad Preysing to bring attention to the particular persecution of the Jews.[35] The majority of church personnel, however, focussed on their own losses, routinely pointing to examples of Nazi restrictions on the Church and the current plight of Christian refugees who had been forced to flee from their homes in Eastern Europe at the end of the war. In August 1945, Bishop Marahrens of Hannover gave a somewhat unwilling statement about Nazi crimes in which he declared, 'however greatly we may still differ in our faith from the Jews, and *although they have brought a series of serious harm upon our people*, they still shouldn't be attacked in an inhumane fashion'.[36] His words betrayed the persistence of anti-Semitism and concepts of the Jews as 'Other', and echoed some of the scapegoating that had occurred at the end of the First World War, with the Jews blamed for the country's current misfortunes. It is Germany that is being presented as the victim here.

In December 1945, a letter by the Protestant Bishop Theophil Wurm also relativized Nazi crimes amid a critique of Allied occupation policy. He argued, 'the military conquest and occupation of our country was accompanied by the very same acts of violence against the civilian population about which such just complaint has been made in the countries of the Allies'.[37] Speaking of the recent division of Germany, he added, 'to pack the German people into a still more narrow space, to cut off as far as possible the material basis of their very existence, is no different, in essentials, to Hitler's plan to stamp out the existence of the Jewish race'.[38] Reflecting on church statements during the immediate postwar era, Robert Ericksen and Susannah Heschel conclude that 'the German churches were unable to muster even a strong *condemnation* of the murder of the Jews, much less an expression of responsibility for its horrors'.[39]

Reforming members of the EKD, however, continued to press for a critical engagement with Christianity's own historic relationship with the Jews and in 1948, a meeting in Darmstadt of the Council of Brethren of the Protestant Church issued a 'Message Concerning the Jewish Question'. Leaving aside the unfortunate title of this document, which recalled the language used within Nazi discussions on European Jewry, the Darmstadt Declaration showed the church pondering its past errors. It bemoaned the fact that 'the church is not allowed to teach that Jesus is a member of the Jewish people' and urged the Protestant community to take heed of Christianity's 'special relationship' with the Jews. Calling for an end to anti-Semitism, the document also used inclusive terminology in phrases such as 'what we did to the Jews' to demonstrate the Brethren Council's acceptance of a common responsibility.[40]

Building upon the Darmstadt Declaration, the EKD synod in Berlin Weissensee in April 1950 issued a Protestant confession of guilt for anti-Semitism. This event occurred in the wake of a series of desecrations of Jewish cemeteries and against the background of the dedication of a memorial to victims of Nazi racial persecution in the Weissensee

Jewish cemetery on the opening day of the synod. The impact of these contemporary events was evident when the statement included a request for the Christian congregation to help 'protect Jewish graveyards'. As with the Darmstadt Declaration, the Weissensee text called for a rejection of anti-Semitism and recognition of Jesus 'as a person [who] came from the people of Israel'. In reference to the Nazi era, it also accepted that 'by omission and silence we became implicated before the God of mercy in the outrage which has been perpetrated against the Jews by people of our nation'.[41] Hockenos argues that while the synod could have been more explicit in detailing the church's complicity in discrimination against the Jews, and done more to address the centuries of anti-Judaism within Church teachings, this was still a 'momentous' occasion in that it posed the first serious challenge to conventional Christian theology. The Weissensee text also offered a rejoinder to those members of society who continued to relativize Nazi atrocities, stating 'we caution all Christians not to balance what has come upon us as God's judgment against what we have done to the Jews; for in judgment God's mercy searches the repentant'.[42] It is notable, however, that the key figures behind this more self-critical document stemmed from the middle ranks of the EKD, rather than the Protestant leadership.

In general, responses by the German churches during the immediate postwar era remained introspective, focussed on rescuing Christian theology and safeguarding their own status. Early histories and memoirs by church leaders gave an exaggerated account of Christian resistance, with the Protestants emphasizing the actions of the Confessing Church and Catholic bishops depicting a universal image of loyalty to Rome, rather than Hitler. It would take some time before the messages of Darmstadt and Weissensee were developed further; after the initial flurry of statements in the late 1940s, there was a period of relative silence during the 1950s before a more critical literature finally began to emerge during the 1960s and 1970s. Typical of this increased research was John Conway's *The Persecution of the Nazi Churches* (1968), which looked at examples of collaboration between church and state, as well as acknowledging the role of individual resisters at the grassroots of society. In part, this shift was due to a wider development of Holocaust consciousness amid the new wave of war crimes trials, and a new, more critical generation assuming leadership roles within the churches. The death of Pius XII in 1958 and the staging of Rolf Hochhuth's controversial play, *The Deputy*, in West Germany in 1963 also helped fuel new levels of public and academic interest in church behaviour during the Third Reich. Subtitled 'a Christian tragedy', Hochuth's play referenced real-life figures from the Catholic church including Maximilian Kolbe, who sacrificed himself in Auschwitz to save another Catholic; Bernhard Lichtenberg, who was imprisoned after praying for the Jews; and Pope Pius XII. The inclusion of the latter, who was criticized in the play for his silence, became the subject of heated public discussion.[43]

Against this background, the Second Vatican Council of 1965 adopted the 'Declaration on the Relationship of the Church to Non-Christian Religions', known as the *Nostra Aetate* (In Our Age). As with the EKD's Weissensee statement, this document recognized the shared heritage of Christianity and Judaism, rejected anti-Semitism and pushed for interfaith understanding. However, as Randolph Braham points out, it still managed to include negative references to the Jews, demonstrating the difficulties of shaking off the old doctrine. Thus, *Nostra Aetate* still accused some Jews of opposing the spread of the Gospel. It also asserted that many Jews living at the time of Christ had actively pushed for his death, although the document insisted that modern-day Jews should not be held responsible for this.[44] Other key moments within Catholicism's confrontation with the past came with the appointment of John Paul II in 1978 and his official visit to Auschwitz in 1979; and a public statement issued by German Catholic bishops on the fiftieth anniversary of that camp on 27 January 1995. In this text, the bishops expressed regret for the church's failure to speak out against Nazi racial policy and admitted a 'special responsibility' to fight instances of anti-Semitism.[45] On 16 March 1998, the Vatican also issued *We Remember: A Reflection on the Shoah* in which the Pope referred to the Holocaust as 'an indelible stain on the history of the century' and acknowledged the effects of the 'erroneous and unjust interpretations of the New Testament regarding the Jewish people'.[46] Catholics were urged to remember the victims of the Holocaust – yet critics argued that the document still did not go far enough in its condemnation of the past. There remained, they argued, an attempt to distinguish between Christian anti-Judaism and Nazi anti-Semitism, to overstate the strength of Church resistance and to present an overly favourable account of Pius XII's response to the Nazi genocide.[47] Braham agrees that the document is selective in its interpretation of the German Catholic church, preferring to focus its attentions on statements made before Hitler became Chancellor and thereby evading the fact that numerous members of the clergy supported the Nazis' domestic and foreign policies after 1933.[48]

Protestant theology – and the attitudes of individual church leaders – would also be scrutinized heavily. In 1980, for example, Leonore Siegele-Wenschkewitz published her account of Gerhard Kittler, a distinguished Protestant scholar of Judaism who was shown to have entered into discussions on the 'Jewish Question' during the early 1930s. This, in turn, would generate a new wave of literature on the relationship between Christian theology and the Holocaust. Hannah Holtschneider has analysed three key examples of the EKD's own writings on this theme: 'Towards a Renewal of the Relationship of Christians and Jews' (1980); 'About the Misery and Affliction of Theology' (1988); and 'In the Realm of Death there is Life' (1996). These texts typify (belated) postwar efforts to portray Judaism in a positive manner, yet Holtschneider argues that, despite their stated intentions, most Holocaust theologians have still not listened properly to Jewish perspectives.[49]

Restitution, denazification and war crimes trials

Internal church discussions and public pronouncements on Nazism and its impact on Christian theology in the immediate aftermath of the Second World War were accompanied by practical efforts to ease German recovery. Indeed, the churches would play an integral role within Germany's reconstruction, not least with the formation of the Christian Democratic Union of Germany and the Christian Social Union of Bavaria – parties that would become hugely influential in postwar West German politics. In contrast to the silences of the Nazi era, the churches now seemed very willing to speak out and involve themselves in political issues. Key issues in 1945 concerned the restitution payments to victims of Nazi persecution, denazification and the necessity of Allied war crimes proceedings. As the following summary will demonstrate, there could be a significant gulf between institutional expressions of atonement, and the clergy's actual willingness to pursue justice for Holocaust victims in practice.

After the war, German church leaders spoke publicly about the need for restitution to be paid to the victims of National Socialism. During Christmas 1945, 3,000 Marks were collected among German Catholics in Berlin to contribute specifically towards the relief of Jewish suffering and in 1948, the Mainz Katholikentag again reiterated the need for all Catholics to contribute to these welfare campaigns.[50] German bishops declared that there was a moral duty to make donations in order to help right past wrongs. They also presented it as a way to welcome Jewish-converts into the Christian faith and demonstrate the eradication of anti-Semitism from German society.[51] However, as Michael Phayer points out, the scheme was never pursued wholeheartedly; the Vatican did not press the matter and it was left to a few individuals such as Gertrud Luckner, who was attempting to organize a national campaign with the Catholic charity, Caritas, to take the initiative.[52] Again, we actually see a continuity in personnel: those most active in aiding Holocaust victims after the war were the same individuals who had struggled to offer assistance during the Third Reich. Restitution was also made difficult by ordinary Germans who were unwilling to return items of Jewish property and unable to comprehend the experiences of Holocaust survivors. Given that there was already an international relief effort taking place on behalf of the victims of Nazism, rumours circulated that the Jews were among the better off members of society, thereby enabling older stereotypes and prejudices to persist. Even within the church, the primary focus for both Catholic and Protestant relief efforts rested on Jews who had converted to Christianity. The reasoning for this lay with the fact that this was a sector excluded from the international aid agencies. Steven Schroeder notes that the very names of relief organizations such as the Protestant Central Committee of Christian Aid Societies for Racial Persecutees of non-Jewish Faith in Germany distinguished between Christians and Jews. Church correspondence during this period also revealed the persistence of Nazi terms and racial categories, with references to 'non-Aryan Christians', 'Hebrew Christians' and 'Jewish Christians'. Such language, he argues, obstructed the process of reconciliation.[53] Amidst the broader currents of German victimhood, meanwhile, church relief schemes often gave priority to those German Christians who had been expelled from their homes in Eastern Europe at the end of the war. Some churchmen likened their experiences to those of Holocaust victims.[54]

Elsewhere, the churches appeared far more interested in the plight of Nazi perpetrators than their victims as they entered into a growing public criticism of denazification and war crimes trials. Most churchmen had been able to retain their positions after 1945, with the Allies leaving the churches to denazify themselves. Consequently, someone like Siegfried Leffler, who had joined the NSDAP in 1929 and had led the German Christians, was able to become the spokesperson for the Protestant Church in Bavaria.[55] In addition to concealing some of their own indiscretions, Church leaders also helped members of their congregations to evade justice. As we have already seen in Chapter 1, a common way to try and circumvent denazification proceedings was to obtain a character reference, testifying to one's fundamental decency. Churchmen were frequently called upon to fulfil these requests; their willingness to assist in this process is caricatured in the cartoon below, which appeared in the satirical German magazine *Simplizissimus* in 1946. Here, the newly denazified white sheep wear crosses and what look like surplices as they walk under an archway and out towards the light. The banner above them references the Book of Luke in the New Testament with the assurance that 'there will be more joy over one sinner who repents than over ten righteous persons'.[56]

Representatives of both churches also proved sceptical of Allied war crimes proceedings. In December 1946, for example, Cardinal Joseph Frings of Cologne used his New Year's Eve sermon to express his dissatisfaction with the recently concluded IMT at Nuremberg, and the Allies' apparent adherence to a collective guilt thesis. He argued that only God could determine guilt and that the Allies were 'pagan and naive' if they thought otherwise.[57] Both churches also involved themselves deeply in the fate of German nationals who had been sentenced by Allied military tribunals or other foreign courts. Ronald Webster documents how a number of Protestant churchmen actively campaigned for convicted war criminals held in foreign custody.[58] Key figures here included Bishop Hans Stempel who became the official EKD representative for German prisoners held in Western Europe, and Bishop Theodor Heckel who represented the interests of POWs held in Soviet captivity. The latter's own recent history made him a questionable choice for this role. During the Third Reich, Heckel had been the representative of the EKD abroad, yet had ignored humanitarian appeals made to him by foreign Protestants. He had also

FIGURE 5.1 *'Black Becomes White, or Automatic Denazification'*, Simplissimus, *September 1946 © bpk – Bildagentur für Kunst, Kultur und Geschichte, Berlin.*

had a close relationship with the Reichssicherheitshauptamt (RSHA).[59] Stempel, meanwhile, had devoted his life to POW issues, having himself been captured during the First World War. Having served as prison chaplain to German soldiers sentenced by Nazi courts during the Second World War, he had also had more than his fair share of observing condemned men and their executions. Unsurprisingly, he was vehemently opposed to the death penalty and would spend the postwar years lobbying for the commuting of sentences for persons condemned by the Allies.[60] However, the prisoners that Stempel and his colleagues would be working with after 1945 were not 'mere soldiers', despite their insistence to the contrary. Those held in French, Belgian and Dutch prisons included Holocaust perpetrators: individuals who had participated in the mass shootings of Jews and partisans; worked in concentration camps and who had participated in the rounding up and deportation of West European Jews to Poland. Among the figures that Stempel was concerning himself with, for example, were former members of Natzweiler concentration camp.

During the late 1940s and 1950s, the EKD campaigned vigorously for the repatriation of German prisoners. These efforts gained particular momentum from 1948, when the last of the POWs were released from detention in Western Europe. Clearly, the church struggled to comprehend how these returning soldiers were in any way distinct from convicted war criminals; instead, they regarded them as further victims of victors' justice. In June 1950, Pastor Theodor Friedrich, a close colleague of Stempel, claimed that if the French carried out the death sentences against Natzweiler personnel, 'National Socialism will have its martyrs'.[61] In appealing for their release, churchmen questioned the legality of the war crimes proceedings, alleged that the prisoners had not been informed of the charges against them and criticized the fact that the courts had refused to accept that these defendants had been following orders and 'only' doing their duty. The accused, they argued, were just 'little men' and it was not fair to punish them for the decisions of their superiors. Sources highlighted by Webster suggest that Stempel and his colleagues were far too willing to accept the apologetic statements made to them by the prisoners. One former SS man, for instance, insisted that he had only been at Natzweiler to 'look after clothing questions'. Exactly what was meant by this remained unexplored and, as Webster notes, there was no recognition of the fact that the man's SS membership was sufficient for the courts to find him complicit in war crimes.[62] Similarly, EKD representatives were too eager to accept claims of a postwar religious conversion among the war criminals. This spiritual redemption, they argued, demonstrated a prisoner's essential good character and proved that they should be released.

The efforts of the EKD thus went beyond offering mere spiritual guidance to German prisoners abroad. They entered into personal expressions of sympathy for the accused, raised funds to support war criminals' wives and families back in Germany and lobbied FRG and West European political leaders to intervene on behalf of these figures. The EKD also established a special agency to pay for lawyers. Webster argues that these Protestant churchmen were so invested in the accused that their actions were 'at times positively embarrassing to other Germans'.[63]

Within Germany, meanwhile, particular attention was focussed on the fate of seventy-four former SS personnel convicted during the Malmédy Trial of spring 1946. All but one of the defendants had been found guilty of murdering Belgian civilians and US POWs during the Battle of the Bulge in December 1944. Forty-three of these men were sentenced to death. Almost immediately, though, various accusations were levelled by the defence, members of the public – and church leaders – about the legality of these proceedings. It was claimed that the Americans had used torture to extract false confessions, investigators had been biased and that the accused had not been properly informed of the nature of the charges. Much was made of the fact that the accused were 'ordinary soldiers' and that any deaths that had occurred in Malmédy were the result of battle, rather than cold-blooded murder. Jerome Legge argues that the presence of Jewish members of the prosecution team further fuelled accusations that the trial was about revenge, rather than a genuine enquiry into guilt and innocence.[64]

Criticism reached such a level that Congress was forced to launch an investigation into US military practice in occupied Germany. Johannes Neuhäusler, the Auxiliary Bishop of Munich, and Cardinal Frings of Cologne played a leading role in the campaign against the Malmedy sentences, as did Theopil Wurm for the EKD. Neuhäusler, for example, petitioned US Congressmen to suspend the death sentence and called for the establishment of a clemency board to review alleged procedural irregularities. Neuhäusler himself had been interned in Dachau and Oranienburg during the Third Reich and this status may well have helped to legitimize his postwar campaigns. Protests also spilled over into the German press. In November 1948, Neuhäusler published an article in a Munich Catholic newspaper condemning the trials and calling for a stay of execution until the guilt of the Malmédy defendants could be proven beyond doubt.[65] The Malmédy case quickly became the impetus for a wider public critique of Allied justice in general. In October 1948, Bishop Wurm issued a statement that questioned why Allied atrocities were not being similarly punished before courts of law. Looking further back, he also launched a series of criticisms of the IMT, including the fact that the Soviets had been allowed to sit in judgement.[66] Frings, meanwhile, used another of his New Year's Eve sermons to discuss the suffering of all those German nationals who had been sentenced by Allied courts as war criminals.[67]

In 1949, the Catholic Church established the Committee for Church Aid to Prisoners, complementing a similar organization already set up by the Protestant community. That same year, Rudolf Aschenauer, a German lawyer who had previously served as part of the defence counsel during the

Ohlendorf and the IG Farben trials, began producing a periodical entitled *The Other Side*, which expressed the churches' views on war crimes trials.[68] In February 1952, officials from both the Catholic and Protestant churches also met with representatives from the Federal Ministry of Justice to discuss the German prisoners still being held in France.[69]

Although the eventual amnestying of Nazi war criminals in West Germany can be explained by a number of factors, Jerome Legge argues that the campaigns undertaken by the German churches were 'influential' in granting clemency for the Malmedy defendants – and for preventing their scheduled execution.[70] For Buscher and Phayer, the attitude of Catholic bishops to postwar trials can be linked to their previous failure to speak out during the Holocaust. They argue that 'Catholic bishops were first and foremost German nationals who proved unwilling to exercise their moral authority either during the war or thereafter.'[71] However, the churches' stance on the war crimes issue did evolve over time and, amid the Frankfurt Auschwitz trial of the mid-1960s, the EKD involved itself in a broader political and legal debate about the application of West Germany's Statute of Limitations for Nazi atrocities. During its 1963 synod in Düsseldorf, the EKD added its voice to those urging continued war crimes investigations, producing a seven-page document that was disseminated from the pulpit and to the wider public through the religious and secular West German press. This document spoke of a collective responsibility for Nazi crimes and proclaimed that 'in any society evil must be recognized as abominable and must be punished accordingly'.[72] Admittedly, some of the older criticisms of war crimes trials persisted, with the EKD commenting on the role of terror that affected people's power to resist Nazi policy, and the 'cunning propaganda' that induced them to participate in atrocities. It also expressed legitimate concerns about the courts' ability to uncover the facts so long after the events in question. At the same time, though, the EKD also drew repeatedly on inclusive terminology to insist upon a widespread guilt and responsibility for the Holocaust, stating:

> In these trials... crimes that were committed by members of our people against millions of Jews and other ethnic groups, against men, women and children, once again rise before us in their enormous extent and their entire brutality. It is imperative that, through this, we challenge the discussion of the Nazi past of our people that we have previously neglected or taken too lightly.[73]

Conclusion

The responses of the German churches to the Nazi past after 1945 were imperfect and characterized by moments of self-justification and myth-making. Far from being completely silent, their responses generally reflected the sentiments of wider German society, and reflected the prevailing social and political concerns of the period. In many ways, they had a particularly difficult task: there was a need to balance the behaviour of individual priests and pastors during the Third Reich with broader theological considerations that would affect the entire Christian community. The Holocaust challenged existing church teachings and traditions; it would take some time for the church to come to terms with that and find a way of recalling faith after Auschwitz.

6

Memorializing the Holocaust

Since German reunification in 1990, there has been a veritable boom in the construction of memorials to the Nazi past. Some, such as the Memorial to the Murdered Jews of Europe, which stands in central Berlin, have been specially commissioned to commemorate the Holocaust, reflecting its place within the nation's historical consciousness. Other existing monuments, such as the Neue Wache, which is also located within Germany's reconstituted capital, have been subject to a redesign and rededication, reflecting the shifting political culture after the fall of the Berlin Wall. Such revisions demonstrate the challenges of incorporating formerly distinct East and West patterns of remembrance into a united, German memorial discourse. Elsewhere, there have also been public discussions over how best to mark those sites indelibly associated with National Socialism, most obviously the former concentration camps. This chapter presents examples of some of the different types of Holocaust memorials that have been erected since 1945 and highlights the difficulties in designing a suitable commemorative space for the Nazi genocide.

The problem with Holocaust memorials

The term 'memorial' is multifaceted. It may refer to a physical monument, a sculpture, statue, stone, plaque or garden of remembrance constructed in specific remembrance of a historical event or personality; or it might refer to a museum, archive or documentation centre established with a mission to commemorate a particular past. Examples of the latter include the United States Holocaust Memorial Museum, Berlin's Jewish Museum or the House of the Wannsee Conference. During the 1980s, Pierre Nora coined the phrase *lieux de mémoire* (site of memory) to refer to physical, historical locations as well as symbols of the past and places that exist only in the collective imagination. These can serve as memorials in themselves, preserving the landscape and inviting visitors to reflect upon what happened within a particular space.[1] In Germany, such sites encompass not only the former concentration camps, but also the 'euthanasia' centres, former Nazi prisons and the NSDAP parade grounds in Nuremberg.[2] Jewish cemeteries, sites of former synagogues and homes once owned by the victims of the Holocaust constitute further, crucial spaces for remembrance, enabling people to recall individuals and reflect upon the destruction wrought by National Socialism. Bebelplatz in Berlin, the scene for the Nazis' burning of Jewish books in 1933, offers just one example here.

Given the broad nature of memorials, the literature on this topic cuts across a wide range of disciplines, including history, art history, architecture, cultural geography and museum studies. The majority of works on physical monuments to the Holocaust have tended to analyse the memorials as part of a specific national culture. James Young's *Texture of Memory*, for example, has separate chapters detailing particular monument forms in Germany, Austria and Poland, while Peter Carrier has compared and contrasted the construction of national memorials in France and Germany.[3] Given the proliferation of Holocaust memorials, though, Harold Marcuse has called for a greater consideration of them as a genre in their own right. The scale of the Holocaust was such that memorials to it are necessarily speaking to transnational audiences. Consequently, since the 1960s, they have tended to draw upon a particular set of visual imagery, including barbed wire, chimney stacks, urns and figures in mourning, that are easily recognizable as symbols of the concentration camps.[4]

One of the most discussed Holocaust memorials in recent years has been Berlin's Memorial to the Murdered Jews of Europe.[5] Designed by the American artist, Peter Eisenman, it covers a space of 20,000 metres and consists of a field of stone blocks, or *stelae*, reminiscent of tombstones. Those on the outermost edge of the memorial space are little more than paving slabs, with the effect that the casual visitor can be drawn into the memorial before they realize it. Stones towards the centre of the memorial, on the other hand, reach beyond head height, enabling the audience to become immersed in the memorial. Symbolically, the memorial represents the blot of the Nazism on human history; some visitors may find the experience of walking through the stelae claustrophobic but their passage through the memorial and back into the sunlight represents the act of working through the past. Likewise, the ground beneath the visitors undulates so that it becomes difficult to walk through the memorial in any relaxed fashion. Below the field of stelae there is an Information Centre, which documents the history of the Nazi persecution of the Jews, giving a chronology of racial policy and presenting extracts from victims' diaries and letters. Photographs and family biographies enable visitors to trace the fate of individuals from right across Nazi-occupied Europe, giving a human face to the victims that is missing in the monument above. A 'Room of Names' develops this further, reading out the names and brief biographical information of individual victims; the accompanying guide to the Information Centre informs visitors that it would take six years, seven months and twenty-seven days to read out the names of every single person killed in the Holocaust.[6]

Analyses of Holocaust memorials – including that in Berlin – tend to traverse several key issues: purpose, form and effect. How and why have people chosen to represent the Holocaust? What impact have such memorials had upon popular understandings of the past? Memorials are frequently associated with mourning and paying tribute to deceased compatriots, yet they also tend to have celebratory overtones, fitting into a nation's preferred historical narrative of courage, determination and triumph over adversity. Few countries choose to commemorate the darker aspects of their history. In Britain, for example, it has been much easier to build memorials to abolitionists than to acknowledge the nation's role in promoting slavery. Why, then, does Germany have so many Holocaust memorials?

Speaking at the unveiling of Berlin's Memorial to the Murdered Jews of Europe in May 2005, Lea Rosh celebrated the fact that 'no where to date on this planet has a people recognized its greatest crime, making it for ever visible in the centre of its capital, so clearly and unmistakably honouring the memory of those it murdered'. Quoting her husband and co-sponsor of the memorial project, architect Jakob Schulze-Rohr, she summed up the monument's significance: 'now it's easier to live in this country'.[7]

Memory, as James Young argues, is never pure and the construction of physical memorial to the past may stem from a variety of motives.[8] Guilt, as well as a state's need to explain the past to itself, may play a role here. There may also be – as Rosh's statement implies – a keen desire to show the rest of the world that the nation is bravely facing up to its crimes. The very act of constructing a memorial, in other words, might be taken as evidence of a nation's rehabilitation.

Holocaust memorials are also usually the result of an enjoinder to remember the victims, reflect on man's inhumanity to man and ensure that nothing similar ever happens again. Over time, our greater distance from the events in question has also sparked an increased awareness of the need to educate future generations about these terrible events; memorials can thus have an important pedagogic function. This was again evident at the unveiling of the Berlin Holocaust memorial in 2005 when the president of the German Parliament, Wolfgang Thierse, commented:

> What today can still be narrated vividly by contemporary witnesses must in future be transmitted by museums, by works of art. We are at the moment within a change in generations, a shift in the tides, as some may phrase it. National Socialism, war and organized genocide will become less and less the living experience of contemporaries to the events. They will become ever more events of history. There is a shift

under way from personal memory, individually certified, to a collective memory transmitted by knowledge. The memorial is the expression of that transition.[9]

Memorials serve the needs of the present; debates over their design usually reveal much more about current political culture than the past. A memorial may thus be used to foster a sense of shared experience, destiny or collective identity – a comforting sense of belonging after the turmoil of war and division. Hence, we see initial postwar memorials presenting the victims of Nazism in universal terms – everybody is united in their experience of suffering. Pride too can play a part. Both Germanys, as we will see, used memorials to celebrate the defeat of fascism, the endurance of the German people and the laying of the foundations for the new democratic or socialist state. Consequently, the extent to which the Holocaust was being truly remembered is questionable.

Indeed, the extent to which the presence of any memorial constitutes an act of engagement with the past remains a thorny issue. Some scholars, such as James Young, have argued that the erection of a memorial can actually have the opposite effect; it does the memory work so we do not have to. The sheer presence of a memorial posits that we *have* remembered, but then enables us to move on and focus on something else once the building process is complete. As Young explains, 'once we assign monumental form to memory, we have to some degree divested ourselves of the obligation to remember. In shouldering the memory work, the monument may relieve viewers of their memory burden.'[10] A memorial, then, can actually displace memory.

Consequently, the ways in which people interact with monuments and sites of memory has become a source of much fascination among scholars in recent years. Do memorials simply blend, unnoticed, into the ordinary landscape? How many people will stop, deviate from their purpose and pause to contemplate the meaning of a monument? To some extent, Berlin's Memorial to the Murdered Jews of Europe has circumvented one of these problems: its immense scale and prime location near the Brandenburg Gate, Tiergarten and the Reichstag means that it is not easily ignored. Instead, it is regularly humming with visitors, with people wandering between the stelae, taking photographs and queuing to enter the Information Centre located below the memorial. Coaches deposit tourists at the edge of the memorial, guides conduct tours in multiple languages through the site, and most Berlin guidebooks list the memorial as a 'must see' item. Souvenir shops across the city sell a variety of postcards depicting the memorial from different angles.

Do visitor numbers, however, equate to a genuine act of remembrance? Irit Dekel points out that, unlike the memorials established within the former concentration camps, the Berlin monument does not lie in an 'authentic space'.[11] Its abstract design means that its meaning is not immediately apparent to the casual visitor and its title also leaves room for ambiguity.

It may be dedicated to the Murdered Jews of Europe, but nowhere (above ground) does it explain who murdered them, where, when, how or why. That task is left to the accompanying Information Centre. The president of the Central Council of the Jews in Germany commented on this fact during the memorial's unveiling, stating, 'the memorializing of those murdered spares the observer any confrontation with questions of guilt and responsibility'.[12]

A small plaque on the edge of the memorial does, however, list a series of 'rules of conduct' for visitors entering the site, forbidding loud noise, alcohol, barbeques, dogs, bicycles, skateboards and roller-blades. Visitors are also asked not to climb upon or jump between the stelae, and patrolling security guards are kept busy trying to enforce this. Clearly, this is supposed to be a quiet, contemplative space; in reality, it is frequently populated by young people playing hide and seek between the stone columns, and groups seemingly more interested in posing for a quick photograph than anything else. Is this appropriate behaviour? Should memorials, and especially those dedicated to the victims of genocide, occupy a sacred space, demanding a particular set of reverent responses from their visitors?

Linked to these questions, has come a wave of literature into the so-called 'dark tourism', examining the motives and behaviour of visitors who flock each year to sites of atrocity. Tim Cole has emphasized the 'voyeurism' that characterizes people's visits to Auschwitz.[13] Jenny Edkins has similarly written about the desire of visitors to Dachau to see things as they were.[14] These sites hold an important pedagogic value, but for some they are simply another stop on the tourist trail. Reflecting on his experience as a tour guide at Dachau in 2002–3, Charles Hawley wrote:

> on any given day, the historically initiated formed only about half of my tour participants. The rest were there for the second main reason tourists visit Dachau: Because it is on the Munich tourist to-do list.... It was as if, after reading 'Let's Go' and 'Fodors', the Holocaust became something to sandwich in between a quick art museum visit in the morning and a session at the Hofbrauhaus in the evening. In short, they didn't know what they were getting into.[15]

In a similar vein, there have been regular criticisms within the media of visitor behaviour at the Berlin Holocaust memorial. In 2006, the *Süddeutsche Zeitung* bemoaned the fact that 'at night loving couples bill and coo in the Stelenfeld, in the morning, children play hide and seek there, school classes gather for group photos and often people bring their lunch to the border of the memorial to the Murdered Jews of Europe'.[16]

An additional challenge within Holocaust commemoration is deciding just what form a memorial should take. Scholars have long debated the aesthetic possibilities of representing the enormity of the Holocaust. Figurative monuments can be seen as simplifying events, reducing the Holocaust to clichés. Abstract memorials may invite a greater amount of memory work on the part of the viewer, but they can also lead to confusion and misinterpretation. Young recalls the oft-repeated complaint among survivors that 'we weren't tortured and our families weren't murdered in the abstract'; for them, a more literal form has often been regarded as the more appropriate tribute to the victims.[17]

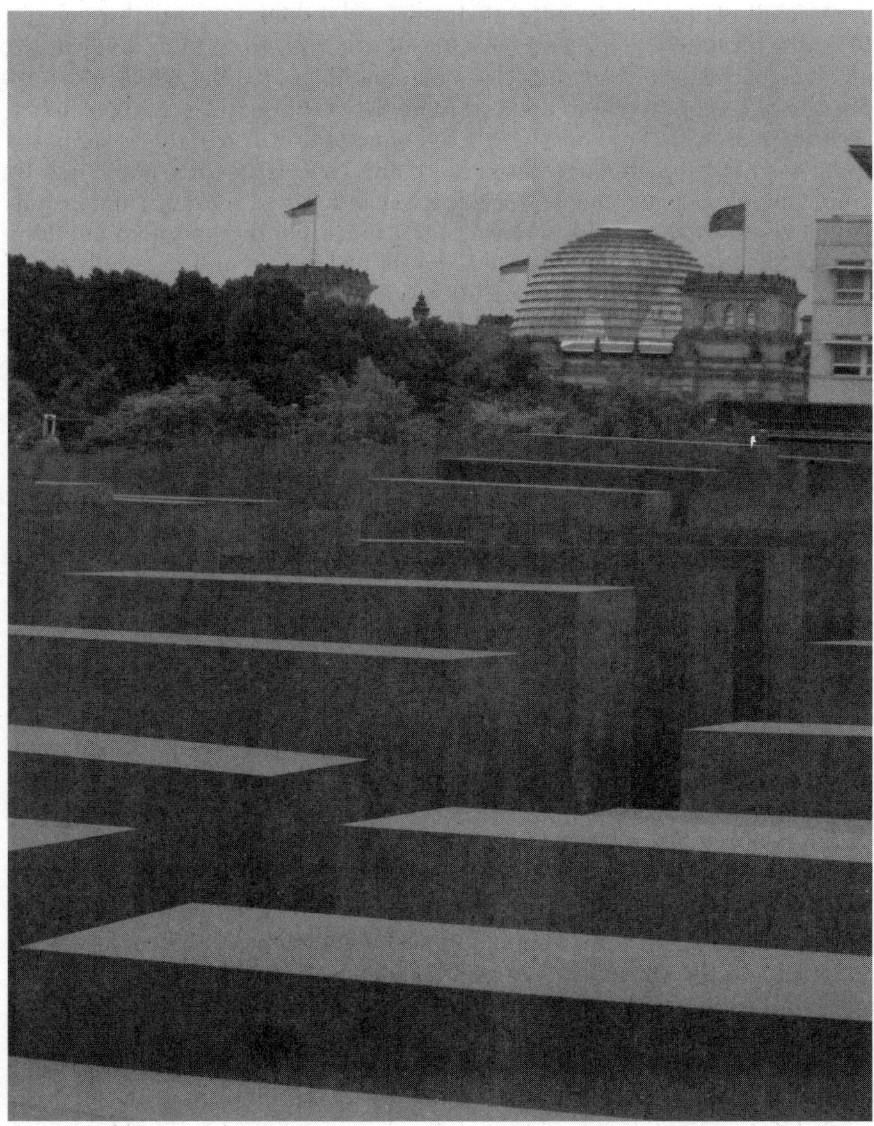

FIGURE 6.1 *Photograph of the Berlin Memorial to the Murdered Jews of Europe (author's own).*

The design process itself can also be protracted and heavily politicized; Berlin's Memorial to the Murdered Jews of Europe took almost seventeen years to complete, from its initial conception in 1989 to its eventual unveiling in 2005. The initiative for this venture came from a citizens group, 'Perspective for Berlin', led by the German television journalist Lea Rosh and the historian Eberhard Jäckel. In 1993, the then German chancellor lent his support to the campaign and pledged that part of central Berlin would be given over to the memorial. The origins of the memorial played out against the background of German reunification and the relocation of the Federal Republic's capital from Bonn back to Berlin.

Between 1994 and 1998, two international competitions were held to try and find a suitable form for the memorial.[18] The eventual winning design by Eisenman was praised for its lack of sentimentality and the demands that it placed upon visitors to navigate the past. Brigitte Sion argues that the memorial with its narrow, uneven paths, cold stone, muffled sound and sense of confinement encourages a 'multi-sensory experience'.[19] James Young, who sat on the project's selection committee, has called it an 'audacious' design, with a 'pointedly anti-redemptory' message about the past.[20] Critics, however, have argued that the memorial is simply too large and likely to attract graffiti. The memorial is, in fact, coated with an anti-vandalism paint, and further controversy came when it emerged that the company supplying this was a subsidiary of that which had produced Zyklon B for the gas chambers. Elsewhere, while some argued that no memorial could ever hope to encapsulate the horror of the Holocaust or warned that it could even stifle discussion about the Nazi past, the German novelist Martin Walser attacked the relentless depiction of Germany's shame. Echoing some of the sentiments of the Historikerstreit of the 1980s, he argued for the formation of a more positive national identity.[21] Dekel points out that the Memorial to the Murdered Jews is also located in the former 'death strip' beside the Berlin Wall, commenting that the positioning of the memorial in this particular landscape 'serves to recall and transform experience of this and other historically charged grounds and to make it habitable' – but can the Nazi past be rendered 'habitable'?[22]

For some commentators, the difficult discussions over memorial designs were themselves crucial acts of memory work. James Young, for instance, declared himself in favour of a continual debate over the form and function of a central Holocaust memorial as offering a better act of remembrance in reunified Germany than any eventual monument. Writing during the early 1990s, he reflected, 'Holocaust memorial work in Germany today remains a tortured, self-reflective, even paralysing preoccupation. Every monument, at every turn, is endlessly scrutinized, explicated and debated .... Memory is strenuously rolled nearly to the top of consciousness only to clatter back down in arguments and political bickering, whence it starts all over again.'[23]

One of the persistent controversies surrounding the Berlin Memorial, though, is the fact that it focuses on Jewish suffering to the exclusion of other persecuted groups. At the end of 2004, the Jewish writer Rafael Seligmann criticized the Foundation for the Murdered Jews, the organization set up to oversee the memorial project, for 'monopolizing' the remembrance of the victims. 'To select them!' he exclaimed, 'wasn't it bad enough that the Nazis separated their handpicked victims from those they kept alive? Do we today have the right to decide who is remembered where? Does a murdered handicapped person count less than the highly educated Edith Stein?' Describing his encounter with the project's managing director, Hans Haverkampf, Seligmann added: 'when I ask why the foundation couldn't bring itself to include the other victims of Nazi persecution as well, Haverkampf runs into intellectual trouble. You cannot lump all the war dead together. No. But didn't the Gypsies suffer just like the Jews? Weren't they murdered in Auschwitz just like the Jews?'[24]

Berlin has subsequently added separate memorials to the other victims of the Holocaust. A sculpture dedicated to the memory of the homosexuals persecuted by the Nazi regime was unveiled in the Tiergarten, just over the road from the Memorial to the Murdered Jews of Europe, in 2008. Designed by Michael Elmgreen and Ingar Dragset, it consists of a single, grey concrete block that is reminiscent of the Eisenman memorial, suggesting the victims' experiences were similar, yet separate, to those of the Jews. It also invites visitor interaction; a small window gives people the opportunity to peer inside the memorial and view a film. As of 2014, the video in question depicts two men kissing, but the aim is to have new films commissioned every few years, thereby ensuring that the memorial remains active.

A memorial to the murdered Sinti and Roma, meanwhile, lies in another section of the Tiergarten opposite the Reichstag – a busier section of the park. Unveiled by Chancellor Angela Merkel in 2012, it comprises of a pool of water, with a triangular plinth in the middle onto which fresh flowers are laid each day. Artist Dani Karavan described the thought process behind his design:

> A quaint, unimposing site, withdrawn from the bustle of the city. A site of inner sadness, a site for feeling pain, for remembering and not letting the annihilation of the Sinti and Roma by the National Socialist regime fall into oblivion. Is such a place possible? Or is it only found in emptiness, in nothingness? Do I have the strength to create a site of nothingness? A site deprived of everything. No words, no names, no metal, no stone. Only tears, only water, surrounded by the survivors, by those who remember what happened, by those who know the horror as well as those who never experienced it. They are reflected, upside down, in the water of the deep, black pit, covered by the sky – the water, the tears. Only a small stone, which sinks and rises, again and again, day after day. And on it every day a new blossom, so that each day we can remember anew, constantly, to all eternity.[25]

FIGURE 6.2 *Photograph of the Berlin Memorial to the Homosexuals Persecuted under the National Socialist Regime (author's own).*

Visitors to the site may be drawn in by the sight of the water, or the sound of recorded violin music playing over hidden speakers. They may not immediately notice that some of the paving stones they are standing on around the edge of the pool are engraved with the name of a concentration camp. Thus, they become part of the memorial before they are fully aware of

FIGURE 6.3 *Photograph of the Berlin Memorial to the Sinti and Roma of Europe Murdered under the National Socialist Regime (author's own).*

it. Interestingly, there is more on-site information here about the persecution of Sinti and Roma than there is at the memorial to the homosexuals. Panels around the edge of the site document the various stages of Nazi racial policy – and act as a fence between the memorial and the rest of the park.

Finally, in September 2014, another memorial was opened in Berlin to recall the disabled victims of the Third Reich. Built upon the site of the administrative headquarters of the T4 'euthanasia programme', it consists of a 24-metre-long wall of blue glass set into grey concrete. The latter material again invokes continuities with the Memorial to the Murdered Jews and the Memorial to the Homosexuals, underscoring the enormous effects of National Socialism. An accompanying outdoor exhibition provides visitors with background information on the killings.[26]

All four memorials – that to the Jews, homosexuals, Sinti and Roma, and the disabled – are managed by the Foundation Memorial to the Murdered Jews of Europe that was set up in 1999. Connections between them are underscored at each site by the availability of free leaflets for each of the other memorials. A casual visitor to the Memorial to the Murdered Jews of Europe can therefore learn about the existence of the other memorials and perhaps be inspired to go and look at them as well. In contrast to earlier postwar narratives of the past, there is thus an emphasis on the experiences of multiple victim groups.

Counter-monuments

One effort to resolve both problems of audience engagement and finding a suitable memorial form for representations of the Holocaust came during the 1980s with the development of the 'counter-monument' (*Gegen-Denkmal*) in West Germany. These were abstract memorials that challenged conventional memorial forms and demanded an element of audience participation. The designs were fully conscious of the fact that they were being constructed many years after the Holocaust, and used this temporal distance as an integral part of the memorial, encouraging visitors to reflect upon the role of memory and their own relationship to the Nazi past.[27] A leading example of the counter-monument trend is the Harburg Monument Against Fascism, a 12-metre-high sculpture that was unveiled in 1986. The artists, Jochen and Esther Gerz, were determined to avoid producing anything that had a fixed message; this would be a memorial to make people think. They also broke with convention by rejecting the town's offer to construct the monument in a park setting, preferring a grittier, urban location. The memorial, then, was not to be hidden away but placed right in the midst of people's daily lives. Its very placement was to become a blot on the landscape, just as the Nazi past continued to cast its shadow over West Germany. Once in position, passers-by were invited to sign the memorial; as more names were added, the monument was slowly lowered deeper into the ground. The idea was that the more active people were in participating with the memorial, the quicker it would disappear from view. The Harburg memorial broke down the traditional relationship between monument and audience. The latter could not remain passive, but had to bear the brunt of the memory work for themselves.[28]

Another example of a counter-monument constructed during this period is the Aschrott fountain in Kassel. It is based on a previous fountain donated to the city in 1908 by a Jewish businessman, and destroyed by the Nazis in 1939. In 1987, the local authorities decided to rebuild the fountain, in its original location, and turn it into a site of memory. The obelisk that had lain at the heart of the fountain was now recreated as a hollow shell, turned upside down and buried in the ground so that the water would run down into a deep well. The aim was to symbolize loss, most notably the deportation of 3,000 Jews from Kassel to the extermination camps during the Holocaust. Corinna Tomberger suggests, however, that the memorial could also be used to mourn German suffering, invoking the upheaval of the war years.[29]

The meanings of memorials are not static. Subsequent generations can impose their own interpretation on a memorial so that its significance may alter over time. Changes to the prevailing ideological climate also affect the preferred historical narrative and this was especially evident in the memorialization of former Nazi concentration camps after 1945.

Sites of memory: Former concentration camps in German memorial culture

There were seven major concentration camps located in Germany. Dachau, the very first camp to be constructed by the Nazis, opened on 22 March 1933 near Munich. It would be followed by Sachsenhausen in 1936; Buchenwald in 1937; Flossenbürg and Neuengamme in 1938; Ravensbrück in 1939; and Bergen-Belsen, which held prisoners of war from 1940 and Jews from 1943. Each camp was responsible for the deaths of tens of thousands of prisoners. Today, these sites recall the multiple groups persecuted by the Nazis and attract thousands of visitors each year, yet this has not always been the case. The ways in which these sites were recalled after 1945 were complicated by the division of Germany, as well as their postwar usage by the Allies. During the period of Soviet occupation, Buchenwald and Sachsenhausen, for instance, became 'special camps', holding first former Nazis awaiting trial for war crimes, and then anyone opposed to the Soviet takeover. Parts of Ravensbrück continued to be used by the Soviet military during the GDR, with troops only leaving in 1994 while, in the West, sections of Dachau likewise remained under US Military Control until 1972. These sites were thus associated with a continued military presence, while the fact that some of the camps were closed to the public gave visitors a false impression of its scale.[30] The Western Allies also used former concentration camps to house displaced persons after the war. Flossenbürg, for example, became a centre for German expellees from 1947, and during the 1950s, its grounds were even sold off to make way for family homes to house this population. Neuengamme, in Hamburg, meanwhile, became a prison after 1948. The authorities there stressed that this institution would follow the rule of law and be a model penal institution, offering a pointed contrast with the civil rights abuses that had occurred under the Third Reich. However, as Bill Niven points out, 'it was not just the penal environment that was criminal in Neuengamme camp, but the fact that people had been imprisoned there in the first place'.[31]

These postwar uses would cloud subsequent commemorative activities, blurring the identities of the prisoners who had passed through these camps and facilitating further narratives of German victimhood. This became especially evident in the wake of reunification when Germany tried to acknowledge the victims of both Nazi and Soviet detention. During the early 1990s, the discovery of mass graves in the woodland surrounding Buchenwald and Sachsenhausen produced immense shock and dismay. The graves held the remains of those who had died through starvation or disease during their internment by the Russians – people who were now depicted publicly as the innocent victims of totalitarianism. There were local initiatives to mark the burial spots with individual, hand-made wooden crosses and site administrators began to weave the horrors of Stalin's 'special camps' into their museum exhibitions. A new entrance sign added to Sachsenhausen in 1992 stated:

> Dear Visitor! This memorial site was built and designed by the Communist power holders before perestroika and the turning point [of 1989] in order to commemorate the victims of Nazi criminals. The end of Communist domination, and the unification of our country in peace and freedom, makes it possible also to commemorate those who, under the Soviet occupying power and under the lawless GDR state after 1945, sacrificed their freedom, health, and their lives in resistance. The necessary redesigning of this memorial site is now underway.[32]

The sign played down the Nazi past in favour of emphasizing the more recent GDR experience. Similarly, a stone memorial was added inside the camp inscribed to the memory of the 'victims of Stalinist arbitrariness, 1945–1950'.[33]

As a result of these actions, the boundaries between the Nazi and the Soviet camp were blurred. The particular horror of Nazi persecution was diminished and there was no recognition of the fact that former SS personnel and other Holocaust perpetrators had been among those killed in the Soviet camp.[34] Protests from Holocaust survivors, however, led to the establishment of a historical commission to try and resolve the problem of representing this 'double past'. This body agreed that commemoration of the Nazi and Soviet period within these sites should be kept physically separate. A new building was established at Buchenwald to represent the latter and the controversial Sachsenhausen entrance sign was taken down in 1993.

To some extent, previous memory work within these camps can be seen as more advanced in the GDR than the FRG, with Buchenwald, Sachsenhausen and Ravensbrück becoming key sites within national commemorative culture as early as 1959. Remembrance here was driven by the state and the camps opened as memorial sites before any of the FRG ones.[35] In the West, it was largely survivors' groups that steered the memorialization process, lobbying for recognition and the establishment of suitable monuments and museums, a process that necessarily took more time. Sarah Farmer also stresses the distinction between attitudes in the FRG, where the former camps tended to be regarded as 'sites of national shame', and those in the GDR where, thanks to the emphasis on resistance, they became 'sites of national pride'.[36] From 1961, Buchenwald, Sachsenhausen and Ravensbrück were all afforded the status of National Sites of Admonition and Remembrance (*Nationalen Mahn- und Gedenkstätte*).

Both Germanys, however, were slow to recognize the suffering of particular victim groups. In the GDR, the emphasis, as always, was on

Communist resistance. Buchenwald, for instance, became a celebratory story of 'self-liberation', on the basis that the camp's underground movement had stormed the gates in April 1945 as the SS began to withdraw. This moment was depicted in the first major memorial to be constructed on the site – a sculpture depicting eleven prisoners bearing arms or waving their fists in a clear display of defiance.[37] The opening of the Ravensbrück memorial in 1959, meanwhile, included a speech by Ernst Thälmann's widow, Rosa, in which she declared that 'the legacy of the dead and the great ideas of the anti-fascist liberation struggle' had finally been realized through the establishment of the GDR.[38]

In 1961, a government statute proclaimed that preserving the former concentration camps would demonstrate:

a) the struggle of the German working class and of all democratic forces against the fascist threat;
b) the role of the KPD as the strongest and leading force in the struggle against the criminal Nazi regime;
c) the antifascist resistance in the years between 1933 and 1945 in Germany and the European countries;
d) the SS terror in the camps and the lack of respect for human life;
e) the common struggle of the members of European nations, especially the Soviet POWs, against the SS terror and the special role of international solidarity in this fight as well as the measures that led to the liberation of the camps;
f) the resurrection of fascism and militarism in West Germany;
g) the historical role of the GDR.[39]

Closer analysis of the postwar treatment of Ravensbrück demonstrates some of these themes in practice. At first, the camp appeared to have been rather forgotten after the war, used as a source of building materials for the local community but little else.[40] During the occupation period, any commemorations at the site tended to be organized by the former prisoners, although even here, notes Robin Ostow, a narrative was being generated of Communist struggle with the singing of songs from the 1917 Russian Revolution.[41] Later, commemorations were organized by the VVN and the Democratic Women's Federation, marking the International Day of the Victims of Fascism each September. During the 1950s, there was also increasing observation of the anniversary of the camp's liberation on 30 April 1945. These moments of reflection became important propaganda opportunities for the GDR, with the singing of the national anthem and speeches that spoke to Communist ideology. In 1955, for example, members of the Free German Youth swore a public oath on the site in remembrance of both the victims of Ravensbrück, and the Red Army that had liberated the survivors, declaring: 'your blood was not shed in vain. Its stream flows united with the blood shed by the glorious heroes of the Soviet Army who liberated our nation and all the nations of Europe from the yoke of Hitler's fascism. Today, the nations of the Soviet Union stand by us as our closest, dearest friends. And you, too, are standing next to us, you brave mothers, admonishing and strengthening us'.[42]

Once Ravensbrück had been established as an official memorial site in 1959, participants within commemorative ceremonies increasingly appeared in uniform, be it that of the East German army, or of the state's youth groups. All ceremonies began with the laying of a wreath to the fallen Soviet soldiers, ensuring that their fate was remembered before that of the camp's prisoners.[43] Photographs displayed within the camp's museum likewise included many representations of the atrocities committed during the occupation of the USSR.[44] In 1977, a Soviet tank memorial was added on the approach to Ravensbrück, reminding visitors of the Red Army's role as heroic liberators but also using the site to commemorate the sixtieth anniversary of the Russian Revolution.[45] Eschebach notes that the Stasi were also routinely present during commemorative activities to maintain the peace and ensure that people adhered to the party line. 'Provocative behaviour' would be dealt with, and politically incorrect entries in the visitors' book would be removed. Likewise, a careful eye was maintained on the floral tributes being left at the site. In 1986, wreathes left in remembrance of lesbian victims of the Third Reich were removed as they did not fit into the preferred rhetoric about the past.[46]

Given that Ravensbrück had primarily held female prisoners, it is not surprising that it was the figure of the heroic, female anti-fascist fighter that assumed centre stage within the memorialization of the camp. In 1959, a sculpture entitled the *Burdened Woman* was unveiled at the site, depicting a female prisoner carrying another, emaciated woman. The monument symbolized compassion and solidarity between the prisoners of the camp; a visitors' book produced between 1959 and 1989 affirmed: 'it is a memorial to the women of strong will, to the women with knowledge, who stood firmly together and who supported and sustained their weaker comrades, the defenceless victims; it is a monument built here to the everlasting glory of our heroines, who fought here to the very last breath'.[47] As with the wider GDR discourse on victims of fascism, the emphasis within the Ravensbrück commemorations was on the people who had fought back.

In contrast, it took time for the former concentration camps in the FRG to enter into popular memorial consciousness. Bill Niven records that there were actually instances where these spaces, rather than being preserved as sites of memory, were appropriated for commercial causes. The former SS canteen at Flossenbürg, for example, was transformed into a restaurant while, in 1973, parts of Neuengamme, including the canal that had been constructed by the camp's prisoners, were leased to a wharf company. This prompted a 'constant struggle' among survivors' groups to try and reclaim the sites in remembrance of the victims.[48]

Such commemorations as there were before the 1960s tended to speak in terms of universal victims of National Socialism and there was also a striking use of Christian imagery, despite the fact that the majority of the dead in all of the camps had been Jewish.[49] In Dachau, the only memorial to be constructed before 1949 was a large wooden cross, seemingly put up by non-Jewish Polish DPs. During the early 1960s, work also began for the construction of both a Carmelite monastery and a Protestant Church of Conciliation.[50] Flossenbürg too, saw the opening of a Catholic chapel in 1947, although a sign erected on the site that same year did include the word 'Jews' within a roll call of the dead, a list otherwise populated by nationalities.[51] The first memorial to be established at Neuengamme, meanwhile, came as the result of pressure from French survivors during the early 1950s, anxious to commemorate their murdered compatriots. In 1953, a column was built on the edge of the site with the simple dedication, 'to the victims, 1938–1945'.[52] There was no effort to explain who these people had been or how they had been killed.

The only real exception to this rule was Bergen-Belsen, which had become the largest centre for Jewish DPs after the war. On the first anniversary of the camp's liberation, in April 1946, Jewish survivors mounted a two-metre column inscribed, in Hebrew and English, as follows: 'Israel and the world shall remember thirty thousand Jews exterminated in the concentration camp of Bergen-Belsen at the hands of the murderous Nazis. Earth conceal not the blood shed on thee!'[53] A year later, the British occupying authorities began work on another, larger memorial, a twenty-metre obelisk that was formally unveiled in November 1952 before representatives of the Jewish community and the West German president, Theodor Heuss. It included an inscription, in Yiddish and Hebrew, that stated:

> This monument testifies to the incomparably horrific acts that the German 'Third Reich' committed against the Jewish people in the years 1939 to 1945, when the Nazi terror horribly and cruelly murdered five million of its sons and daughters. The world should never forget the innocently shed blood of these sacred victims that soaks this soil.[54]

Further interest in Belsen as a site of Jewish suffering was evident from 1957, when the publication of Anne Frank's diary generated thousands of visitors to the site where she had died.

For the most part, though, Jewish suffering was not particularized within West German commemorative culture before the 1960s. Marcuse offers an extensive documentation of the eventual emergence of Jewish memorials at Dachau from 1963, but argues that even then, Jewish commemoration within the other western camps remained 'very low-key, rare or non-existent'.[55] Visitor numbers to the former concentration camps did, however, increase dramatically in the wake of the American television series *Holocaust* broadcast at the end of the 1970s.[56] The role of the younger generation was also significant in raising the profile of the former concentration camps. Marcuse notes that, from 1953, the youth wing of the German trade union association began holding its annual commemorations at Dachau, attracting thousands of young attendees each year. Similarly, Niven stresses the role of an international youth camp in helping to both research and maintain Neuengamme during the early 1980s, prompting the Hamburg authorities to belatedly place a preservation order on the site.[57]

Indeed, it was really only during the 1980s that either German state began to address a wider range of victims within the concentration camp memorials. At Ravensbrück, for example, the fate of Jews, Sinti and Roma, and lesbians began to be recalled alongside the tales of antifascist resistance. Memorialization has also become more coordinated since the turn of the century. In 1999, the Bundestag passed the *Gedenkstättenkonzeption des Bundes* (Federal Strategy for Memorial Sites), which formalized the definition of a 'national' memorial site, confirmed the division of responsibilities for memorial sites between central and regional governments and set out the framework for increased national funding for their upkeep. The measures stemmed, in part, from the need to integrate the GDR experience into collective German historical memory. They also reflect the increased significance being attached internationally to Holocaust commemoration during this period. In 2008, the *Gedenkstättenkonzeption* was amended to take into account, among other initiatives, the newly established Memorial to the Murdered Jews of Europe.

In setting out its criteria for supporting memorials, it was clear that the *Gedenkstättenkonzeption* was looking for sites that would either illustrate a particular aspect of Nazi racial policy, or serve to represent the fate of a particular set of victims. Reflecting on four of the former concentration camps in western Germany, for example, it stressed Dachau's importance as the very first camp and a name synonymous with Nazi terror, and Bergen-Belsen's significance as the end point for tens of thousands of victims on the death marches during the last phases of the war. Neuengamme and Flossenbürg were highlighted for their ability to document 'extermination through work' and the exploitation of slave labour.[58] Learning from the controversies of the early 1990s, the document also made an explicit distinction between memorials to the GDR, and those to the Holocaust.

Reusing old memorials

So far, this chapter has focussed on those memorials that have been constructed specifically in response to the Holocaust or that have emerged from former Nazi sites. However, the meaning of memorials continues to evolve over time, with each generation viewing a monument in a different way, and changing political cultures affecting the preferred public narrative. In Berlin, the establishment of a national Holocaust memorial was accompanied by the reworking of an existing monument on Unter den Linden, one of the oldest thoroughfares in the city's centre. The Neue Wache was part of the old Prussian guardhouse and had been used for state ceremonies during the Kaiserreich. It glorified militarism and the Prussian tradition. After the First World War, the site became a memorial to fallen German soldiers and, from 1933, was appropriated by the Nazis to perpetuate heroic narratives of military sacrifice. After 1945, the Neue Wache became part of the Soviet sector of the city and was almost included in a general demolition of Prussian architecture that was taking place during the occupation period. In 1948, though, the memorial was reoriented as a monument to Soviet-German friendship. Statues of Prussian military heroes were removed and replaced with images of Communist leaders and tributes to Josef Stalin.[59] From 1957, the site was dedicated as a Memorial to the Victims of Fascism and Militarism. The authorities, though, did more than simply swap political portraits around. References to the Holocaust were also – literally – embedded in the memorial as ashes from Buchenwald, Sachsenhausen and Ravensbrück were transferred to Berlin and buried in the Neue Wache.[60]

Following German reunification, the Neue Wache underwent yet another transformation. At the same time as Lea Rosh was campaigning for the construction of a central memorial to European Jewry, Chancellor Kohl decided that the new Germany also needed a central place in which dignitaries could pay their respects to the nation's dead. To some extent, this decision showed that lessons had been learned after the unfortunate use of Bitburg during the fortieth anniversary commemorations of the war's end in 1985. No other world leader would face the risk of visiting a cemetery containing SS graves when they wanted to demonstrate international friendship with Germany. The repositioning of the Neue Wache in this manner can be seen as representing the 'normalization' of German history after 1990. However, Kohl's actions generated extensive public debate – the first post-unification expression of what Vergangenheitsbewältigung now meant for Germany.[61]

Controversy sprang from several issues including the site's rededication as a Memorial for Victims of War and Tyranny – a title that merged victims of both world wars together with those killed during the GDR – and the inclusion, at the centre of the memorial, of a sculpture by Käthe Kollwitz. This artwork depicted a mother mourning her dead child. It had been originally designed by Kollwitz in 1937 while coming to terms with the loss of her own son in the First World War. Critics noted that it had never been designed to take account of something of such magnitude as the Holocaust, and also drew attention to the ways in which it reflected

Christian iconography; Kollwitz's sculpture seen as a Pieta figure, cradling her lost child in a manner reminiscent of Mary holding the body of Christ after his crucifixion. There was also some disquiet at the fact that Kohl had announced the new memorial form without any consultation or design process as is customary in Germany.

The site was unveiled on 14 November 1993. Commemorative plaques – in multiple languages – recall much of the wording of Richard Weizsacker's 1985 speech as they endeavour to highlight the plurality of wartime suffering. The dedication reads:

> We honour the peoples who suffered from the war.
>
> We remember their citizens who were prosecuted and who lost their lives.
>
> We remember those killed in action in the World Wars.
>
> We remember the innocent who lost their lives in war and as a result of war in their homeland, in captivity and through expulsion.
>
> We remember the 6 million Jews who were murdered.
>
> We remember the Sinti and Roma who were murdered.
>
> We remember all those who were killed because of their origin, their homosexuality or because of sickness and weakness.
>
> We remember all who were murdered, whose right to life was denied.
>
> We remember the people who had to die because of their religious or political convictions.
>
> We remember all those who were victims of tyranny and met their death, though innocent.
>
> We remember the women and men who sacrificed their lives in resistance to despotic rule.
>
> We honour all who suffered death rather than acted against their conscience.
>
> We honour the memory of the women and men who were persecuted and murdered because they resisted totalitarian dictatorship after 1945.[62]

This, then, is a memorial in which all suffering has been blended together. It is an inclusive memorial, encouraging people to identify themselves with at least one of the named groups, and ultimately it is a memorial that, with all its emphasis on conscience and heroic sacrifice, enables Germans to take collective pride in their country. The perpetrators of all this suffering, on the other hand, are absent from the memorial text. As such, the Neue Wache does little to challenge older interpretations of the past or inspire a critical reflection on how the Holocaust was made possible.

Recalling absence

One problem that perhaps comes with relying on memorials to engage people about the past is that in a lot of cases, the audience needs to go out of their way to see them. Not everyone, for instance, will be willing to visit a former concentration camp, or necessarily spend time contemplating the meaning of an abstract counter-monument in their town. The final stages of this chapter therefore turn to an alternative form of Holocaust memorial that hopes to both jar people out of their complacency, and foster new ways of thinking about the victims of National Socialism.

Since the 1990s, Germany has witnessed a variety of *Stolpersteine* (Stumbling Stones) projects – small stones or street signs placed in unexpected locations to draw attention to a past event. One of the most successful of these was created by the artist Gunter Demnig with stones, measuring just ten centimetres square, set into pavements across the Federal Republic. These blocks are covered with a brass coating engraved with the name of a Holocaust victim, and the dates of their deportation or death. Placed in front of the house or apartment block where that person once lived, the stones help to recall a once flourishing community, and remind present-day locals of their neighbourhood's Nazi past.[63] Each stone is crafted by hand and this, together with the actual naming of the dead, restores a sense of individuality to the victims of the Holocaust – something that can be lost in more conventional genocide memorials. This is a memorial that can take people by surprise and make them think. Its effects, as Michael Imort explains succinctly, are highly symbolic:

> The brass plate inscribed with the name and life dates of the victim never tarnishes, as friction from shoe soles continually burnishes the material to an almost golden gleam and so visually refreshes the memory. The text is manually stamped into the brass in lettering that ... evokes uncanny comparisons with the typescript of the memoranda in which the Nazis meticulously recorded their mass murder. The inscription itself is rather small, so passers-by must stoop down a bit to be able to read – and thus perform what can be seen as a respectful bow to the victim .... On a more metaphorical level, this handcrafting of remembrance also creates a counterpoint to the industrial methods and scale of the killing.[64]

The Stumbling Stones project is also notable for the way it inspires memory work at the grassroots of society. While most Holocaust memorials are officially sanctioned affairs, the impetus here can come from any group or individual who wishes to sponsor a stone. The project feeds into Holocaust education, with school classes frequently conducting their own research into the lives of the commemorated individual. It also encourages people to view the deceased as more than just passive objects; focussing on their last 'voluntary residence' rather than the scene of their murder, and fostering reflection on what their lives may have been like before the rise of Nazism.[65]

Since the project's inception in 1995, the number of stumbling stones across Germany has flourished. As of 2008, Cologne, for example, had 1,500 of them on its streets, and Hamburg some 2,500.[66] Some people have embraced the project with great enthusiasm; others have accepted it somewhat hesitantly. Critics, however, have questioned whether the whole act does not constitute a trivializing of the Holocaust. In Munich, the city council continues to refuse permission for such an installation, citing a fear of detracting from other, existing memorials, and the difficulties of deciding just which victims should be chosen for commemoration. In 2004, the mayor of Munich argued, 'we want to keep all the Holocaust victims in our hearts and not among the dirt of the street. We do not want the victims to be trampled over every day, and we want to remember all of them, not just one or two'.[67] Imort, however, believes that the council's stance owes more to the fact that the current Chair of the Jewish Community in Munich is hostile to the project than anything else. Since October 2013, something of a compromise measure has been reached with the launch of a stumbling stone app. People can now access digital biographies of 8,000 Jews as they wander through the city, bringing Holocaust memorials firmly into the twenty-first century.[68]

7

The Holocaust on Screen: Representations of the Nazi Genocide in German Film and on German Television

One of the most frequently cited moments in the history of Germany's Vergangenheitsbewältigung is the screening of the American television series, *Holocaust*, in January 1979. Broadcast in the FRG by Westdeutsche Rundfunk (WDR), yet also watched by millions in East Germany, *Holocaust* has been routinely celebrated for bringing details of the Nazi genocide to the masses, generating an intense emotional reaction among the German population and inspiring an unprecedented, critical public discussion of the recent past. On a smaller scale, much of the public interest in the 1961 Eichmann trial has likewise been credited to the fact that the proceedings were relayed through nightly, prime-time news reports on German television, turning the Holocaust into what Jean-Paul Bier describes as a 'painful actuality' for West Germans.[1] Information on the Nazi era was steadily reaching bigger audiences, extending into people's own homes. Such broadcasts, as well as related feature films being screened in East and West German cinemas, ensured that the past was becoming more accessible than ever before. However, these productions were not without controversy and there was much debate over both the aesthetics and wisdom of screening representations of the Holocaust. This chapter explores some of these issues, analysing the particular resonance of *Holocaust* in 1979, but also paying attention to the development of other films about Nazi atrocities in East, West and reunified Germany.

Representing the unrepresentable?

When reflecting upon representations of the Holocaust in film, art or literature, scholars will frequently cite Theodor Adorno's famous declaration that to 'write poetry after Auschwitz is barbaric'.[2] Fundamentally, this refers to the notion that the Holocaust is unrepresentable. The event was so enormous and so horrific that it defies conventional cultural forms. Words cannot do justice to people's experiences; nor can we hope to describe the final moments of those who perished in the gas chambers. Consequently, people like Thomas Elsaesser have argued that the Holocaust 'defies representation'.[3] Even survivor testimony, argued Primo Levi, has its limits: 'We, the survivors, are not the true witnesses [...] we are those who by their prevarications or abilities or good luck did not touch bottom. Those who did so, those who saw the Gorgon, have not returned to tell about it.'[4]

Cinematic or televisual representations of the Holocaust have been especially contested, not least because of the tension between documenting what actually happened, and keeping the audience entertained. Lawrence Baron points out that commercial interests and the role of films as popular entertainment mean that filmmakers are constrained from offering anything too graphic or depressing. As a result, he notes, 'the annihilation of the majority of the targeted population usually serves as the backdrop for uplifting stories about potential bystanders and persecutors who mustered the courage to resist the transgressions of their peers'.[5] Such narratives may leave the audience in a happier frame of mind, but they fail to represent the majority experience of the victims. Wulf Kansteiner, for example, notes that the boom in West German television programming on the Holocaust during the 1980s was typified by an emphasis on the triumphant survival of 'exceptionally lucky, resourceful, cunning and gifted individuals ... often blessed with exceptional virtue'.[6]

On screen, the adherence to dramatic conventions can also be regarded as trivializing the Holocaust.[7] The use of cliff-hangers before commercial breaks (as happed during the American broadcast of *Holocaust* in 1978), or structures more usually suited to mainstream thrillers, runs the risk of treating the Holocaust as a subject like any other, a reduction that can be seen as disrespectful to the victims.

However, Berel Lang suggests that even 'bad' representations of the Holocaust can be useful in the fact that they raise public interest in the topic.[8] Wulf Kansteiner would seem to agree with this point, noting that 'television played a crucial role in the process of coming to terms with the Nazi past, because the medium relayed to a larger national audience the interpretations of Nazism .... In this process, scriptwriters, directors and TV administrators served as conduits between the intellectual elite, to which they belong by training and social origin, and the mainstream national public, which they serve.'[9]

Screening the Holocaust before *Holocaust*

In their study of postwar German cinema, Carol and Robert Reimer argued that West German film directors 'bracketed out consideration of the Holocaust and the persecution of the Jews.... Most of the films do not acknowledge it, even if some do not entirely conceal it. Before the American miniseries "Holocaust"... played to a wide audience on German television in 1979, German Nazi-retro films made only vague or obscure references to the systematic killing of Jews that occurred under Hitler's rule. Movies made prior to this watershed year depict isolated instances of anti-Semitism but do not place them in the context of a government policy.'[10]

Such statements are in keeping with conventional historical narratives that emphasize the unprecedented impact of *Holocaust* in 1979. Yet, as scholars such as Christine Haase and David Bathrick are quick to point out, this assessment of postwar German filmmaking is not strictly true.[11] In fact, there were several instances where film and television in both the FRG and the GDR began to address the crimes of the Third Reich almost as soon as the war was over.

In East Germany, the state-owned production company, Deutsche Film-Aktiengesellschaft (DEFA), made around 100 anti-fascist films between 1946 and 1992, constituting 13 per cent of the total film output in East Germany.[12] The first, *Die Mörder sind unter uns* (The Murderers among Us, 1946) examined public knowledge of Nazi atrocities, tracing the relationship between a former military surgeon and a concentration camp survivor and their discovery of a Nazi perpetrator now operating as a successful businessman. However, there was little mention of the Jews in this production. Shots of civilian graves at the end of the film are marked with crosses, suggestive of a Catholic, Polish identity instead. One year later, *Ehe im Schatten* (Marriage in the Shadow) traced the story of a non-Jewish man and his Jewish wife who choose to commit suicide rather than be deported. The film thus placed the persecution of the Jews at its centre. Covering the introduction of the Nuremberg Laws, Kristallnacht and forced labour, it highlighted the development of racial policy – and critiqued the impassivity of the German populations.[13] The film was screened in all four sectors of Berlin and attracted more than ten million viewers, making it one of the most successful films DEFA ever made.[14]

These early examples of East German films 'created a complex historical imaginary that involved mass death, destruction and defeat, as well as German responsibility and antifascist renewal'.[15] There was, at first, some scope for representing Jewish suffering on-screen. However, this initial period of relative artistic freedom soon gave way. Anti-zionist campaigns in the Soviet Union by the start of the 1950s meant that East German filmmakers began to avoid the Holocaust. Instead, the focal point became the state-determined narratives of Communist resistance and Marxist-Leninist interpretations of fascism. When Nazi crimes against the Jews did re-enter

East German cinemas, it was usually only as a means to attack the FRG.[16] In 1950, for example, *Der Rat der Götter* (Council of the Gods) traced the role of German chemical engineers in the development of Zkylon B. Based upon the transcripts of the IG Farben trial that took place in Nuremberg between 1947 and 1948, the film reflected official, ideological narratives on the relationship between big business and National Socialism.[17] Towards the end of the decade, there were also a growing number of films that pointed to the FRG's failure to enact a thorough denazification after the war. In 1958, for example, it released *Der Prozess wird vertagt* (The Trial is Postponed), depicting the story of a Jewish man who discovers that the person who murdered his sister during the war is now a high-ranking member of the postwar judiciary. Similarly, Mark Wolfgram argues that one of the most significant representations of the Holocaust on GDR television came in 1963 with the broadcast of the trial (in absentia) of Adenauer's State Secretary Hans Globke from East Berlin. As he puts it, 'the narrative of persecution during the Nazi years was useful not so much for educating the public about the past, but rather as a polemical hammer to use against West Germany'.[18] Further reference to the Globke scandal was evident in the 1961 film, *Aktion J*, a production that – while documenting the effects of the Nuremberg Laws and the persecution of the Jews – went so far as to superimpose images of the West German chancellor, Konrad Adenauer, with those of Goebbels and Hitler.[19] Another film, *Mord in Lwow* (Murder in Lvov, 1960), adopted similar measures in depicting Theodor Oberlander and in 1964, the film *Jetzt und in der Stunde meines Todes* (Now and in the Hour of My Death) used the backdrop of the recent Eichmann trial to emphasize the number of former Nazis that remained at large within West Berlin.[20]

The relationship between Nazism and capitalism – and present-day West German industrialists – was again underscored in 1966 with a five-part television series entitled *Dr. Schlüter*. Like *Der Rat der Götter* before it, the programme focussed on a chemist working in Auschwitz, and culminated in the protagonist emigrating to the GDR after the war, unable to withstand working alongside former Nazis in the West.[21] The timing of the broadcast was also significant, presumably inspired by the recent conclusion of the trial, in Frankfurt, of twenty former Auschwitz guards.

Six years later, East German television returned to these themes with the four-part series, *Die Bilder des Zeugen Schattmann* (The Pictures of the Witness Schattmann, 1972). The programme was based around the premise of the titular character testifying at Globke's trial. It included scenes shot at the Auschwitz site and placed particular stress on antifascist resistance. The programme proved enduring, screened again in 1979 as daytime viewing for schools, and broadcast as a prime-time feature film in 1982.

Criticism of West Germany within DEFA films persisted right up to 1989 when the documentary *Der Mann an der Rampe* (The Man on the Ramp) condemned the FRG as a haven for Nazis.[22] However, the late 1980s also saw conventional GDR versions of the past being challenged by filmmakers. More critical representations of Soviet atrocities began to appear, along with discussion of East German guilt for Nazi crimes. Depictions of Jewish suffering also re-emerged, particularly in the run up to the fiftieth anniversary of Kristallnacht. In 1988, the documentary *Die Lüge und der Tod* (Lies and Death) drew upon actual Nazi footage from 1941 that showed Jews being readied for deportation eastwards. That same year saw the release of *Jeder konnte es sehen* (Everyone Could See It), which referenced the assassination of Ernst vom Rath – the trigger for the 1938 pogrom against the Jews.

Despite the overarching political narratives within DEFA films, Fox argues that East German artists actually did more to confront the Holocaust than their Western counterparts.[23] Certainly, the majority of FRG productions tended to focus on the non-Jewish wartime experience, with anti-Semitism or the concentration camps used primarily as a back story. Yet, here too, there were a number of filmmakers who were trying to give expression to the Holocaust.

The first West German film to deal directly with the Holocaust was *Lang ist der Weg* (Long is the Road) in 1948. Following the experiences of a Jewish family during the Third Reich, it showed deportations, ghettoization and the concentration camps. However, the film did not find a distributor and so its public impact was necessarily limited, confined during the 1950s to a few independent film clubs. Those who did manage to see its 1948 premiere in West Berlin were also largely hostile. Reports indicate that some audience members applauded when the crematoria at Auschwitz were depicted on-screen; others shouted that 'there weren't enough that went in'. In the Soviet zone, the press criticized the pro-zionist message embedded within the film.[24]

Lang ist der Weg remained the only West German film to adopt a central Jewish perspective for the next thirty years.[25] Other notable West German releases during the postwar period, however, included the 1965 film *Zeugin aus der Hölle* (Witness to Hell), which depicted a Jewish woman asked to testify at the trial of a doctor accused of human experimentation within a concentration camp. Produced by Artur Brauner, himself a Holocaust survivor, it reflected the horrors then being documented in the Frankfurt Auschwitz trial.[26]

Auschwitz was also the setting for *Aus einem deutschen Leben* (Excerpts from a German Life), released in 1977. This film followed the life of a fictional camp commandant, Franz Lang, during the Second World War. It was a remarkable piece of West German cinema in that it adopted a perpetrator as the central character, one that was very much based upon the real-life Auschwitz commandant, Rudolf Höss. The filmmakers had used Höss's memoirs as the basis for their script, and the character's name was the pseudonym used by Höss when trying to flee the Allies at the end of the war.[27] The film offered a careful documentation of the killing process, with Lang describing the technicalities of the gas chambers to Heinrich

Himmler. In the process, it emphasized the bureaucratic nature of Nazi racial policy. Lang himself was depicted over the course of several years so that he was presented not solely as an SS monster, but also as an ordinary family man keen to do his duty to the nation. Wolfgram argues that it made for an intriguing character study, but the slow pace failed to capture the imagination of the audience.[28]

Meanwhile, on the small screen, West German audiences were exposed to the Nazi past through a variety of documentaries, plays and dramas. Andrei Markovits counts more than 900 documentaries on the National Socialist period shown in cinemas or on West German television before 1979.[29] In 1957, the news programme *Panorama* used excerpts from Alain Resnais's *Nacht und Nebel* (Night and Fog) as a basis for discussing Nazi atrocities.[30] Further representations of the Holocaust came with *Das Dritte Reich* (The Third Reich), a fourteen-part series produced by Nord- und Westdeutsche Rundfunkverband (NWRV) between 1960 and 1961 – and repeated in 1963. In her memoir about growing up in postwar Germany, Sabine Reichel describes the impact this programme had on her:

> by the time I was sixteen, I had some idea of what the Third Reich looked like. There had been snippets here and there on TV and in magazines for as long as I could remember. Still, when I saw those images as part of a continuous and coherent narrative, the concentrated horror sent shivers down my spine and my arms had goose bumps all over.[31]

Experiencing a range of emotions over the course of the series, amused by the sight of marching stormtroopers or Hitler's 'comical' moustache, scared by the marching uniforms and bombs and shocked by the concentration camp footage, Reichel added,

> The documentary had initially seemed like a promising and entertaining thriller, but the ending had come as a shock. This was no movie; I couldn't go home laughing, shaking it all off. The Third Reich actually happened. I was stuck with that bitter truth.[32]

Reichel's memoir is also interesting for the description of her parents' behaviour during the programmes. It is her father who shouts at her to come and watch the series with him, yet he is unable to cope with her judgements:

> 'Jesus, were you all blind?' I blurted out with a look at my father. 'You don't understand,' he replied. 'It was a different time, people saw thing differently. It's not comprehensible today.'[33]

Reichel's mother, on the other hand, was initially reluctant to watch with the rest of the family, protesting 'that's too much for me, I don't need to see that again'. Drawn back into the room amid the coverage of the air raids, however, she started to reminisce about her own experiences of the bombing in war-torn Berlin and Hamburg:

> 'All done by the Tommies and Amis!' Mom added reproachfully, but as she spoke another image appeared on the screen and her expression changed…'I can't watch this!' My mother almost gagged and ran out while my father and I remained in our chairs, silent.[34]

The images in question were scenes from within the concentration camps.

Zweites Deutsches Fernsehen (ZDF), meanwhile, broadcast more than 1,200 television programmes on the Third Reich and the Holocaust between its on-air debut in 1963 and 1993.[35] Of these, 31 per cent were devoted to the history of the Second World War, 16 per cent to the consequences of war and Nazism, and 18 per cent to Nazi crimes. The remaining topics encompassed the Nazi movement (10 per cent), resistance (9 per cent), collaboration (9 per cent), emigration (4 per cent) and European fascism (3 per cent).[36] In his analysis of ZDF's output, Wulf Kansteiner pinpoints the 1960s and 1970s as the pinnacle of historical broadcasting about the Third Reich, with an average of 1,600 prime-time minutes devoted to that period.[37] He argues that there were two key phases of engagement with the Nazi past: 1963–71 and 1978–86. The former consisted of programmes made and watched by those who had been adults at the end of the war and, while the programming was anti-Nazi, there were nevertheless various techniques to 'lift the moral burden of Nazism' from the audience's shoulders.[38] Within these programmes, there was an emphasis on the German conservative resistance and the role of the 'clean' soldier.[39] As with West German feature films, Jewish experiences were generally marginalized with little direct focus on the Holocaust during this period.[40] Instead, there was an emphasis on philo-Semitic programmes, which documented the history of Jewish culture in Germany; films imported from Eastern Europe that detailed the effects of Nazi occupation and racial policy there; and tales of rescue.[41] The last type frequently focussed on the efforts of heroic churchmen, but quietly omitted the churches' institutional silence during the Third Reich. Kansteiner argues that such programmes offered role models to younger West Germans and endeavoured to 'restore hope in humanity, especially German humanity'.[42] He also notes that even when historical programming began to disappear from prime-time slots at the start of the 1970s, ZDF continued to demonstrate its commitment to Vergangenheitsbewältigung with related shows in afternoon or late night slots.[43]

It was only from the late 1970s that coverage of the Holocaust began to be expanded, with a rapid rise in interviews with survivors living both in West Germany and around the world.[44] Until then, argues Wolfgram, 'if one simply were to look at German film narratives about the persecution of Jews during the Nazi regime without any outside knowledge, it would be difficult to truly piece together what was actually going on. The threat of death is certainly pervasive, but the true scope and scale of the mass murder as well as how it functioned would remain largely a mystery.' This, he claims, is why *Holocaust* had such an impact in 1979; people finally heard about the genocide in detail.[45]

The impact of *Holocaust*

Between 22 and 26 January 1979, the American television series, *Holocaust*, was screened in four instalments on WDR. It was not broadcast on GDR television (despite Western pressure to do so), but many East Germans were nonetheless able to pick up the WDR programme; approximately 90 per cent of East Germans watched FRG television during the 1970s.[46]

The programme had already generated international publicity when it was broadcast on US stations in 1978, and had been quickly bought up by other countries including the UK and Israel.[47] The series, starring Meryl Streep and Sam Wanamaker, followed the lives of two families during the Third Reich: the Jewish Weiss family, and the Dorfs who would become increasingly involved in the killing process. Opening in September 1935, it traced the impact of the Nuremberg Laws, Kristallnacht, the 'euthanasia' programme, deportation, ghettoization and, ultimately, the extermination camps.

The screening of this series in the FRG has been routinely cited by historians as constituting a crucial turning point in the nation's confrontation with the Nazi past. Andreas Huyssen notes that it 'opened up an understanding of the Holocaust which all the enlightened, rational and objective discourses and representations of the past decades failed to produce'.[48] Jean-Paul Bier argues that it 'destroyed a taboo', with the nation's 'truly emotional outburst' giving rise to a new willingness to talk about the past.[49] Observers writing at the time for *Der Spiegel*, meanwhile, described *Holocaust* as the 'catharsis of the nation'.[50] Viewing figures for the series, combined with extensive media coverage and letters and telephone calls from members of the West German public, quickly established *Holocaust* as a national viewing event.

Initial responses to the series, however, were largely negative. Having purchased the broadcast rights to *Holocaust* in autumn 1978, WDR made the decision to screen it on the Third Programme, the home of serious productions that usually attracted a much smaller audience than the two main channels. Each episode would be followed by a panel discussion, but the screenings were scheduled in such a way that these debates would go on beyond midnight. Neither the channel nor the timing of the broadcasts was especially conducive for attracting a mass audience.[51] Moreover, in the run up to the broadcast, numerous criticisms were levelled at the series. Some conservatives accused WDR of only buying the programme under political pressure from the SPD; the broadcaster strenuously refuted such allegations.[52] Others took issue with the fact that the programme was an

American production, seeing it as little more than a 'foreign' critique of German guilt.[53] Similarly, there was a keen awareness that US television had recently enjoyed significant success with *Roots*, a series examining slavery. Producing a new set of programmes on the Holocaust was regarded by some as a blatant commercialization of the past, exploiting human suffering in search of a profit. The CDU politician Franz Josef Strauss referred to it as a 'fast buck operation'.[54]

The majority of criticisms, however, took their lead from Elie Wiesel's own condemnation of the series in April 1978 when he accused the programme makers of 'trivializing' the Holocaust. Writing in the *New York Times*, Wiesel took issue with factual errors (both in terms of the development of Nazi racial policy and Jewish religious customs), the stereotyping of Jews and Germans and the depiction of the European Jews as passive victim. Questioning efforts to show the inside of the gas chambers, he argued that 'Auschwitz cannot be explained nor can it be visualised'; 'untrue, offensive, cheap ... the film is an insult to those who perished and to those who survived'.[55] Before they had even seen the series for themselves, a number of West German journalists and intellectuals echoed these aesthetic concerns, viewing the impending WDR broadcast with significant scepticism. Supporters of the series, however, insisted that the FRG had a moral obligation to screen *Holocaust* and argued that the format would, at least, help to make the topic more accessible for the general public. *Die Zeit* viewed the aesthetic criticisms with some cynicism, commenting, 'the wish not to remember these events, especially when the impulse to do so comes from abroad, hides behind a high-minded disapproval of form. The need to repress the past couldn't find a better alibi.'[56]

Similarly, in the hours before the first episode was shown on 22 January 1979, WDR received numerous telephone calls from people complaining that the series was even being shown in Germany.[57] At the extreme, Neo-Nazis planted bombs outside regional television stations in Koblenz and Münster in an effort to try and halt the broadcast.[58] Others appeared to have little to no interest in watching any programmes on the genocide. On 18 January, WDR aimed to prepare viewers for *Holocaust* by screening a documentary on the Holocaust. Twenty-two per cent of the audience switched on for this, and ratings dropped to a mere 19 per cent within the first ten minutes of the programme.[59]

Given these reactions, the eventual success of *Holocaust* took many observers by surprise. Werner Sollers records that the viewing figures were 'exceptional' in the history of the Third Programme, averaging more than 30 per cent of the audience (around 11 million viewers) for the first episode. This rose to 41 per cent (15 million people) by the final night of the series.[60] In fact, the Third Programme received more viewers than the First and Second Programmes combined.[61] Almost half of the West German population watched at least one episode of the series.[62] The WDR panel discussions attracted approximately 30,000 telephone calls over the course of the four nights of an increasingly emotional and personal nature, and West German newspapers and magazines were similarly deluged with thousands of letters from members of the public, eager to share their thoughts on the series.

Some of these responses remained in the negative, with people taking issue with historical inaccuracies to critique, in turn, American knowledge and understanding of Nazi Europe. One oft-cited issue here was the wearing of Hitler Youth summer uniforms in winter.[63] For some, the main concern was whether *Holocaust* would simply stir up anti-German sentiments in other countries; others preferred to draw attention to Allied atrocities, or subsequent wars and genocides such as Vietnam and Cambodia. Elsewhere, people continued to talk of a Hollywood 'kitsch', critiquing the soap opera format and the use of American narrative patterns including the use of cliff-hangers to sustain viewers' interests. For the most part, though, West Germans concentrated their criticisms on the scheduling of the series, with some demanding that it be re-shown on one of the main channels at prime time.[64] The West German press, meanwhile, shifted its previously cautious tone to one of widespread praise for the series. *Der Spiegel* demonstrated a particular turnaround in opinion. Huyssen notes that many left-wing commentators critiqued the series for not providing a sufficient explanation of either National Socialism or anti-Semitism.[65] Like Wiesel, many people also condemned the programme's narrow focus on just two families, a factor that served to reduce the Holocaust to a handful of people, and left insufficient space for the contemplation of perpetrator motivation. Markovits notes that the series ignored the 'grey areas' of behaviour and instead reduced the Holocaust to a simplistic dichotomy between 'Nazis/ Jews, Evil/Good, Tormentors/Martyrs'.[66] Consequently, there was little incentive for viewers to think about how they would have behaved in the situation.

The primary response to *Holocaust* was one of intense emotion. Describing the deluge of calls to WDR, Julius Schoeps commented:

> Most calls revolved around the concepts of 'forgetting', 'guilt' and 'How could it have come to that?' I could not help feeling that many callers felt the need to talk with someone to let out their feelings of sadness, consternation, and shame. When I asked some of the young people who were busy answering the constant stream of calls for their first impressions, they said they had never experienced anything like it, they almost had the feeling they were offering 'spiritual counselling'.[67]

Suddenly, people began to talk more openly about the past than ever before. Rather than hiding behind protestations of complete ignorance about Nazi crimes, a number of West Germans offered a self-critical reflection on their past behaviour and the issue of public knowledge about Nazi atrocities came to the fore. The editor of *Der Spiegel*, Rudolf Augstein, for instance, now declared:

> We all knew Dachau. Dachau stood for incarceration and Nazi brutality – for all concentration camps. I came home from the war on the eastern front knowing nothing about gas chambers or the systematic murdering. War had made me insensitive. I suddenly realized that all the time my one concern had been my own and my family's fate. I had lost sight of the fate of the Jews.[68]

Similarly, Henri Nannen, editor of *Stern* magazine, stated:

> I, at any rate, I knew that in Germany's name defenceless people were being exterminated in the way vermin are extinguished. And unashamed, I wore the uniform of an officer in the German air force. Yes, I knew about it and was too cowardly to resist.[69]

Recalling the reactions to the panel discussions, Markovits states, 'each evening more people called, admitting shamefully that they had not wanted to know what was going on, and that they had purposely remained oblivious to the whole experience. Many callers insisted that because of the show, they were able to talk about World War II for the first time with their families'.[70]

Others used the panel discussions to try and learn more about the circumstances of the time. Among the most popular historical questions were queries about the lack of resistance, the silence of the churches and the failure of the international community to intervene. Some enquired about the 'passivity' of the Jews.[71] Others pondered why it had taken an American rather than a German company to make the series, how much the ordinary German population could have known about the Holocaust at the time and, quite simply whether things really had been 'that bad'.[72] A survey of 1,800 people by the Bundeszentrale für Politische Bildung one week after the broadcast found that 73 per cent of respondents expressed a positive reaction to the show. Sixty-four per cent found the show 'deeply upsetting', 39 per cent felt ashamed that such crimes had been committed and tolerated by Germans. Twenty-two per cent admitted that there had been scenes in which they had almost cried. Only 2 per cent of those questioned dismissed the show altogether.[73]

The effects of *Holocaust* were multifaceted. Fundamentally, the series served to popularize the very term 'Holocaust' for describing the Nazi policy of extermination. Sollers notes that, up until this point, West Germans had frequently relied upon Nazi vocabulary to reference these events.[74] Similarly, Zielinski states that 'for many days [after the screening] words like Nazi-crimes, concentration camps, antisemitism, Auschwitz, Neo-Nazism and finally the term "Holocaust" itself, pervaded and satiated the daily life of most West Germans. What had formerly been the province of a few educated circles and certain political groupings became a public event of the first order.'[75] The fate of the Jews necessarily gained greater recognition, but so too did the experiences of other victim groups including

Sinti and Roma, political prisoners and homosexuals.[76] In the aftermath of the broadcast, a wide range of educational initiatives were devised to help younger people learn more about the Nazi period. Several schools began to organize 'anti-fascist' weeks, or to invite survivors to talk to students. Many communities began to conduct greater research into their history, collating oral testimonies and staging exhibitions on local Jewish life. New editions of Anne Frank's *Diary* were published, newspapers reproduced survivor testimonies and visits to the former concentration camp sites also increased. Cinemas organized special series of screenings, re-showing *Holocaust* and older West German productions, as well as examples of foreign Holocaust documentaries including Alain Resnais's *Nacht und Nebel*. On television too, there were a number of follow-up programmes including a film about Auschwitz commandant Rudolf Höss that attracted 31 per cent of the audience.[77] The Bundeszentrale für politische Bildung found its background information brochure on the persecution of the Jews in huge demand, sending out 235,000 copies.[78] Neo-Nazi activity within the FRG came under greater scrutiny, with a number of critical newspaper articles on the theme, and there were a flurry of prosecutions for extremist activity.[79] At the same time, public support for the continued prosecution of Nazi war criminals grew; *Holocaust* was routinely referenced throughout the final round of Bundestag debates over the Statute of Limitations for Nazi crimes and has been credited for inspiring the eventual abolition of the statute in 1979. Observers within other countries were delighted at the level of West German engagement, with the *New York Times* describing reactions to *Holocaust* as 'wholesome'.[80] Many asserted that the silence surrounding the Nazi past had finally been shattered.

Why did *Holocaust* succeed where previous efforts to represent the Nazi past had failed? In part, the much-derided soap opera format of the series had to play a part here. In following the plight of one family, television viewers were encouraged to recognize the victims of the genocide as individuals, rather than anonymous statistics. The programme encouraged a sense of empathy – and thus sparked a highly emotional response. WDR representative Peter Märthesheimer explained the public reaction as follows:

> This narrative strategy places us ... on the side of the victims, makes us suffer with them and fear the killers. It thus frees us from the horrible, paralyzing anxiety that has remained repressed for decades, that in truth we were in league with the murderers. Instead we are able to experience, as in the psychodrama in a therapeutic experiment, every phase of horror – which we were supposed to have committed against the other – in ourselves ... to feel and suffer it – and thereby finally in the truest sense of the word to deal with it as our own trauma.[81]

Huyssen points out that public empathy was made easier by the fact that the fictional Weiss family were assimilated German Jews.[82]

The timing of the series also had an effect on public responses. Thirty-four years after the war's end, the nation was arguably in a better position to be able to look back on the Nazi era in a critical fashion. The postwar era had come to an end and a new generation had come of age with no direct experience of the Third Reich. Furthermore, the months immediately prior to *Holocaust* had seen a number of controversies in the FRG with regard to the Nazi past. Concerns were mounting, for instance, about the number of young people joining right-wing extremist groups and the distribution of Neo-Nazi literature within schools.[83] At the same time, the so-called 'Hitler wave' was taking place with a growing number of publications appearing on the Third Reich. The medievalist historian Hellmut Diwald attracted widespread criticism, for example in 1978, when he claimed that a number of questions about the Holocaust remained 'unexplained'. Among his shocking assertions in *Geschichte der Deutschen*, Diwald suggested that Jews had been deported only to work in the armaments factories and that the crematoria at Auschwitz Birkenau had been designed to tackle a typhoid epidemic.[84] A further scandal had occurred when the CDU politician, Hans Filbinger, sought to justify his role in the killing of German prisoner of war in 1945 on the grounds that 'what was right in the Third Reich cannot be wrong today'.[85] Herf argues that these incidents, together with the ongoing debate about the statute of limitations for Nazi war crimes, meant that *Holocaust* would be broadcast in the midst of growing public criticism of the nation's handling of the past.[86] The time was ripe for a more critical engagement.

Furthermore, it is perhaps worth noting the extensive preparations that had been laid for *Holocaust* in the FRG since WDR had announced its acquisition of the broadcasting rights in October 1978. Aesthetical debates in the press, together with the fortieth anniversary commemorations of Kristallnacht in November 1978 had already helped to raise awareness of the topic. In early January 1979, Channel One had also screened two related documentaries, *Antisemitism* and *Final Solution*.[87] Zielinksi, meanwhile, stresses the fact that people in the FRG were already keenly aware of the ways in which *Holocaust* had been received in other countries – and that international observers would soon be paying close attention to their own responses.[88] Arguably, some sort of reaction was to be expected.

However, there remained some limits to *Holocaust*'s effects and, as Jeffrey Herf argues, even in the midst of all the media coverage, there remained significant distortions within West German narratives of the past. In the months prior to the broadcast, Herf notes that West German conservatives generally adopted their usual position vis-à-vis the Nazi past: don't mention it.[89] Liberals and social democrats, while harbouring some concerns about the format of the series, were usually vocal in their support for it to be shown.[90] The New Left, however, was perhaps more concerned with critiquing the culture industry than engaging with the past.[91] Herf identifies four key themes within the post-broadcast responses of the Left: that *Holocaust* served American and Israeli interests; that the series failed to show the persistence of authoritarian structures after 1945; a criticism of the lack of wartime resistance and a comparison between the Holocaust and the My Lai massacre in Vietnam.[92] Thus, for all of the public sensation surrounding *Holocaust*, reactions tended to reflect older political ideologies. Herf also reflects that the renewed public engagement with the past was not enough to prevent the election of former Nazi Karl Carstens to the position of Bundespräsident later that year.[93] In addition, there is some opinion poll evidence that anti-Semitism returned to pre-broadcast levels within a few months.[94] Harold Marcuse, meanwhile, stresses that, while it can be easy to regard *Holocaust* as an isolated event, it actually needs to be recognized as the culmination of a number of prior developments. Younger people's investigation into the Nazi past, as well as growing numbers of visitors to historic sites such as Dachau, was underway before 1979.[95]

Representations of the Holocaust since 1990

Fifteen years after *Holocaust*, another American production generated renewed, international interest in Nazi atrocities. Steven Spielberg's *Schindler's List* opened in Germany in March 1994. Within the first four days of its release, it had been seen by 98,000 people, despite only being available in forty-five cinemas. By the end of the week, audience numbers had increased to 371,482.[96] After fifteen weeks, it had been viewed by 5.719 million people, while Thomas Keneally's book, *Schindler's Ark*, had also become a bestseller. German critics praised the film's techniques and labelled it a masterpiece but, as Niven argues, 'for the most part it was the perceived value of Spielberg's film as a therapy against collective amnesia, not its value in aesthetic or cinematographical terms, which prompted the positive reaction'.[97] The British newspaper, the *Guardian*, observed that the film was provoking 'the same kind of soul searching debate on national identity and collective guilt that the Holocaust television series unleashed 15 years ago'. Reporting on the film's premiere in Frankfurt, it quoted a middle-aged couple who were wary of their fellow Germans' responses. 'There will be resistance precisely because it's objective and there will be shock', they said, adding concern that it might also bolster political extremism among younger people.[98]

The timing of *Schindler's List* was, in fact, deemed quite fortuitous by many in the West German media. The early 1990s had seen a number of Neo-Nazi incidents across Germany, and opinion polls were again revealing a lingering anti-Semitism. In February and March 1994, EMNID reported that a fifth of the population held negative attitudes towards Jews, and that 52 per cent of Germans felt that a final line really should now be drawn under the Nazi past. Thirty-seven per cent of those questioned claimed that the Holocaust, having happened fifty years before, was no longer significant.[99] Consequently, the appearance of *Schindler's List* was greeted with relief in many quarters of the German media amid the hope it could shore up historical memory and revive dwindling interest in the past. There was also a keen expectation that the film could serve to protect youngsters from the dangers of political extremism. One newspaper spoke of the 'sheer necessity' of the film at a time when a 'dirty renaissance of fascism' was taking place on the streets of Germany.[100] In March 1994, the KMK officially recommended *Schindler's List* to schools, declaring it would help students learn important lessons about tolerance and respect for human rights.[101] In a couple of instances, members of the German-Jewish community accompanied students to screenings and discussed the subject with them afterwards.[102] The leading German tabloid, *Bild-Zeitung*, meanwhile, gave away 200 free tickets to the film.[103] However, when youths set fire to a synagogue in Lübeck on 24 March 1994, there was some concern that the film might also be stirring up old hatred.[104]

Amid the media coverage of *Schindler's List*, there was a re-emergence of some familiar names – and rhetoric about the past. Ernst Nolte, a leading figure in the Historikerstreit of the mid-1980s, appeared on television to express his objections to the film. In particular, he critiqued the fact that Spielberg had made no effort to place National Socialism within a broader context of totalitarianism.[105] Calling for a cinematic representation of Stalin's gulags, Nolte thus persisted in his efforts to relativize Nazi atrocities. Resistance myths, meanwhile, were both challenged and bolstered by the film. Much of the press coverage quickly became fixated upon Schindler's personality. Newspapers labelled him an opportunist, a drunk, a womanizer and a black-market profiteer. On the one hand, this raised some tricky questions about the failure of other people to take action against the persecution of the Jews. As Niven puts it, 'if even *Schindler* could do something [despite all his faults], why could other people not have done more?'[106] On the other hand, though, Schindler could also be depicted as a man of inherent contradictions, an atypical individual who managed to combine an act of heroism with some damning personal traits. Viewed in this guise, he became more of a fantasy figure, a distant, unrealistic personality with little in common with the majority population who, in turn, had no need to berate themselves for not behaving in the same manner.[107] At the same time, a flurry of stories in the German press about other acts of rescue during the war had the potential to produce the opposite effect, reaffirming claims of widespread opposition to Nazism and impeding any further, critical reflection on the past.[108]

Among the notable post-reunification German productions about the Nazi era was Oliver Hirschbiegel's *Der Untergang* (*Downfall*), released in 2004. Focussing on the final twelve days of the Third Reich, the film depicts Hitler huddled in his Berlin bunker as the Russians advance on the capital. It was one of the most expensive German productions ever made, and starred leading German actors; the script was based upon historian Joachim Fest's 2002 book, *Inside Hitler's Bunker*.[109] *Downfall* won multiple awards, and was nominated for the Oscar for Best Foreign Language Film. John Bendix argues that this film constituted an opportunity to lay Hitler, and the Nazi past, to rest.[110] He notes that the focus on the final days in the bunker meant that the filmmakers chose not to focus on other aspects such as Nazi ideology, or the Holocaust:

> One could argue that many of these aspects were well known to the public or prospective audiences already, or that other dramatic films about this era that have had wide circulation – The Diary of Anne Frank, Sophie's Choice, Jacob the Liar, Schindler's List, The Pianist, etc. – address precisely these themes. Yet, these are not dramatic films made by German directors and producers – or even made in German.[111]

The film attracted criticism for some of these omissions, and for trivializing the past. In particular, the ethics of representing Hitler and other high-ranking members of the Nazi leadership was challenged. Some feared that it could serve to 'explain away' Nazi crimes; others that it might glamourize Nazism. Film director Wim Wenders attacked *Downfall*, stating:

> The film has no opinion about anything, especially not about fascism or Hitler … Himmler and Göring are shown no differently than all the other war criminals, put on the same plane as the other nice people, the Traudls and little Peters, so by the end seducers and victims are unified by an arbitrary lack of attitude … . Viewers are led into a black hole in which they are (almost) imperceptibly brought to see this era from the point of view of the perpetrators, or at least are asked to bring a certain understanding for them.[112]

In the end, Wenders implied, viewers were being encouraged to think more about the tragic collapse of Nazism, than the suffering of its victims.[113]

Haase notes that while *Downfall* attracted much praise among foreign critics, German reviewers were 'underwhelmed, if not contemptuous or uninfuriated'. *Der Spiegel* labelled the film 'banal'.[114] Some critiqued the film for failing to explore the causes of Nazism or go beyond merely stating the facts. Haase adds that,

> The film reconstructs the history of the Third Reich and the Holocaust as a cruel and crazed but linear and readable story emanating from Adolf Hitler as its centre. In doing so, it not only unduly simplifies, it also echoes the old revisionist model of primarily implicating a small group of fanatic madmen, thus tracing the existence and crimes of Nazi Germany to one rather confined – and largely uniformed – field of force.[115]

Four and a half million Germans went to view the film within the first three months of its release.[116] Audiences were left 'stunned', with many departing from the cinema in silence. Bendix comments that 'most disturbing for many Germans was their feeling they were facing Hitler … physically imploding but still capable of towering rage when he hears what he does not like, and yet also capable of being kind to his naive secretary. This was Hitler, the real human being that you were facing, intimately and at eye-level.'[117]

Like *Schindler's List* in 1994, *Downfall* quickly became essential viewing for many schools. Surveys of younger Germans, however, raised concerns as to the impact the film had on understandings of Hitler and, by extension, the National Socialist past. A poll of 400 students revealed that those who had seen the film were more inclined to see Hitler in a 'human light' and 'had less of a negative reaction to him than students who had not [seen the film]'.[118] Bendix, however, notes that responses to Hitler have always been 'complex' and the results of this poll should not be considered too alarming:

> Polls from the 1950s to 1970s asking: 'which great German, in your opinion, has done most for Germany?' found virtually no support for Hitler, as compared with, say, Chancellor Adenauer or Bismarck. Yet, polls in the same period that asked the more suggestive question: 'would you say Hitler was one of Germany's greatest statesmen, had it not been for the war?' found a third of the respondents agreeing…. A 2004 poll among 2,500 respondents, found 17 per cent in the West (7 per cent in the East) of those without a Gymnasium education, and 10 per cent in the West (3 per cent in the East) of those with one, agreeing with the statement: 'Had it not been for the extermination of the Jews, Hitler would be regarded as a great statesman.' Other polls consistently indicate that 'almost nobody would vote again for a man like Hitler' if given the same choice again, yet when asked the more suggestive question: 'Do you think Nazism was a good idea that was badly implemented?' 26 per cent of those in a 1994 poll said it was.[119]

In other words, there have always been a minority in postwar Germany willing to separate the 'positive' achievements of the Third Reich from its atrocities.

Questions of German guilt, finally, were revived yet again in spring 2013 when ZDF broadcast the home-grown, three-part miniseries, *Unsere Mütter, unsere Väter* (Our Mothers, Our Fathers), tracing the experiences of five young Germans between 1941 and 1945. Historians' opinion of this production was divided. Norbert Frei praised it, insisting that 'the film is … a step forward because we have never seen the war against the Soviet Union on German television in such an unvarnished way. The advantage of this three part [series] are its shades of grey. No one-dimensional, idealized figures, no invitation to easy identification, no melodrama, but broken characters, aware of their complicity.'[120] Hans-Ulrih Wehler liked the way in which the war was recognized as having a brutalizing effect on people. Others, however, including Martin Sabrow and Habbo Knoch, noted that a focus on protagonists in their twenties ensured that the 'real' perpetrators were left strangely absent in this representation of the war. Throughout the series, there was little sense of the older Germans who had voted Hitler into power or helped in the construction of the Third Reich.[121] An element of distance was thus retained as viewers observed events through the lives of apolitical youngsters. Ulrich Herbert criticized the way in which, by the end of the series, the five characters had become either victims or opponents of the regime – an experience that was, all postwar mythologizing aside, hardly typical of the German population in 1945.[122]

Regardless of these concerns, *Unsere Mütter, unsere Väter* was regarded as a success among the viewing public with each episode attracting around 7 million viewers. Reflecting on the series' popular appeal, *Der Spiegel* commented:

> The contemporary witnesses, the war generation of perpetrators and victims, the collaborators, followers and members of the resistance, are dying. As they pass away, they take their actual experiences from Germany and Europe with them. But the past refuses to disappear. Like the undead, demons from the darkness of abstract history are constantly coming to life again. And even if they no longer torment grandparents and parents, because soon there will no longer be any contemporary witnesses left to tell their stories, they will continue to haunt the imaginations of their children and grandchildren.
>
> World War II ended 68 years ago. It has certainly taken time to grapple with the history of that period, but by now virtually everything has been studied, examined and said. For future generations, enlightenment no longer occurs through knowledge and confrontation with the hard facts of real barbarism, but through emotions. It's as if the Germans, even the very young, to whom tales of the Nazis must feel as if extraterrestrials were at work, still shudder when they think about what their grandmothers and grandfathers were capable of. As if they were afraid that certain patterns of character and behaviour could be passed on to future generations.
>
> ... The reactions of 15-year-old schoolchildren who have seen the ZDF series show how important it is to bring the whole of history into the individual's world of perceptible experience. The culture of remembrance, in its ritualized repetition, creates distance and with it sometimes tedium, just like the repetitious knowledge derived from schoolbooks. The SS thugs and the clamour of Hitler and Goebbels are taken out of time and space, and sterile instruction points to a different world, one that has become unreal. Nazism then turns into a grotesque theatre, an impression that filmmakers like Quentin Tarantino can successfully exploit.

By contrast, a series like 'Our Mothers, Our Fathers' offers the antidote – an experience of emotional awakening. It attempts to provide an answer to the incredulous question asked by young people today: Grandpa and grandma were there when that happened?[123]

Conclusion

Today, representations of Nazism and the Holocaust show no signs of abating within popular culture. Although some programmes may contain aesthetic or factual flaws, it is evident that television and film remains a key means for engaging the public in history and, as recent productions such as *Unsere Mütter, unsere Väter* have shown, they continue to foster moments of intense public discussion. In this way, the past continues to be remembered.

8

Holocaust Education in Germany

Since the turn of the twenty-first century, the Holocaust has come to occupy a central position within school curricula around the world. The International Holocaust Remembrance Alliance (IHRA), established in 1998, has placed education at the heart of its activities, promoting pedagogy in schools, universities and communities in order to (1) 'advance knowledge about this unprecedented destruction'; (2) 'preserve the memory of those who suffered'; and (3) 'encourage educators and students to reflect upon the moral and spiritual questions raised by the events of the Holocaust and as they apply in today's world'.[1] To this end, numerous studies have been launched into the current state of Holocaust education, and each member of the IHRA has produced a detailed report reflecting on Holocaust pedagogy in their own nation. Various compilations of educational resources have been digitized and made available to schools to download, and opportunities for specialist teacher training on the Holocaust continue to be developed to facilitate teaching and learning on this sensitive topic.[2] The establishment of an international day of remembrance for the victims of the Holocaust has also fostered a range of educational activities, from commemorative school assemblies, film screenings and talks by survivors, to research projects conducted by the students themselves. Beyond the classroom, permanent museum exhibitions on the Nazi past, or school trips to sites of atrocity constitute further, important pedagogic tools. Such developments are evident not only in Germany, but much of Europe and North America. Holocaust education is now booming, but teaching about the National Socialist period has not always been held in such high regard. Political ideologies and postwar mythologies have affected the extent and mode of Holocaust representation within school textbooks, while frequent scandals have erupted in the media both in Germany and abroad about students' apparent lack of historical knowledge. This chapter highlights some of these issues as they relate to Germany, as well as some of the general criticisms that have been levelled against Holocaust education over the years.

The problems of Holocaust education

The form and extent of Holocaust education has generated significant scholarly criticism over the years, notably from the likes of Lucy Dawidowicz, Karen Shawn and Samuel Totten.[3] Concern, for instance, has been routinely expressed about the practicalities of Holocaust education including the actual amount of time given over to the teaching of this topic within schools, teachers' own knowledge and understanding of the subject matter and the availability of specialist educational resources to aid lesson planning.[4] There has been debate too as to the appropriate age for students to receive lessons on the Holocaust and the type of materials that should be utilized within the classroom. Most current Holocaust teaching, for example, takes place within secondary schools, targeting fifteen- and sixteen-year-olds. However, in Germany, as well as other countries such as Scotland, there has been some discussion about introducing much younger pupils to the topic.[5]

As the last of the contemporary eyewitnesses pass away, there have been extensive discussions on the best ways to teach people about the Nazi period once there are no longer any survivors to invite into classrooms. Investigations have consequently been launched into the effects of digital technology, as well as the pedagogic value of students visiting museums and sites of atrocity.[6] Other crucial methodological issues highlighted by scholars include the risk of oversimplifying or misrepresenting the Holocaust, and whether teaching should be grounded in a purely historical approach, focussing on the facts; or based upon an emotional and moral approach to the topic.[7] In countries like Britain, Holocaust education has frequently been bound up in Citizenship lessons, with the notion that learning about the Nazi persecution of the Jews will leave today's students better placed to combat racism in modern society.[8] This is in keeping with the standard refrain that those who do not remember the past are condemned to repeat it; the concept of 'never again' is at the centre of Holocaust education.

In Germany too, Holocaust education has been firmly linked to proving the democratic and moral qualities of the younger generation and, by extension, the nation itself. During the GDR, for instance, education became yet another means of proving the antifascist credentials of the East German state. In the West, teaching has been routinely connected to the liberal democratic values embedded within the Basic Law, the founding document of the FRG. This was exemplified through the 1982 Bavarian Law on Education and Teaching which stipulated that schools should educate pupils 'to exercise freedom responsibly, to show tolerance, a peaceful attitude and respect for other people'.[9] Examining how such principles have been destroyed in the past was considered an essential part of this. Likewise, the wave of xenophobic violence that erupted shortly after reunification during the early 1990s prompted the Standing Conference of the Ministers of Education and Cultural Affairs of the Länder (KMK), which oversees education in each of the German states, to issue a statement affirming the importance of Holocaust education for promoting intercultural understanding.[10] In short, since the Second World War, education has been routinely used to demonstrate Germany's 're-civilization'.

As Ieva Gundare and Pieter Batelaan noted succinctly in 2003, approaches to teaching about the Holocaust depend not only upon a nation's educational culture, but also that country's particular experience of National Socialism and the Second World War.[11] This has provoked significant scholarly interest in the treatment of the Holocaust within territories occupied by, or allied to, the Nazis, with notable recent works focussing upon Holocaust education in Poland, the Baltic States, Romania and the former Czechoslovakia, exploring silences or distortions within school textbooks and the impact of victimhood narratives upon representations of the past.[12] Bystander nations too have come under scrutiny. In Britain, a nation physically remote from the killing sites, scholars have felt compelled to underscore the fact that the Holocaust should, nonetheless, be regarded as an essential part of the country's history, encouraging schools to undertake a critical reflection on attitudes to Jewish refugees during the 1930s and government responses to reports on mass killings during the early 1940s.[13] Again, the message here is that the Holocaust constitutes an important moral lesson for all of humanity. As in Germany, however, the development of pedagogic initiatives within these other countries has been a slow process. Holocaust education, as we understand it today, really only began to emerge during the late 1980s and 1990s.

Teaching the Nazi past in East and West Germany, 1945–90

During the Third Reich, the Nazis had placed a strong emphasis on education to promote their ideology and ensure the long-term future of the regime. Textbooks and other teaching materials reflected the National Socialist worldview, with maps pointing to Germany's 'intrinsic' right to the territory lost after the First World War, anti-Semitic stories and images and, in the case of maths books, problems that encouraged students to calculate the cost of sustaining disabled people for the Volksgemeinschaft.[14] Such resources were, of course, removed after the Second World War as the Allies launched a programme of re-education to put Germany back on the 'right' track.[15] The aim was to eradicate all traces of National Socialism, as well as the militarism and aggressive nationalism that was deemed responsible for leading Europe into two world wars. Nazi textbooks were replaced with historical accounts that would demonstrate the inherent criminality of the National Socialist state.

Schools began to be reopened from autumn 1945. At first, though, teaching was difficult given the shortage of available classrooms (many schools had been damaged during the war and needed to be rebuilt), materials and staff. The majority of educators, having been members of the National Socialist Teachers' League during the Third Reich, were now facing denazification procedures. Seventy-five per cent of teachers were dismissed by the Military Government in the French zone during the summer of 1945, and 65 per cent of primary school teachers in Bavaria.[16] However, as the Allies struggled to find enough politically reliable staff for the reconstituted schools, and denazification itself began to be wound up, many of these dismissals ultimately proved short-lived. By 1947, at least 85 per cent of Bavarian teachers, for example, had returned to their posts.[17] This continuity in personnel would have an impact on the amount of teaching postwar students would receive on the Nazi period and, in particular, the crimes of the Third Reich.

Although it would take time before historiography addressed the Holocaust in its own right, early German teaching of the Third Reich could nevertheless illustrate Nazi atrocities by drawing upon the extensive documentation that had been compiled during the first wave of war crimes trials, as well as records produced by survivors such as Eugen Kogon. Bodo von Borries argues that, by 1949, there were at least six examples of Nazi crimes that could be discussed in schools: the acts of aggression against the Soviet Union, the so-called Commissar Order to kill partisans in Eastern Europe, the use of slave labour, the mass shootings conducted by the *Einsatzgruppen*, the deportation and ghettoization of the European Jews and the mass killing through the use of poison gas.[18] The extent to which these themes were addressed in the classroom, and the way in which they were interpreted, though, would be affected by both Cold War politics and teachers' own ability to talk about the past.

In the East, school teaching about the Nazi period reflected official commemorative rhetoric with the emphasis on 'victims of fascism'. Teachers were compelled to adhere to the Marxist-Leninist theory of history, accentuating the relationship between capitalism and fascism, as well as the centrality of class struggle. In August 1949, the SED issued its guidelines for ensuring a 'democratic' education within East Germany. Calling upon schools to transform youth 'into fighters for the unity of Germany, for a just peace and for a peaceful and amicable coexistence between nations, especially with the Soviet Union', the SED argued that such goals could only be met 'if every teacher and educator combats all reactionary and neo-Fascist, militaristic, war mongering and especially anti-Soviet influences and theories, any religious, national and racial hatred'.[19]

State controls meant that there was just one standard textbook in the GDR that would be updated every few years. Thus, as Borries points out, there were only around seven textbooks produced during the course of the East German state.[20] Within these texts, stark reference was made to the extermination camps, but the dead tended to be listed primarily by nationality. There was no mention of persecuted homosexuals, Sinti and Roma, or Jehovah's Witnesses, or the murder of the disabled. The statistics for those killed also tended to be erroneous, with a 1952 textbook referring to 'tens of thousands of human beings'.[21] While another textbook from the early 1950s did use the phrase 'millions', special emphasis was placed upon Soviet suffering, with the statement, 'from 9.5 million Jews in Europe, about 5 million were murdered. Nazi racial persecution had an *even more* horrible effect on the Slavic peoples, on Poland and above all on the Soviet Union'.[22] Borries argues that it was only in 1988 that Jewish victims began to receive more attention although even then, the plundering of businesses and the plight of the forced labourers continued to take precedence in the historical narrative.[23]

Instead, the main feature of East German textbooks was the emphasis on the struggle between 'socialists' and 'imperialists'. Stalin's signing of the Non-Aggression Treaty with Germany in 1939 was presented as a defensive measure that would give him time to prepare for war in two years' time, while the Western Allies were critiqued for not helping Poland or opening up a second front to aid Russia, as well as committing their own war crimes in the bombing of innocent East German civilians at Dresden.[24] Furthermore, when Nazi crimes against humanity were addressed, it was often as a means for critiquing the West German companies that had profited from the use of forced labour and the appropriation of vital resources.[25] In describing the extermination process, for instance, one textbook stated:

> The nazis had invented the extermination of human beings on a large-scale, industrial basis: in order to be able to kill quickly and to kill as many people as possible, they administered gassing. They guided the naked prisoners into a room into which they caused poison gas to be poured... German capitalists profited from this mass murder. Thus, in only one year, just one company, Tesch-Stabenow, supplied 190,000 kilos of this poison gas. The main supplier of the poison gas was the company IG-Farben.[26]

Likewise, revised GDR textbooks issued during the 1960s were quick to capitalize upon the presence of former Nazis then occupying a prominent position within West German public life. The scandal surrounding Hans Globke, for example, was relayed to East German students in a 1963 textbook through a reference to the Nuremberg Laws 'for which Adenauer's current Secretary of State, Dr. Globke wrote the interpretative commentary'.[27]

Analysing textbooks in both East and West Germany after 1945, Bodo von Borries has identified four key strands within early postwar representations of Nazism: a long-standing belief in Germany's 'Divine Mission', the central role of Hitler, the role of political and social elites in facilitating the Nazi rise to power and the notion that National Socialism and Bolshevism constituted a similar brand of totalitarianism.[28] Although Nazism was being condemned, each of these themes reflected the vested interests of the two German states, or the Allies. Talk of a history of fanatical nationalism, for example, pointed to the long continuity of German history, suggesting that the German people did, indeed, bear a collective guilt for what had happened under Hitler and needed to be directed towards the 'right' path of development. This particular theme was mostly evident during the occupation period, reflecting the Allies' ambitions for re-education. It disappeared from school textbooks once control over education had been restored to the Germans. By contrast, an emphasis on Hitler's omnipotent rule, for example, served to demonstrate the futility of resistance during the Third Reich and present Nazism as an aberration in an otherwise healthy history. The remaining themes reflected the different ideological stances of the GDR and FRG. Emphasizing the role of the conservative elites reflected the Comintern definition of fascism, while the stress on totalitarianism reflected the general Cold War rhetoric of the West.

In the FRG, up to thirty different textbooks could be available at any one time, but these too were characterized by certain omissions. Pagaard argues that 'textbooks in the 1950s … were characterised … by their general neglect of the Holocaust and by a tendency to absolve the German people as a whole of responsibility, a feat usually accomplished by focusing on the Nazi terror state'. There was also use of perpetrator documents, an emphasis on the 'honourable' German soldier and a tendency to dwell on the plight of the expellees and victims of Soviet atrocities.[29] Michael Kater describes them as 'carelessly' rewritten and notes that, as late as 1965, the popular upper-school text, *Grundriss der Geschichte*, contained the following passage:

> Hitler was gifted in a variety of ways, but he was lazy, capricious and without stamina. Full of ideas, he was too flighty to make anything of them. His only passions were reading the papers and politicizing. Although he read much, he did so indiscriminately and unsystematically. In any discussion he would scream as soon as he got agitated and would berate his opponents endlessly. Even in that early period, he was showing his manic tendency toward monologues, as well as a one-sidedness that bordered on the psychopathic.[30]

Such descriptions imposed a useful sense of distance between Hitler and the rest of population, focussing solely on his character defects rather than contemplating the popular support he had enjoyed, or the consensus and collaboration that had enabled racial ideology to be implemented to such sinister effect.

Examining a 1956 textbook, *Kletts geschichtliches Unterrichtswerk*, Borries notes that there were no statements on the persecution of the Jews before 1939, nor the deportations, mass shootings and industrial killings that took place during the war. The genocide 'was not clearly recognisable' in this book, although examples of conflict between the church and state were exaggerated.[31] Moreover, descriptions of the Second World War focussed on Hitler's mistakes, suggesting that the conflict might have been waged more forcefully to smash Bolshevism. Borries sees this text as essentially giving Hitler belated advice on how he might have won the war and achieved his foreign policy ambitions, adding 'this sort of talk might have been common among groups of regulars in German pubs, but it should not have been included in a history textbook'.[32]

By contrast, Borries counts just forty-seven words (fifty-seven when translated into English) on the Holocaust within this same textbook:

> The Jews in Hitler's sphere of control fared even worse. From the beginning of the war, harsher and harsher measures were taken. Hitler ordered the 'Final Solution' of the Jewish question. In the Empire and in the conquered territories some millions of Jews were arrested. They met a terrible death in the gas chambers of the Einsatzkommandos.[33]

The victims are rendered passive objects of Nazi persecution and there is no effort to explain just who was carrying out these orders, and why. Instead, the continual focus on the central role of Hitler placed all the guilt firmly on the Nazi leadership. An additional quote, drawn from the IMT, was used to 'prove' collective German innocence and legitimize postwar mythologies:

> The German nation and the general public of the world heard about these crimes only after the occupation of Germany in 1945. At Nuremberg…an American judge later on testified: 'The statements of those who participated in this terrible planned mass extermination show with great plausibility that no more than a hundred persons were informed about what was happening in general or in any way.'[34]

This was a comforting and reassuring version of history that spared students – and, moreover, their teachers – from having to consider issues of consensus and collaboration.

Kletts geschichtliches Unterrichtswerk was revised in the early 1960s. New passages were added dealing with the persecution of the Jews, including two additional pages detailing Auschwitz, and one mention of mass shootings. The ghettoization of the Jews, however, continued to be omitted and the efforts to excuse the wider German population from the crimes of the Third Reich also persisted. The book stated, 'as some protests became known, the leadership invented less conspicuous methods and increasingly hid the horrible acts of annihilation from its own (German) people'. In this simple line, the textbook thus adhered to the usual narratives of resistance, while highlighting the population's powerlessness to prevent the regime from simply developing new killing tactics.[35]

In keeping with the broader narratives of Vergangenheitsbewältigung and the development of Holocaust historiography, the 1960s are usually pinpointed as the moment in which the teaching of the Nazi past began to improve in both German states. Certainly, the Eichmann trial of 1961 appears to have given new impetus to Holocaust education, with textbooks in both Germanys being updated to say more about the deportation of the Jews. It was also against the backdrop of the Eichmann hearings that a conference of the EKD issued a public statement in July 1961 calling for improvements in history education:

> Parents and teachers should break the silence so far kept on this matter as far as the younger generation is concerned. In the present state of affairs of world politics, the attempt to clear ourselves and to throw the blame for our own failure on other people endangers not only one particular group of people, but the life of every one of us. Again and again, young people complain that they have been insufficiently informed (if at all) about the events in Germany relating to the Jews. We owe youth a frank enlightenment in this matter, even though in doing so we will be compelled to confess our own failure and our wrong thinking.[36]

However, there were also some crucial moments during the late 1950s too that revealed both a growing interest in the Nazi past among German youth, and the growing influence of a new generation of school teachers. One such moment came with the publication of Anne Frank's diary in West Germany in 1956. This book quickly became an important and popular instrument for teaching about the Holocaust and it was of no coincidence that the number of school trips to the site of Bergen-Belsen increased dramatically at this point.[37] Some students also seized the opportunity provided by the publication to voice their own opinions on the prevailing state of education within the FRG. A Christian-Jewish youth group from Bielefeld, for example, reproduced extracts from Anne Frank's diary in their newsletter and juxtaposed them with the cry,

> 11 years after Germany's defeat, 12 years after July 20 1944, 17 years after September 1939, 18 years after November 9 1938, 23 years after January 30 1933, German boys and girls know hardly anything about those dates.... Ask your teacher about Stauffenberg and Julius Leber, about the November pogrom and the Jew badge – they will not answer. Or will they? Just ask. Ask your parents about the concentration camps and the gas chambers. Ask them. And go to the libraries. Get yourselves the books that will tell you all about those days.[38]

Two years later, the prosecution of former Einsatzkommando personnel in Ulm prompted further interest in the recent past. In the aftermath of the trial, the town initiated its own research project into the fate of the local Jewish population between 1933 and 1945. The resultant book, *Documents Relative to the Persecution of the Jewish Citizens of Ulm/ Danube*, listed the names of all Jews who had been resident in Ulm at the time of Hitler's appointment as chancellor, as well as the date and destination of each person deported between 1941 and 1943. In this way, the book helped to individualize the victims of the Holocaust. Copies were presented to every school leaver in the district in the hope that future generations would be able to learn from the mistakes of the past. An introductory comment by the mayor of Ulm outlined instead the town's hopes for the future:

> The history of every nation has its bright side and its shadows. Perhaps the deepest shadows are to be found in that chapter of German history which recounts the persecution of the Jews in the years 1933 to 1945. What was done then by a criminal regime cannot be compensated. More and more opinions are voiced that one should not stir up the past, that one should turn one's back on the injustice and horror. But the voice that warns against forgetfulness of this heavy guilt, no less than of the misery, tears and blood of the victims, should not go unheard. By this carefully produced documentation concerning its own boundaries, Ulm desires to contribute to the illumination of the past, to confess the wrong it has committed and to warn future generations so that such events cannot happen again.[39]

An epilogue by the book's editor, Heinz Keil, also made a direct appeal to the West German youth, stating:

> With the end of the war in 1945, we were faced with a tragic reckoning. 332 out of the 530 Jews of Ulm had successfully emigrated. The remainder who could not emigrate were, for the most part, murdered in the concentration camps. This shows how a people can vote for a system of government which abuses people and civil rights and produces terror and horrors. The youth who did not live through this time should address this theme coolly and soberly.[40]

Elsewhere, university students were also beginning to challenge prevailing public discourse about the past. In 1959, a group of students in Karlsruhe mounted a touring exhibition on Nazi justice including a list of the current whereabouts of 206 judges and prosecutors who had worked for the People's Courts during the Third Reich – many of whom remained within the West German judiciary. One of the key organizers behind this event was himself the son of a former Nazi judge, suggesting that the younger generation were already questioning their parents' behaviour.[41]

One of the most important moments in West Germany's attitude to history education came in the winter of 1959/60 when a rash of swastika graffiti swept across the FRG. The sight of Nazi insignia daubed upon public buildings in several different cities generated outrage in the national press, and fears that the country was facing a renewed threat from Right-wing extremists. The events, though, were quickly attributed to ignorant youths and public attention duly turned to the state of education. A survey conducted by the Hesse state government in 1959 revealed that 57 per cent of graduating high school students had not discussed the Nazi era; and as many as 79 per cent had not studied the Weimar republic.[42] Further investigations conducted during the early 1960s also cast doubt on students' understanding of the Third Reich, revealing a widespread emotional detachment from the Holocaust. Observers noted that pupils would recite the facts by rote as if they belonged to ancient history; there was little sense that this was a topic of any relevance to them. Harold Marcuse argues that this response owed much to the students' teachers, educators who had themselves generally come of age in the early 1940s and found it difficult to talk about the Nazi period. Many avoided it altogether, preferring to focus on the history of the Kaiserreich instead. One woman who taught in the FRG during this period reflected that her history education was 'thorough up until 1919' but then 'blocked out until 1949'.[43]

By the start of the 1960s, then, critics were beginning to attack the existing textbooks, pointing out that praising the construction of the autobahns and the eradication of unemployment during the 1930s amounted to a glorification of National Socialism.[44] West Germany would need to think more seriously about the ways in which it was presenting this period to the younger generation and, in 1962, the education ministers of the German federal states agreed that Nazism should be included in history and social studies curricula in all West German schools.[45] A new range of educational activities, and better quality textbooks were introduced throughout the decade yet, even then, there remained some gaps in the historical narrative. Reinhold Boschki argues that 'the relationship between the majority of the populace and the Jewish minority was neither addressed nor discussed. This encouraged a view of history from the perspective of the perpetrators, while the role of the victims remained underrepresented.'[46]

In 1966, Theodor Adorno gave a speech entitled 'education after Auschwitz' in which he urged that the primary role of education was to ensure that there could be no repeat of the horrors of Nazism. By education, what Adorno meant was referring to two aspects: '(1) education in childhood, especially early childhood, and (2) general enlightenment that creates a spiritual, cultural and social climate that permits no repetition of such monstrous action, thus a climate in which motives that have led to the horror become conscious to some degree'.[47] To begin with, Adorno's words seemed to have little impact. It was only during the student protests, two years later, that people began to take up his cry and call for a more open and honest discussion of the recent past.

That said, there were examples of other educational initiatives taking place on a local level throughout the 1960s. Trips to observe war crimes proceedings, for example, became an interesting educational tool during this period. Various reports note how the public gallery for such trials were invariably populated by younger people; indeed sometimes school classes were the only visitors in attendance.[48] The extent to which these students were genuinely engaged in the case, though, remained questionable. Writing about the audience at the Frankfurt Auschwitz trial, Emmi Bonhoeffer noted: 'I am shocked by the apparent callousness with which young people listen in occasionally on the hearings. Quite frequently the judge has to call them to order as they sit there among the audience in shirt sleeves, with legs crossed high and chewing gum as if they were looking at a movie thriller.'[49] Gita Sereny recalled similar scenes at other trials: 'the seats for the public are often filled with boys and girls – school classes brought by young teachers. The children munch sweets and chocolate. They chat and giggle.'[50] Again, Sereny's reference to the age of the teachers here can be taken as evidence of the ways in which a younger generation of school staff was trying to effect a better understanding of the Nazi period during this period.

Some schools followed up trips to the local courtroom with further educational events focussing on the Holocaust. One year on from the end of the Auschwitz case, a series of school and public lectures were given in Frankfurt by survivor and trial commentator Hermann Langbein, and towards the end of the Cologne Sachsenhausen hearings in 1965, two of the trial witnesses, one Polish, the other a member of the local Cologne population, were similarly invited to speak to pupils at a nearby school. The juxtaposition of these witnesses offered a reminder of German suffering in the city during the Nazi era, thereby recalling resistance mythologies, but also demonstrated a keen awareness of the fate of other nationalities at the hands of the regime. The visit was reported in the local press, and it emerged that the class concerned had already conducted some background research into the subject by reading *Der Sternkinder*, a book which, like the *Diary of Anne Frank*, dealt with the plight of Dutch children during the occupation of Holland. The classroom itself was 'overcrowded' for the occasion and at the end of the session, one child was reported as saying:

> We were always shaken anew and could not grasp at all that people planned and carried out such atrocities. We all want to contribute so that such terrible events are no longer possible in the future. We thank you for coming.[51]

Another crucial moment in West German attitudes to Holocaust education came in during the late 1970s with the so-called 'Boßmann shock'. In 1977,

Dieter Boßmann invited school students from across West Germany to write an essay on the theme 'what I have heard about Hitler'. Over 3,000 responses were received from 110 schools across ten West German states. The results were relayed in the press and generated outcry when it appeared there was much to be desired in terms of what younger people knew about the Nazi period; Boßmann himself declared the results an 'utter disaster'.[52] Many of the students made reference to their grandparents' experiences, or presented the events of the Third Reich as occurring without agency. There were also frequent references to Hitler's alleged sexual depravities. The response of one sixteen-year-old, that they had heard 'nothing, unfortunately' about Hitler made the by-line of *Der Spiegel*. A 14-year-old student confessed, 'I've never listened when being told about Adolf Hitler. Politics doesn't interest me. If we were to go over Hitler in school, I wouldn't pay attention.'[53] There were also a number of apologetic responses, with students insisting that those who did not join the NSDAP were 'slaughtered', or that Hitler only wanted to do good for the German people.[54] Others reflected on the 'benefits' that Hitler could bring if he was alive today, restoring Germany to a position of great power. Considering the differences between Nazi and West German domestic policy, meanwhile, one student bemoaned the fact that criminals were no longer shot.[55]

The results of Boßmann's study generated concern for the future of the FRG, and prompted the West German president, Walter Scheel, to warn 'we are in danger of becoming a country without history'.[56] At the same time, though, a survey conducted by EMNID found that the majority of 16- to 24-year-olds – 53 per cent of those questioned – considered themselves to be 'reasonably informed' about the Nazi past.[57]

The following spring, in April 1978, the KMK passed a resolution stressing the need for schools to 'actively work against uncritical acceptance of portrayals that trivialize or even glorify the Third Reich and its representatives, characterized as it was by dictatorship, genocide and inhumanity'.[58] Three months later, in July 1978, the Minister of Education and Cultural Affairs for North Rhine-Westphalia issued a decree in which it insisted that 'even many decades after Auschwitz, recalling the causes and consequences of National Socialism is one of the most pressing tasks facing school'. Arguing that 'nobody has the right to forget', and pointing to growing right-wing radicalism within the FRG, the minister argued:

> A constructive treatment and discussion of the recent German past should strengthen an understanding of the connection between National Socialist megalomania and its unscrupulous policy of violence, between racist discrimination and genocide, between intolerance towards minorities and 'eradication' .... It seems ... that for us developing sensitivity towards every form of oppression, segregation and intolerance is a commensurate form of 'Vergangenheitsbewältigung'. We should set a living example of behaving towards minorities in our society in a manner differing radically

> from the way that the National Socialist 'Volksgemeinschaft' treated those whom they expelled as alien to the community.[59]

It was the impact of the television series *Holocaust* in 1979, though, that arguably had one of the biggest effects on West German education. In the wake of the broadcast, the Bundeszentrale für politische Bildung (Centre for Political Education) was inundated with requests for educational materials on the Nazi genocide as teachers tried to deal with increased student interest in the topic. Once again, a series of measures were introduced to improve the coverage of the Nazi period in school textbooks. These reflected new historical research methods with the addition of more primary sources to enable students to analyse the evidence for themselves. There was a pedagogic shift from the recitation of facts towards a more analytical exploration of human behaviour and the structure of the Third Reich. Greater emphasis was also placed on *Alltagsgeschichte* (the history of everyday life) and regional case studies. Moreover, the war itself was now recognized as one of extermination. Killing centres such Auschwitz received more attention, and the persecution of Sinti and Roma also received brief mention. The myth of the 'clean' Wehrmacht, however, persisted.[60] Nazism was also now chosen as one of the possible topics for the annual 'President's Prize', a nationwide school essay writing competition. In 1980, students were able to tackle the theme, 'everyday life under National Socialism' and the number of entries to the competition almost tripled.[61]

A further resolution by the KMK in December 1980 again emphasized the need for students to gain a basic knowledge of the Nazi period in both history and political education classes. Noting the need to take note of the new trends in historical research, the KMK used the resolution to speak primarily about the teaching of German wartime resistance:

> Today we do not only know about the existence of systematic, programmatic resistance by political groups (e.g. the Goerdeler circle, the Kreisau circle, Neubeginnen etc.), but also about widespread resistance among the population. This expressed itself in forms of non-conformism, individual refusal, and frequent instances of passive resistance. It is also evident that resistance arose from various ideological and political motives. This resistance cannot be reduced to a single common denominator; it should therefore not be regarded from only one angle and no single group should be portrayed as having a claim to represent the resistance. All forms of resistance however share a common point of departure: objection to the total National Socialist political invasion of everyday life; moral repugnance over violations of law; solidarity with the persecuted; the attempt to preserve a minimum of moral responsibility in a totally controlled state, even if only within the closest circle of family, community, Church; and, with the increasing duration of war, growing awareness of the senselessness and the murderous character of that war.[62]

Although clearly calling for a more nuanced depiction of the resistance to Hitler, the KMK nonetheless managed to echo the popular postwar myth of widespread opposition. The document continued:

> The local and regional historical environment is a particularly suitable medium for treating the resistance. It must be shown that capitulation to dictatorship frequently began not with spectacular defeats but with small, everyday acts of cowardice. By the same token, it must be shown that everyday life was also the special province of silent resistance without which no image of life in the Third Reich would be complete. However, it must also be demonstrated how fear and conformism were able to arise, robbing many of the courage to even recognise injustice, let alone to oppose it . . . . The examination of the resistance should strengthen respect for human rights, political and moral responsibility and active support for a system in which various political and ideological directions can coexist and interact. The forces of resistance, as varied as they were, manifest a common will to express one's moral identity even in a hopeless political situation. Therefore, in bringing the resistance alive in teaching and political education we are providing a key to the future of our democratic system.[63]

The situation in modern Germany

Since reunification and the end of the Cold War, there has been no further question of ideological competition between two German states. Likewise, the greater temporal distance from the events in question means there is perhaps less concern about the effects of personal confrontation between students and their parents or grandparents. Instead, textbooks produced since the 1990s have reflected a new interest in the 'history of mentalities' with students are frequently asked to research their own community or to participate in role-playing activities to consider the range of responses and experiences in the past. The textbook *Rückspiegel*, published in 1996, contains ninety pages on the Third Reich and the Second World War, stressing the criminal character of the conflict and the murder of the European Jews. Photographs and a map of the concentration camps are included, as well as a table detailing the different stages in the killing process. There is also a section that considers the ways in which older Germans responded to defeat and Nazism at the end of the war.[64]

The Holocaust has been a compulsory subject for students aged 14–16 in all sixteen states (*Länder*) since 1995. Some pupils do explore the persecution of the Jews at an earlier age, but this is not mandatory. Students preparing for university will encounter the subject again when they are eighteen.[65] The teaching of the Holocaust typically occurs across multiple subject areas including history, social studies, German literature, music, art, biology and religious education. Between sixteen and twenty lessons are typically scheduled for looking at the Nazi period but within this, it is up to the individual teacher to decide how much time to devote to the Holocaust, it is not treated as a subject in its own right. Various opportunities for teacher training are offered by state organizations for political education, trade unions, museums and memorial institutions.[66] Since the 1960s, the KMK has regularly underscored the need to confront the Holocaust within German schools, with reference not only to an understanding of the nation's historical responsibility, but also to the need to remember the victims. A report in 1997 declared, 'dealing with these topics in education and socialization work is of the utmost importance for the Federal Republic of Germany as a democratic state based on the rule of law'.[67]

Stephen Pagaard's 1995 case study into history teaching within North Rhine-Westphalia, the largest of the federal states, gives some useful insight into the form that Holocaust education takes in practice. There, the *Hauptschule* (lower secondary school) curriculum sets out a programme for fourteen- and fifteen-year-olds entitled 'Only Twelve Years', which covers such themes as the collapse of the Weimar Republic, Nazi ideology, the experience of German youth during the Third Reich, resistance and the persecution of the Jews. The latter traces the evolution of Nazi racial policy including the 1935 Nuremberg Laws, Kristallnacht and Auschwitz. Pagaard reports that 'student motivation is encouraged through discussions, documentary films, group work, project days, eyewitness accounts and local history investigation through field trips. Discussion topics such as "But what has the Holocaust to do with me?" and "It wasn't the German people as a whole but a handful of criminals" are suggested in the curriculum guide.'[68] A similar pedagogic approach exists with the *Realschule* and the *Gymnasium*, although the latter covers topics in greater depth and places more emphasis on document analysis.[69]

In Bavaria, meanwhile, state educators encourage an interdisciplinary examination of the longer history of Jewish–non-Jewish relations, encouraging students to appreciate the richness of Jewish history and culture, rather than viewing Jews merely as the objects of Nazi violence. This is seen as a necessary precondition for promoting understanding, tolerance and respect. Thus secondary school curricula in Bavaria encompasses Jewish life in medieval society and emancipation and assimilation since the Enlightenment, as well as the history of modern anti-Semitism and persecution.[70] Since the 1980s, *Gedenkstätte* (memorial sites) have come to occupy a central place within Holocaust education and initiatives within both Bavaria and North Rhine-Westphalia reflect this. Pagaard, for instance, records how schools in the later state will visit the Alte Synagogue or the former Gestapo prison in Cologne.[71] Students in Bavaria, meanwhile, are likely to visit Dachau or Flossenbürg concentration camp.[72]

However, some challenges remain within the field of Holocaust education, not least Germany's own background as the 'land of the perpetrators'. The

Nazi era is not abstract history, but one that has the potential to recall family experiences and behaviour; thinking about perpetrator motivation or the popular consensus behind Hitler can remain painful, despite our ever-growing distance from the events in question. In compiling its country report for the IHRA, the German government noted that some students may still feel that there is an 'implicit accusation of guilt' being levelled at them, and be compelled to defend themselves, sometimes resulting 'in a rejection of dealing with the topic'.[73] Furthermore, Stephan Marks argues that for both teachers and students, the Holocaust 'is burdened with unconscious content and emotions such as guilt and shame, which were transgenerationally transmitted from one's ancestors. The majority of today's teachers and students are descendants of those millions of men and women who were bystanders or perpetrators – standing by, agreeing to, or actively participating in National Socialism. So, most teachers as well as students may, in one way or another, embody "the sins of their fathers", mothers, grandparents, or ancestors even further back.' Consequently, Marks argues that Germans need to reflect carefully on their teaching and learning experiences to reduce overreactions and misunderstandings and evasions.[74] He suggests that even today, there is a risk that students may become the focus of their teachers' unresolved conflict with their own parents, routinely given the message that they should feel ashamed of the older generation.[75]

Further complications may ensue from the fact that the Holocaust is today a permanent feature of public culture, prompting some students to feel that they are already sufficiently informed about the Holocaust, and need not concern themselves too much with it in school as well. Teachers, concluded the report, must find new ways to motivate these students for studying the topic in greater depth. Indeed, some critics have questioned the impact of schools on students' interpretations of the past, arguing that by the time they come to study the Nazi period, their opinions have already been formed by the media and family ties.[76] At the same time, it was noted that the history of the Holocaust is competing with many other modern topics. It can therefore be difficult to ensure that the curriculum devotes sufficient space to this period. The report argued, 'continuing efforts are needed to convince curriculum designers, teachers, and the public of the extraordinary significance of the Holocaust'.[77] In today's multicultural society, there is also some concern as to the best ways to integrate the history of the Holocaust into the experiences of immigrants from other countries who may question the relevance of the subject to themselves.[78]

Boschki argues that 'while National Socialism remains one of the most studied phenomena of our history, there are virtually no attempts to design teaching about this period in such a way that it does not merely convey information and cognitions, but also sensitizes students against wrongdoing'.[79] In some cases, it can even appear that education has the opposite of its intended effect, alienating teenagers and inadvertently passing on nationalist ideas.[80] Describing an ill-fated research experiment in Freiburg in 1998, Stephan Marks notes that some students, having interviewed former Nazis, found it difficult to suppress their fascination with these figures, or to summarize testimonies with the necessary critical distance.[81]

Reflecting on Holocaust education

The place of the Holocaust within German history teaching has thus undergone significant developments since the late 1970s. In the aftermath of the 'Boßmann shock' and the broadcast of *Holocaust*, there has also been an increased effort among pedagogic researchers to reflect critically on the impact that teaching about the Nazi era is having in Germany. A wave of investigations into teaching materials and student responses demonstrates ongoing concerns about younger people's knowledge of the past, and the need to find new ways of engaging students. The expression of Neo-Nazi and anti-Semitic sentiments, as well as outbreaks of racist violence in Germany since 1990, has been a significant motivating factor in this, prompting fears that Holocaust education is not working.

In 1992, shortly after Germany's reunification, Borries questioned 6,500 students aged between 12 and 18 across eastern and western Germany. Participants in this survey were presented with a list of twelve different concepts and asked to rate them according to what they associated with National Socialism. The results revealed that young people had clear opinions on the Nazi past, and highlighted strong connections between Nazism and negative concepts such as war crimes, concentration camps and the murder of Jews and Sinti and Roma. Positive concepts, such as full employment and civic order – features that had often been highlighted among previous cohorts of West German students – held little sway for this generation. However, a similar survey conducted just two years later found that associations were weakened; Borries has questioned whether this might constitute a 'normalization' of history in modern Germany.[82]

In 2000, meanwhile, there was further controversy when Aphons Silbermann and Manfred Stoffers produced a survey entitled 'Auschwitz: I Have Never Heard of It'. They proclaimed that 'millions' of Germans had very little understanding of the Holocaust and that Germany was in danger of forgetting the past. Other scholars, however, have criticized the survey for being based upon an unrepresentative sample. Having surveyed just 2,197 people, it was hard for Silbermann and Stoffers to justify their accusation of widespread ignorance. In truth, as Borries points out, their own data actually offered a more positive assessment of public knowledge. Sixty-nine per cent of those questioned (and 73 per cent of 18- to 20-year-olds) knew that Auschwitz was an extermination camp; 62 per cent knew that it was in Poland and 81 per cent of 14- to 17-year-olds questioned were able to give 'almost correct' dates for the period of the camp's operation. Eighty-four per cent of 14- to 17-year-olds and 89 per cent of 18- to 20-year-olds were also able to connect Auschwitz with the persecution of the Jews.[83]

Scholars, however, are never entirely satisfied with the way in which history is taught, and there is particular fear about us becoming too complacent within the field of Holocaust education. In 2007, Stephan Marks went so far as to speak of a 'crisis' in German teaching about the Holocaust, arguing that 'students are confronted with the facts and data, as well as the suffering of the victims, while the motives of the Nazi perpetrators and onlookers are, in general left out'. For him, such an omission ran the risk of creating a 'dangerous vacuum'; youngsters need to understand why so many people were attracted to the Nazi movement.[84] A comment by one student sums up this gap in historical understanding:

> For hours and hours our history teacher told us about the Jews, the Communists, the gypsies, the Russians – all those victims, nothing but victims. I never really believed him. Who knows whether it was all that bad? One of my classmates once asked him: 'What was so great about that time? Why did so many people cry Hurrah and Heil Hitler? Why were they all so excited? There must be a reason?' At that point, the teacher looked quite foolish and started to call him a neo-nazi. But we would not let it go. Finally, somebody had raised the all-important question of what had really happened. After all, in the movies he had shown us you could see children laughing, and the women's eyes all lit up. Hundreds of thousands of people in the streets were rejoicing. Where did all this excitement come from?[85]

Other scholars including Michael Kohlstruck, Olaf Jensen and Harald Welzer have explored responses to Nazism and the Holocaust through interviews with different generations of family members, examining the distinction between official, public representations of the past and private cultures of remembrance. Welzer records that even when some of the interviewees told their families about their behaviour as perpetrators during the war, it did not necessarily provoke any great emotional reaction. Instead, 'it is as though such tales were not heard by the family members present. Apparently, ties of family loyalty do not permit a father or grandfather to appear as one who killed people a few decades earlier.'[86] In this way, older narratives of 'Nazis' and 'Germans' can continue to hold sway and, for all of the developments within Holocaust education over the last decades, it remains difficult to effect a critical engagement with the past.

Conclusion: How the Holocaust Looks Today

Since the end of the Second World War, the Nazi past has found multiple forms of expression within Germany, from the construction of physical memorials, through to museum exhibits, films, television programmes, works of literature and plays. Questions over financial restitution to the victims of Nazi persecution or the continuance of legal investigations into suspected war criminals have generated intense political and media debate, while war crimes trials themselves have had the potential to inspire educational initiatives, research into local history under the Third Reich and further cultural representations of the Holocaust. Germans, in other words, have been anything but silent with regard to the legacy of the Third Reich.

However, the precise place of the Holocaust within this discussion has not always been so clear. Much of the early, postwar dialogue about the Nazi era, articulated during the late 1940s and 1950s, remained focussed primarily upon concepts of non-Jewish, German suffering. This encompassed a range of experiences, from forced mass expulsion from the eastern territories, to the devastating effects of Allied wartime bombing. The extent of the German resistance against Hitler was much mythologized while, during the occupation period, food shortages and the Allied denazification programme offered the population further opportunities for presenting themselves as victims. Germany's division into two, ideologically opposed states up until 1989/90 meant that the past also tended to be used very much to meet the needs of the political present; the GDR routinely critiqued the West's handling of former Nazis, while the FRG often used the example of the East German state to talk generically about the dangers of totalitarianism. Reunification, meanwhile, brought its own set of challenges as the country had to try and integrate these disparate postwar experiences into a national historical memory and devise ways to recall the victims of the so-called 'double past' – that of the Third Reich and the GDR.

The experiences of minority groups that had been racially persecuted by the Nazi regime, by contrast, received little serious attention for many years. It was not until the 1960s that Jewish suffering received greater acknowledgement, while other groups such as homosexuals, Jehovah's Witnesses, and Sinti and Roma have had to wait even longer to secure their place within German memorial culture. Even today, there remains much work to be done in this area. Such work as has been done owes much to the determination of survivors' groups, representatives of the political Left, zealous prosecutors, crusading journalists and the younger generations.

Furthermore, there was no easy path to achieving Vergangenheitsbewältigung. It is not sufficient to say that Germany suddenly embarked upon a critical engagement with the past from the 1960s. Alternative versions of the past have continued to circulate, as evidenced by controversies such as the Historikestreit in the mid-1980s, debates over how best to commemorate the fiftieth anniversary of the war's end in 1995, and the efforts to build a museum to the expellee experience at the turn of the century. In private too, reactionary or apologetic views of the past have been articulated that contrast with the official, public discourse of atonement.

Yet analyses of Germany's relationship with the Nazi past need to take note of the extent to which there are similarities between the FRG experience and the development of a Holocaust consciousness within other Western nations. There too, there was a failure to address the fate of the Jews or fully engage with the Holocaust until the 1960s. War fatigue, pressing economic problems and the need to fulfil their own reconstruction needs after 1945 meant that nations such as Britain also required some space before they could start to look back on these events. Postwar politics too affected the Allies' interest in pursuing suspected war criminals and completing the denazification programme. As the United States and the USSR began to carve out their respective alliances, it soon became evident that continued punitive action against the Germans could deny them a useful, strategic ally in the Cold War conflict. This was especially evident in the FRG, where West German rearmament and the maintenance of former Nazi civil servants during the early 1950s was predicated on not asking too many awkward questions about the recent past. In the GDR too, though, there were certain silences, and the threat of exposure as a former Nazi by the Stasi became a useful tool for moulding the 'good' East German citizen.

Today, Germany is held up as a model for the rest of the international community in terms of its work in Holocaust education, research and remembrance and, more generally, in post-conflict reconciliation. The nation's engagement with the Nazi past, despite its belated beginnings, has been remarkable and shows no sign of abating seventy years after the war's end. In March 2008, Chancellor Angela Merkel addressed the Knesset in Jerusalem as part of the celebrations marking the sixtieth anniversary of the founding of the state of Israel. Emphasizing a special relationship between the two nations, Merkel necessarily had cause to reflect on the Holocaust. She stated:

> The mass murder of 6 million Jews, carried out in the name of Germany, has brought indescribable suffering to the Jewish people, Europe and the entire world. The Shoah fills us Germans with shame. I bow my head before the victims. I bow before the survivors and before all those who helped them so they could survive.[1]

This was a historic speech, but Merkel went further still, describing her own experiences of growing up in postwar Germany, critiquing her country's previous handling of the past, and pledging to keep talking about this painful period of German history:

> I myself spent the first 35 years of my life in the German Democratic Republic, a part of Germany where National Socialism was considered a West German problem. But the GDR did not recognize the State of Israel until shortly before its own demise. It took more than 40 years before Germany as a whole acknowledged and embraced both its historical responsibility and the State of Israel.
>
> Ladies and gentlemen, I most firmly believe that only if Germany accepts its enduring responsibility for *the* moral disaster in its history will we be able to build a humane future. Or, to put it another way, respect for our common humanity is rooted in our responsibility for the past.[2]

In this way, it is clear that there can be no neat conclusion to this volume. Germany's memory work remains ongoing, as, indeed, does Holocaust engagement within other countries. Ultimately, it is this continual discussion of the past that serves as one of the best forms of remembrance for the victims of National Socialism.

NOTES

Introduction

1 International Holocaust Remembrance Alliance, 'Declaration of the Stockholm International Forum on the Holocaust', https://www.holocaustremembrance.com/about-us/stockholm-declaration.

2 The Holocaust and the United Nations Outreach Programme, A/RES/60/7: 'Resolution adopted by the General Assembly on the Holocaust Remembrance', 1 November 2005, http://www.un.org/en/holocaustremembrance/docs/res607.shtml.

3 Denkmal für die ermordeten Juden Europas, 'Anzahl der Besucher im Ort der Information 2005–2013', http://www.stiftung-denkmal.de/denkmaeler/denkmal-fuer-die-ermordeten-juden-europas/besucherzahlen.html#c2384.

4 Stiftung Topographie des Terrors, 'Dokumentationszentrum Topographie des Terrors', http://www.topographie.de/.

5 *Der Spiegel*, 'Kein Kriegsdenken', 1 March 2014.

6 For an overview of the division of Germany and its relationship to the Cold War, see Rolf Steiniger, 'Germany after 1945: Divided and Integrated or United and Neutral?', *German History*, Vol. 7, No. 1 (1989) pp. 5–18; David Reynolds, 'The Origins of the Cold War: The European Dimension, 1944–1951', *Historical Journal*, Vol. 28, No. 2 (1985) pp. 497–515; Tony Sharp, *The Wartime Alliance and the Zonal Division of Germany* (Oxford: Oxford University Press, 1975).

7 On Heimat, see Celia Applegate, *A Nation of Provincials: The German Idea of Heimat* (Berkeley, California: University of California Press, 1990); Alon Confino, *The Nation as a Local Metaphor: Wurttemberg, Imperial Germany and National Memory, 1871–1918* (Chapel Hill, North Carolina: University of North Carolina Press, 1997); Alon Confino & Ajay Skaria, 'The Local Life of Nationhood', *National Identities*, Vol. 4, No. 1 (2002) pp. 7–24. On similar efforts in East Germany, see Jason James, 'Retrieving a Redemptive Past: Protecting Heritage and Heimat in East German Cities', *German Politics and Society*, Vol. 27, No. 3 (2009) pp. 1–27.

8 David Robb, 'Playing with the "Erbe": Songs of the 1848 Revolution in the GDR', *German Life and Letters*, Vol. 63, No. 3 (2010) pp. 295–310. For more on the construction of usable identities in both states, see Mary Fulbrook, *German National Identity after the Holocaust* (Cambridge: Polity Press, 1999).

9 On the concept of a 'Zero Hour', see Konrad H. Jarausch, '1945 and the Continuities of German History: Reflections on Memory, Historiography

and Politics', G. Giles (ed.), *Stunde Null: The End and the Beginning Fifty Years Ago* (Washington, District of Columbia: German Historical Institute, Occasional Paper No. 20, 1997) pp. 9–24.

10 Jeffrey Herf, *Divided Memory: The Nazi Past in the Two Germanys* (Cambridge, Massachusetts: Harvard University Press, 1997) pp. 1–3; 106–161.

11 Bill Niven, *Facing the Nazi Past: United Germany and the Legacy of the Third Reich* (New York: Routledge, 2002) p. 2.

12 On the impact of these events, see Geoff Eley (ed.), *The Goldhagen Effect. History, Memory, Nazism- Facing the German Past* (Ann Arbor, Michigan: University of Michigan Press, 2000); Robert A. Shandley (ed.), *Unwilling Germans? The Goldhagen Debate* (Minneapolis, Minnesota: University of Minnesota Press, 1998); Lars Rensmann, 'Holocaust Memory and Mass Media in Contemporary Germany: Reflections on the Goldhagen Debate', *Patterns of Prejudice*, Vol. 33, No. 1 (1999) pp. 59–76; Niven, *Facing the Nazi Past*, pp. 143–174; Eve Rosenhaft, 'Facing Up to the Past – Again? "Crimes of the Wehrmacht"', *Debatte*, Vol. 5, No. 1 (1997) pp. 105–118; Hannes Heer & Jane Caplan, 'The Difficulty of Ending a War: Reactions to the Exhibition "War of Extermination: Crimes of the Wehrmacht 1941 to 1944"', *History Workshop Journal*, Vol. 46 (1998) pp. 187–203.

13 For an overview of recent historiographical trends, see Dan Stone, 'Beyond the "Auschwitz Syndrome": Holocaust Historiography after the Cold War', *Patterns of Prejudice*, Vol. 44, No. 5 (2010) pp. 454–468. On the use of the Holocaust to justify present-day military action, see Alan E. Steinweiss, 'The Auschwitz Analogy: Holocaust Memory and American Debates over Intervention in Bosnia and Kosovo in the 1990s', *Holocaust and Genocide Studies*, Vol. 19, No. 2 (2005) pp. 276–289.

14 Tony Kushner, *The Holocaust and the Liberal Imagination: A Social and Cultural History* (Oxford: Blackwell, 1994); Andy Pearce, *Holocaust Consciousness in Contemporary Britain* (London: Routledge, 2014); Caroline Sharples & Olaf Jensen (eds.), *Britain and the Holocaust: Remembering and Representing War and Genocide* (Basingstoke: Palgrave Macmillan, 2013). On the United States, see Peter Novick, *The Holocaust in Collective Memory The American Experience* (London: Bloomsbury, 2001); Lawrence Baron, 'The Holocaust and the American Public Memory, 1945-1960', *Holocaust and Genocide Studies*, Vol. 17, No. 1 (2003) pp. 62–88.

15 David Art, *The Politics of the Nazi Past in Germany and Austria* (Cambridge: Cambridge University Press, 2005); Günter Bischof, 'Victims? Perpetrators? "Punching Bags" of European Historical Memory? The Austrians and their World War II Legacies', *German Studies Review*, Vol. 27, No. 1 (2004) pp. 17–32; M. Bunzl, 'On the Politics and Semantics of Austrian Memory: Vienna's Monument against War and Fascism', *History and Memory*, Vol. 7, No. 2 (1995) pp. 7–40; Robert G. Knight 'Contours of Memory in Post-Nazi Austria', *Patterns of Prejudice*, Vol. 34, No. 4 (2000) pp. 5–11; Heidemarie Uhl, 'Of Heroes and Victims: World War II in Austrian Memory', *Austrian History Yearbook*, Vol. 42 (2011) pp. 185–200.

16 Andrea Mammone, 'A Daily Revision of the Past: Fascism, Anti-Fascism, and Memory in Contemporary Italy', *Modern Italy*, Vol. 11, No. 2 (2006) pp. 211–226; Robert S.C. Gordon, 'The Holocaust in Italian Collective Memory: *Il giorno della memoria*, 27 January 2001', *Modern Italy*, Vol. 11, No. 2 (2006) pp. 167–188; Robert S.C. Gordon, 'Which Holocaust? Primo Levi and the Field of Holocaust Memory in Post-War Italy', *Italian Studies*, Vol. 61, No. 1 (2006) pp. 85–113; Robert Ventresca, 'Mussolini's Ghost: Italy's Duce in History and Memory', *History and Memory*, Vol. 18, No. 1 (2006) pp. 86–119.

17 See, for example, Pieter Lagrou, 'Victims of Genocide and National Memory: Belgium, France and the Netherlands, 1945-1965', *Past and Present*, Vol. 154 (1997) pp. 181–222; Hermann W. von der Dunk, 'The Netherlands and the Memory of the Second World War', *European Review*, Vol. 4 (1996) pp. 221–239; Bella Zisere, 'The Memory of the Shoah in the Post-Soviet Latvia', *East European Jewish Affairs*, Vol. 35, No. 2 (2005) pp. 155–165; Stefan Rohdewald, 'Post-Soviet Remembrance of the Holocaust and National Memories of the Second World War in Russia, Ukraine and Lithuania', *Forum for Modern Language Studies*, Vol. 44, No. 2 (2008) pp. 173–184. See also the special issue of the *Scandinavian Journal of History*, Vol. 36, No. 5 (2011) for articles on the representation of the Holocaust in Norway, Sweden, Finland and Denmark.

18 Ljiljana Radonic, 'Croatia: Exhibiting Memory and History at the "Shores of Europe"', *Culture Unbound*, Vol. 3 (2011) pp. 355–367.

19 See, for example, Caroline Sharples, *West Germans and the Nazi Legacy* (New York: Routledge, 2012); Christoph Classen, *Bilder der Vergangenheit: Die Zeit des Nationalsozialismus im Fernsehen der Bundesrepublik Deutschland, 1955–1965* (Cologne: Böhlau Verlag, 1999); Harold Marcuse, *Legacies of Dachau: The Uses and Abuses of a Concentration Camp, 1933–2001* (Cambridge: Cambridge University Press, 2001).

20 Thomas C. Fox, *Stated Memory: East Germany and the Holocaust* (Rochester, New York: Camden House, 1999); Herf, *Divided Memory*. Another useful overview of the GDR's relationship with the past is offered in Jeffrey M. Peck, 'East Germany', D.S. Wyman (ed.), *The World Reacts to the Holocaust* (Baltimore, Maryland and London: John Hopkins University Press, 1996) pp. 447–474.

21 Wolfgang Benz, 'Nachkriegsgesellschaft und Nationalsozialismus. Erinnerung, Amnesie, Abwehr', *Dachauer Hefte*, Vol. 6 (1990) pp. 12–24; Ralph Giordano, *Die Zweite Schuld oder von der Last ein Deutscher zu sein* (Hamburg: Rasch und Rohring, 1987). Similar sentiments are produced in Ian Buruma, *The Wages of Guilt: Memories of War in Germany and Japan* (London: Vintage, 1995); Siobhan Kattago, *Ambigous Memory: The Nazi Past and German National Identity* (Westport, Connecticut: Praeger, 2001) and Werner Bergmann, 'Die Reaktion auf den Holocaust in Westdeutschland von 1945 bis 1989', *Geschichte in Wissenschaft und Unterricht*, Vol. 43 (1992) pp. 327–350.

22 Robert Moeller, *War Stories: The Search for a Usable Past in the Federal Republic of Germany* (Berkeley, California: University of

California Press, 2001). See also Ulrich Brochhagen, *Nach Nürnberg: Vergangensheitsbewältigung und Westintegration in der Ära Adenauer* (Berlin: Ullstein, 1999); Alf Ludtke, '"Coming to Terms with the Past": Illusions of Remembering, Ways of Forgetting Nazism in West Germany', *Journal of Modern History*, Vol. 65 (1993) pp. 542–572; Alon Confino, *Germany as a Culture of Remembrance: Promises and Limits of Writing History* (Chapel Hill, North Carolina: University of North Carolina Press, 2006).

23 Neil Gregor, *Haunted City: Nuremberg and the Nazi Past* (New Haven, Connecticut: Yale University Press, 2008) p. 11.

24 Ibid.; Marcuse, *Legacies of Dachau*; Peter Reichel, *Das Gedachtnis der Stadt: Hamburg im Umgang mit seiner nationalsozialistischen Vergangenheit* (Hamburg: Döllig & Galitz Verlag, 1997). See also Sven Keller, *Gunzburg und der Fall Josef Mengele: Die Heimatstadt und die Jagd nach dem NS-Verbrecher* (Munich: Oldenbourg, 2003); Gavriel D. Rosenfeld, *Munich and Memory: Architecture, Monuments and the Legacy of the Third Reich* (Berkeley, California: University of California Press, 2000); Gavriel D. Rosenfeld & Paul B. Jaskot (eds.), *Beyond Berlin: Twelve German Cities Confront the Nazi Past* (Ann Arbor, Michigan: University of Michigan Press, 2007).

25 See, for example, Philipp Gassert & Alan E. Steinweiss (eds.), *Coping with the Nazi Past: West German Debates on Nazism and Generational Conflict, 1955–1975* (New York: Berghahn, 2007); Dorothee Wierling, 'Generations and Generational Conflicts in East and West Germany', C. Klessmann (ed.), *The Divided Past: Rewriting Postwar German History* (Oxford: Berg, 2001) pp. 69–89; Elizabeth Heinemann, 'The Hour of the Woman: Memories of Germany's Crisis Years and West German National Identity', *American Historical Review*, Vol. 101, No. 2 (1996) pp. 354–395; J.M. Mushaben, 'Collective Memory Divided and Reunited: Mothers, Daughters and the Fascist Experience in Germany', *History and Memory*, Vol. 11, No. 1 (1999) pp. 7–40.

26 Such events usually appear as a stock list of factors within accounts of Vergangenheitsbewältigung but not necessarily with any detailed analysis of their actual impact upon popular responses to the past. For in-depth accounts of some of these events, see Robert Sackett, 'Memory by Way of Anne Frank: Enlightenment and Denial among West Germans circa 1960', *Holocaust and Genocide Studies*, Vol. 16, No. 2 (2002) pp. 243–265; Devin O. Pendas, *The Frankfurt Auschwitz Trial, 1963-1965: Genocide, History and the Limits of the Law* (Cambridge: Cambridge University Press, 2006); Rebecca Wittmann, *Beyond Justice? The Auschwitz Trial* (Cambridge, Massachusetts: Harvard University Press, 2005); Detlev Siegfried, '"Don't Trust Anyone Older Than 30?" Voices of Conflict and Consensus between Generations in 1960s West Germany', *Journal of Contemporary History*, Vol. 40, No. 4 (2005) pp. 727–744; Carole Fink, Philipp Gassert & Detlef Junker (eds.), *1968: The World Transformed* (Cambridge: Cambridge University Press, 1998); Rob Burns, *Protest and Democracy in West Germany: Extra-Parliamentary Opposition and the Democratic Agenda* (Basingstoke: Palgrave Macmillan, 1988).

27 Jeffrey Herf, 'The "Holocaust" Reception in West Germany: Right, Center and Left', *New German Critique*, Vol. 19, No. 1 (1980) pp. 30–52; Andreas

Huyssen, 'The Politics of Identification: "Holocaust" and West German Drama', *New German Critique*, Vol. 19, No. 1 (1980) pp. 117–136; Wolf Kansteiner, 'Nazis, Viewers and Statistics: Television History, Television Audience Research and Collective Memory in West Germany', *Journal of Contemporary History*, Vol. 30, No. 4 (2004) pp. 575–598.

28 Geoffrey H. Hartman (ed.), *Bitburg in Moral and Political Perspective* (Bloomington, Indiana: Indiana University Press, 1986); Geoff Eley, 'Nazism, Politics and the Image of the Past: Thoughts on the West German Historikerstreit, 1986-1987', *Past and Present*, Vol. 121 (1988) pp. 171–208; Richard J. Evans, 'The New Nationalism and the Old History: Perspectives on the West German Historikerstreit', *Journal of Modern History*, Vol. 59, No. 4 (1987) pp. 761–797. Richard Evans, *In Hitler's Shadow: West German Historians and the Attempt to Escape from the Nazi Past* (London: Pantheon, 1989).

29 Charles Maier, *The Unmasterable Past: Holocaust and German National Identity* (Cambridge, Massachusetts: Harvard University Press, 1988). Similarly, the early 1990s also saw the publication of Buruma's *Wages of Guilt* and Judith Miller, *One by One by One: Facing the Holocaust* (New York: Simon & Schuster, 1990).

30 For an overview of these various political issues and scandals, see Norbert Frei, *Adenauer's Germany and the Nazi Past: The Politics of Amnesty and Integration*, translated by J. Golb (New York: Columbia University Press, 2002). On rearmament and memories of the Second World War, see Alaric Searle, *Wehrmacht Generals, West German Society and the Rearmament Debate, 1949–1959* (Westport, Connecticut: Praeger, 2003).

31 Bill Niven, 'The GDR and the Bombing of Dresden', B. Niven (ed.), *Germans as Victims* (Basingstoke: Palgrave Macmillan, 2006) pp. 109–129; Hans Kundnani, 'Perpetrators and Victims: Germany's 1968 Generation and Collective Memory', *German Life and Letters*, Vol. 64, No. 2 (2011) pp. 272–282.

32 Niven, *Facing the Nazi Past*; Kattago, *Ambiguous Memory*; Klaus Neumann, *Shifting Memories: The Nazi Past in the New Germany* (Ann Arbor, Michigan: University of Michigan Press, 2000).

33 Eric Langenbacher, 'The Mastered Past? Collective Memory Trends in Germany since Unification', *German Politics and Society*, Vol. 28, No. 1 (2010) pp. 42–68.

Chapter 1

1 *Time Magazine*, 'Poland: Vernichtungslager', 21 August 1944. See also *Manchester Guardian*, 'Visit to Nazi Mass Murder Camp a Lublin', 12 August 1944; *New York Times*, 'Nazi Mass Killing Laid Bare in Camp', 30 August 1944.

2 United States Holocaust Memorial Museum, 'Ohrdruf', http://www.ushmm.org/wlc/en/article.php?ModuleId=0006131

3 United States Holocaust Memorial Museum, 'German Civilians Visit Buchenwald', http://www.ushmm.org/online/film/display/detail.php?file_num=22

4 Harold Marcuse, *Legacies of Dachau: The Uses and Abuses of a Concentration Camp, 1933–2001* (Cambridge: Cambridge University Press, 2001) p. 55.

5 Dokument 38: Imre Kertész, 'Beobachtung der Weimarer Bürger im Lager', Manfred Overesch (ed.), *Buchenwald und die DDR oder die Suche nach Selbstlegitimation* (Göttingen: Vandenhoeck & Ruprecht, 1995) p. 109.

6 *New York Herald Tribune*, 'Army Forces Weimar Citizens to View Buchenwald's Horrors', 18 April 1945.

7 Susan L. Carruthers, 'Compulsory Viewing: Concentration Camp Film and German Re-education', *Millennium: Journal of International Studies*, Vol. 30 (2001) p. 753.

8 Donald Bloxham, *Genocide on Trial: War Crimes Trials and the Formation of Holocaust History and Memory* (Oxford: Oxford University Press, 2001), pp. 139–140.

9 Joanne Reilly, *Belsen: The Liberation of a Concentration Camp* (London: Routledge, 1998) p. 71.

10 Morris Janowitz, 'German Reactions to Nazi Atrocities', *American Journal of Psychology*, Vol. 52, No. 2 (1946) p. 143.

11 Ibid.

12 See: Nikolaus Wachsmann & Jane Caplan (eds.), *Concentration Camps in Nazi Germany: The New Histories* (London: Routledge, 2010); Nikolaus Wachsmann & Christian Goeschel (eds.), *Before the Holocaust: New Approaches to the Nazi Concentration Camps, 1933–1939*, special issue of *Journal of Contemporary History*, Vol. 45, No. 3 (2010).

13 Janowitz, 'German Reactions', p. 142.

14 Ibid., p. 144.

15 Robert Gellately, *Backing Hitler: Consent and Coercion in Nazi Germany* (Oxford: Oxford University Press, 2002).

16 Janowitz, 'German Reactions', p. 143.

17 Shlomo Aronson, 'Preparations for the Nuremberg Trial: The OSS, Charles Dwork and the Holocaust', *Holocaust and Genocide Studies*, Vol. 12 (1998) pp. 257–281; Arieh J. Kochavi, 'The British Foreign Office versus the United Nations War Crimes Commission during the Second World War', *Holocaust and Genocide Studies*, Vol. 8, No. 1 (1994) pp. 28–49; S.S. Alderman, 'Negotiating the Nuremberg Trial Agreements, 1945', Raymond Dennett & Joseph E. Johnson (eds.), *Negotiating with the Russians* (Boston, Massachusetts: World Peace Foundation, 1951) pp. 49–100; Bradley F. Smith, *The Road to Nuremberg* (London: Deutsch, 1981); George Ginsburgs, *Moscow's Road to Nuremberg: The Soviet Background to the Trial* (The Hague: Martinus Nijhoff, 1996).

18 Indictment against Hermann Göring et al., reproduced by the *Avalon Project: Documents in Law, History and Diplomacy*, http://avalon.law.yale.edu/imt/count.asp

19 Among the other subsequent Nuremberg proceedings were trials against members of the German judiciary, industry and the *Einsatzgruppen* – the mobile killing squads that had murdered hundreds of thousands of people along the Eastern Front from June 1941.

20 John Cramer, *Belsen Trial 1945: der Lüneburger Prozess gegen Wachpersonal der Konzentrationslager Auschwitz und Bergen-Belsen* (Göttingen: Wallstein Verlag, 2011).

21 Tomasz Jardim, *The Mauthausen Trial: American Military Justice in Germany* (Cambridge, Massachusetts: Harvard University Press, 2012); Joshua M. Greene, *Justice at Dachau: The Trials of an American Prosecutor* (New York: Broadway, 2003); Fern Overbey-Hilton, *The Dachau Defendants: Life Stories from Testimony and Documents of the War Crimes Prosecutions* (Jefferson, North Carolina: McFarland, 2004).

22 Secondary literature on trials in the French and Soviet zones remains relatively scarce, but see Christian Meyer-Seltz, 'NS-Prozesse in der SBZ', *Tribüne*, Vol. 39. No. 155 (2000) pp. 132–137.

23 For an overview of early German trials, see: Nathan Stoltzfus & Henry Friedlander (eds.), *Nazi Crimes and the Law* (Cambridge: Cambridge University Press, 2009).

24 See, for example, George Ginsburgs, *The Nuremberg Trial and International Law* (Dordrecht: Nijhoff Publishers, 1990); Robert Wolfe, 'Flaws in the Nuremberg Legacy: An Impediment to International War Crimes Tribunals' Prosecution of Crimes Against Humanity', *Holocaust and Genocide Studies*, Vol. 12, No. 3 (1998) pp. 434–453; Hannah Caven, 'Horror in Our Time: Images of the Concentration Camps in the British Media, 1945', *Historical Journal of Film, Radio and Television*, Vol. 21, No. 3 (2001) pp. 205–253; Susan Twist, 'Evidence of Atrocities or Atrocious Use of Evidence: The Controversial Use of Atrocity Film at Nuremberg', *Liverpool Law Review*, Vol. 26, No. 3 (2005) pp. 267–302; Lawrence Douglas, 'Film as Witness: Screening Nazi Concentration Camps before the Nuremberg Tribunal', *The Yale Law Journal*, Vol. 105, No. 2 (1995) pp. 449–481.

25 Michael Marrus, 'The Holocaust at Nuremberg', *Yad Vashem Studies*, Vol. 26 (1998) p. 1; Jürgen Wilke et al., *Holocaust und NS-Prozesse* (Cologne: Bohlau Verlag, 1995); Jeffrey Herf, *Divided Memory: The Nazi Past in the Two Germanies* (Cambridge, Massachusetts: Harvard University Press, 1997) pp. 206–208; Bloxham, *Genocide on Trial*.

26 Erich Haberer, 'History and Justice: Paradigms of the Prosecution of Nazi Crimes', *Holocaust and Genocide Studies*, Vol. 19, No. 3 (2005) pp. 487–519, p. 493. See also Donald Bloxham, 'The Missing Camps of Aktion Reinhard: The Judicial Displacement of a Mass Murder', P. Gray & K. Oliver (eds.), *The Memory of Catastrophe* (Manchester: Manchester University Press, 2004) pp. 118–134, and *Genocide on Trial*, pp. 88–9, 124–126; Tony Kushner, *The Holocaust and the Liberal Imagination: A Social and Cultural History* (Oxford: Blackwell, 1994) pp. 205–342; John Fox, 'The Jewish Factor in British War Crimes Policy in 1942', *English Historical Review*, Vol. 92, No. 362) (1977) pp. 82–106.

27 Kushner, *The Holocaust and the Liberal Imagination*, p. 226.

28 Christoph Burchard, 'The Nuremberg Trial and Its Impact on Germany', *Journal of International Criminal Justice*, Vol. 4 (2006) pp. 800–829.

29 Robert Jackson, 'Opening Statement', Proceedings of the International Military Tribunal, Day 2 (21 November 1945).

30 *New York Times*, 'Press in Germany Covers War Trial' (13 December 1945) p. 13.

31 On such reporting, see Alexandra Przyrembel, 'Transfixed by an Image: Ilse Koch, the "Kommandeuse of Buchenwald"', *German History*, Vol. 19, No. 3 (2001) pp. 369–399.

32 Raymond Daniell was a London correspondent for the *New York Times* throughout the Second World War and had followed US troops into Berlin in 1945. He had warned of the dangers of National Socialism and urged his countrymen to fight it before the attack on Pearl Harbor in 1941. *New York Times*, '"So what?" Say the Germans of Nuremberg', 2 December 1945, p. SM3.

33 See, for example, *Neues Deutschland*, 'Sachsenhausenprozeß eröffnet', 24 October 1947.

34 Report No. 16, 'German Attitudes towards the Nuremberg Trials', 7 August 1946, Anna J. Merritt & Richard L. Merritt (eds.), *Public Opinion in Occupied Germany: The OMGUS Surveys, 1945–1949* (Urbana, Illinois: University of Illinois Press, 1970) pp. 93–94.

35 *New York Times*, 'Impact of Nuremberg on the German Mind', 6 October 1946, p. SM5.

36 *New York Times*, 'War Crimes Trial Dull to Germans', 2 January 1946.

37 *Toronto Daily Star*, 'Nuremberg Trial Too Slow Reich Man-in-Street Says', 2 November 1945, p. 7.

38 *Milwaukee Journal*, 'Some Germans Brand War Crimes Trials as Too Slow', 1 November 1945. See also: *The Times*, 'German Views on War Trial', 30 September 1945.

39 *The Times*, 'German Views on War Trial', 30 September 1945.

40 Report No. 16, 'German Attitudes Towards the Nuremberg Trials'.

41 Ibid. For further details on German responses to the IMT, see Caroline Sharples, *West Germans and the Nazi Legacy* (New York: Routledge, 2012) pp. 2–29.

42 *New York Times*, 'Impact of Nuremberg on the German Mind', 6 October 1946.

43 At the end of the trial, British observers expressed concern that allowing the defendants to make final statements before they were hanged meant 'the guilty men have increased in stature among sectors of the German public' – TNA, FO 946/43: German Reaction to Nuremberg Sentences, 'Memorandum by George W. Houghton, Control Office for Germany and Austria', 17 October 1946.

44 *New York Times*, 'Berlin Left Urges Death for 22 Nazis', 3 October 1946.

45 TNA, FO 946/93: German Reaction to Nuremberg Sentences.

46 *The Times*, 'German Public and the Nuremberg Penalties', 3 October 1946.

47 Rebecca West, *A Train of Powder* (London: Virago, 1984), p. 56.

48 *The Times*, 'Acquitted Nazis Should Be Tried in German Court' (3 October 1946) p. 5.

49 *New York Times*, 'Army Investigates Suicide of Göring as Mystery Grows' (17 October 1946) p. 1.

50 *New York Times*, 'German Posters Decry War Trial' (10 November 1946) p. 47.

51 Ibid.

52 TNA, FO 1056/166 Control Commission for Germany, Information Services Control Branch Publicity Material: 'Survey of German Public Opinion No. 8 (Period ending 25 October 1946)'.

53 TNA, FO 1056/93: Control Commission for Germany, Information Services Control Branch: 'Survey of German Public Opinion (Period ending December 1946)'.

54 Mary Fulbrook, *Germany, 1918-1990: The Divided Nation* (London: Fontana Press, 1991) p. 145.

55 Robert Knight, 'Denazification and Reintegration in the Austrian Province of Carinthia', *Journal of Modern History*, Vol. 79, No. 3 (2007) pp. 572–573.

56 Lutz Niethammer, *Entnazifizierung in Bayern: Säuberung und Rehabilitierung unter amerikanischer Besatzung* (Frankfurt: Fischer Verlag, 1972).

57 Wolfgang Friedmann, *The Allied Military Government of Germany* (London: Stevens & Sons, 1947); Michael Balfour & John Mair, *Four Power Control in Germany and Austria, 1945–1946* (Oxford: Oxford University Press, 1956); Constantine Fitzgibbon, *Denazification* (New York: W.W. Norton, 1969). On the American zone see: John Gimbel, *The American Occupation of Germany: Politics and the Military, 1945–1949* (Stanford, California: Stanford University Press, 1968); James Tent, *Mission on the Rhine: Re-education and Denazification in American Occupied Germany* (Chicago, Illinois: University of Chicago Press, 1982).

58 Barbara Marshall, 'German Attitudes to British Military Government, 1945-7', *Journal of Contemporary History*, Vol. 15, No. 4 (1980) pp. 655–684; Ian Turner, 'Denazification in the British Zone', I. Turner (ed.), *Reconstruction in Post-War Germany: British Occupation Policy and the Western Zones, 1945–1955* (Oxford: Oxford University Press, 1989).

59 Perry Biddiscombe, *The Denazification of Germany: A History, 1945–1950* (Stroud: Tempus, 2007).

60 Timothy Vogt, *Denazification in Soviet-Occupied Germany: Brandenburg, 1945–1948* (Cambridge, Massachusetts: Harvard University Press, 2000) p. 2.

61 Mike Dennis, *The Rise and Fall of the German Democratic Republic, 1945–1990* (London: Longman, 2000) p. 18. See also: Norman Naimark, *The Russians in Germany: A History of the Soviet Zone of Occupation, 1945–1949* (Cambridge, Massachusetts: Harvard University Press, 1995).

62 Dennis, *The Rise and Fall of the German Democratic Republic*, p. 19.

63 Marshall, 'German Attitudes to British Military Government, 1945-7', *passim*.

64 TNA, FO 1050/356: German Opinions on Denazification Measures, 'Letter from Hamburg-Harburg, 18 November 1946'.

65 TNA, FO 1050/356: German Opinions on Denazification Measures, 'Letter from Karl L.', 30 November 1947.

66 Ibid.

67 TNA, FO 1050/356: German Opinions on Denazification Measures, 'Letter from unnamed citizen of Hamburg', 27 August 1946.

Chapter 2

1 Statistics taken from Robert G. Moller, 'The Politics of the Past in the 1950s: Rhetorics of Victimisation in East and West Germany', B. Niven (ed.), *Germans as Victims* (Basingstoke: Palgrave Macmillan, 2006) p. 27.

2 Neil Gregor, '"The Illusion of Remembrance": The Karl Diehl Affair and the Memory of National Socialism in Nuremberg, 1945-1999', *Journal of Modern History*, Vol. 75, No. 3 (2003) p. 615.

3 See, for example, Dagmar Barnouw, *The War in the Empty Air: Victims, Perpetrators and Post-War Germans* (Bloomington, Indiana: Indiana University Press, 2003); Alfred-Maurice De Zayas, *The German Expellees: Victims in War and Peace* (New York: St. Martin's Press, 1993); Frank Biess, 'Survivors of Totalitarianism: Returning POWs and the Reconstruction of Masculine Citizenship in West Germany, 1945-1955', H. Schissler (ed.), *The Miracle Years: A Cultural History of West Germany, 1949–1968* (Princeton, New Jersey: Princeton University Press, 2001) pp. 57–82; Neil Gregor, '"Is he still alive, or long since dead?": Loss, Absence and Remembrance in Nuremberg, 1945-1956', *German History*, Vol. 21, No. 2 (2003) pp. 183–203; Atina Grossmann, 'A Question of Silence: The Rape of German Women by Occupation Soldiers', R.G. Moeller (ed.), *West Germany under Construction: Politics, Society and Culture in the Adenauer Era* (Ann Arbor, Michigan: University of Michigan Press, 1997) pp. 33–52; Michael L. Hughes, '"Through No Fault of Our Own": West Germans Remember Their War Losses', *German History*, Vol. 18, No. 2 (2000) pp. 193–213.

4 Eric Langenbacher, 'The Mastered Past? Collective Memory Trends in Germany since Unification', *German Politics & Society*, Vol. 28, No. 1 (2010) sees 1999 as the key turning point in this process. For an overview of historians' discussions of victimhood as a taboo subject, see Stefan Berger, 'On Taboos, Traumas and Other Myths: Why the Debate about German Victims of the Second World War Is Not a Historians' Controversy', Niven, *Germans as Victims*, pp. 210–224.

5 Robert G. Moeller, 'Germans as Victims? Thoughts on a Post-Cold War History of World War II's Legacies', *History and Memory*, Vol. 17, No. 1–2 (2005) p. 154.

6 Elizabeth Heineman, 'The Hour of the Woman: Memories of Germany's "Crisis Years" and West German National Identity', *American Historical Review*, Vol. 101, No. 2 (1996) pp. 354–395.

7 Robert G. Moeller, *War Stories: The Search for a Usable Past in the Federal Republic of Germany* (Berkeley, California: University of California Press, 2001), p. 7.

8 Helmut Schmitz, 'The Birth of the Collective from the Spirit of Empathy: From the "Historians' Dispute" to German Suffering', Niven, *Germans as Victims*, p. 94.

9 Ibid., p. 104. Friedrich's use of Holocaust imagery is similarly highlighted by Bill Niven, 'Introduction: German Victimhood at the Turn of the Millennium', *Germans as Victims*, p. 14; Berger, 'On Taboos, Traumas and Other Myths', in ibid., pp. 219–220.

10 Niven, 'German Victimhood at the Turn of the Millennium', p. 17; Stuart Taberner, 'Representations of German Wartime Suffering in Recent Fiction', Niven, *Germans as Victims*, p. 175.

11 Berger, 'On Taboos, Traumas and Other Myths'; Ruth Wittlinger, 'Taboo or Tradition? The "Germans as Victims" Theme in West Germany Until the Early 1990s', Niven, *Germans as Victims*, pp. 62–75; Hans Kundnani, 'Perpetrators and Victims: Germany's 1968 Generation and Collective Memory', *German Life & Letters*, Vol. 64, No. 2 (2011) pp. 272–282.

12 Kundnani, 'Perpetrators and Victims', p. 274.

13 Ibid., pp. 276–277.

14 Ibid., pp. 274–275.

15 Wittlinger, 'Taboo or Tradition?', p. 64.

16 A. Dirk Moses, 'The Non-German German and the German German: Dilemmas of Identity after the Holocaust', *New German Critique*, Vol. 101 (2007) p. 47.

17 Harold Marcuse, *Legacies of Dachau: The Uses and Abuses of a Concentration Camp, 1933–2001* (Cambridge: Cambridge University Press, 2001) p. 119.

18 Ibid., p. 74.

19 Hermann Lübbe, 'Der Nationalsozialismus im Deutschen Nachkriegsbewusstsein', *Historische Zeitschrift*, Vol. 236 (1983) pp. 585–587.

20 Moeller, *War Stories*, p. 3.

21 Cited in Alexandra Kaiser, 'Performing the New German Past: The People's Day of Mourning and 27 January as Postunification Commemorations', *German Politics & Society*, Vol. 26, No. 4 (2008) p. 44.

22 Moeller, 'The Politics of the Past', Niven, *Germans as Victims*, p. 31.

23 Peter Monteath, 'Organizing Antifascism: The Obscure History of the VVN', *European History Quarterly*, Vol. 29, No. 2 (1999) p. 294.

24 Nonetheless, the VVN continued to exist in the FRG and was expanded, in 1971, to include the Bund der Antifaschisten (Federation of Antifascists or BdA) in an effort to attract more younger people to the cause. In 2002, the

VVN-BdA merged with its former East German counterpart and remains active today in campaigning against Neo-Nazism.

25 Kaiser, 'Performing the New German Past', p. 33.

26 'Decree on Aid Measures for Former Political Prisoners', Ministry of the Interior of Württemberg-Baden, Stuttgart, 17 December 1945 in *German History and Documents and Images*, http://germanhistorydocs.ghi-dc.org/sub_document.cfm?document_id=4477.

27 Cited in X. Peter, 'A Day to Remember: East Germany's Day of Remembrance for the Victims of Fascism', *German History*, Vol. 26, No. 2 (2008) p. 199.

28 Ibid., pp. 199–200.

29 Karl Hauff, 'Memorandum on the Condition of Victims of Political, Racial and Religious Persecution by the Nazi Regime', Stuttgart, 5 February 1947, *German History in Documents and Images*, http://germanhistorydocs.ghi-dc.org/sub_document.cfm?document_id=4503. Hauff, however, emphasized the hardships facing the former victims of Nazi persecution and called for even greater levels of assistance to be made available to them.

30 Konrad Adenauer, 'Policy Statement of the German Federal Government', Bundestag, 20 September 1949. Full text available at *The History Collection*, http://digicoll.library.wisc.edu/cgi-bin/History/History-idx?type=div&did=HISTORY.GPARLIAMENT.ADENAUERK1&isize=text

31 Ibid.

32 Moeller, *War Stories*, p. 22.

33 Hughes, '"Through No Fault of Our Own"', p. 200.

34 Ibid., p. 193.

35 Ibid., pp. 203–204.

36 Cited in ibid., p. 201.

37 Ibid., p. 209.

38 Moeller, *War Stories*, p. 37.

39 Moeller, 'The Politics of the Past', p. 37.

40 Ibid., p. 41.

41 Jan Molitor, 'The Last Soldiers of the Great War', *Die Zeit*, 13 October 1955. Full text reproduced at *German History in Documents and Images*, http://germanhistorydocs.ghi-dc.org/sub_document.cfm?document_id=4562.

42 Moeller, *War Stories*, p. 121.

43 *Tägliche Rundschau*, 'The Equalization of Burdens through Restitution in Kind? A Bone of Contention as a Diversionary Tactic of the Reactionary Contingent', 15 February 1947. Reproduced at *German History in Documents and Images*, http://germanhistorydocs.ghi-dc.org/docpage.cfm?docpage_id=5553.

44 *Der Leuchtturm*, 'Equalization of Burdens Means Equalization of Wealth', No. 5, 1948. Reproduced at *German History in Documents and Images*, http://germanhistorydocs.ghi-dc.org/sub_document.cfm?document_id=4473

45 'German Appraisal of "Lastenausgleich"', Anna J. Merritt & Richard L. Merritt (eds.), *Public Opinion in Occupied Germany: The OMGUS Surveys, 1945–1949* (Urbana, Illinois: University of Illinois Press, 1970) pp. 287–288.

46 Marion Gräfin Dönhoff, 'Homeland in the East', *Die Zeit*, 18 May 1950. Reproduced at *German History in Documents and Images,* http://germanhistorydocs.ghi-dc.org/sub_document.cfm?document_id=4476

47 Daniel Levy & Natan Sznaider, 'Memories of Universal Victimhood: The Case of Ethnic German Expellees', *German Politics & Society*, Vol. 23, No. 2 (2005), p. 9.

48 De Zayas, *The German Expellees*. For critical discussion of de Zayas's work, see the review by Rod Stackelberg in *Central European History*, Vol. 26, No. 4 (1993) pp. 511–3.

49 Brenda Melendy, 'Expellees on Strike: Competing Victimization Discourses and the Dachau Refugee Camp Protest Movement, 1948-1949', *German Studies Review*, Vol. 28, No. 1 (2005) pp. 107–8.

50 Ibid., p. 120.

51 Cited Levy & Sznaider, 'Memories of Universal Victimhood', p. 11.

52 Cited in ibid.

53 Ibid., p. 12.

54 Moeller, *War Stories*, pp. 51–87; 123–170.

55 *BBC News*, 'Berlin Exhibition Stirs Painful Memories', 13 August 2006. Available at http://news.bbc.co.uk/1/hi/world/europe/4788167.stm; *Der Spiegel*, 'The Wounds of World War II: Remembering German Victims', 10 August 2006, http://www.spiegel.de/international/the-wounds-of-world-war-ii-remembering-german-victims-a-431115.html

56 *Der Spiegel*, 'Germany's Expellee Museum: Charges of Historical Revisionism up Berlin', 4 August 2010, http://www.spiegel.de/international/germany/germany-s-expellee-museum-charges-of-historical-revisionism-stir-up-berlin-a-710132.html

57 Kaiser, 'Performing the New German Past', p. 34.

58 Klaus Neuman, *Shifting Memories: The Nazi Past in the New* Germany (Ann Arbor, Michigan: University of Michigan Press, 2000) p. 58.

59 Elizabeth Corwin, 'The Dresden Bombing as Portrayed in German Accounts, East and West', *UCLA Historical Journal*, Vol. 8 (1987) pp. 71–96.

60 Bill Niven, 'The GDR and Memory of the Bombing of Dresden', *Germans as Victims*, pp. 109–129.

61 Corwin, 'The Dresden Bombing', p. 78.

62 Cited in ibid., p. 79.

63 Cited in ibid., p. 84.

64 Ibid., p. 76.

65 Moeller, *War Stories*, p. 171.

66 Dietmar Schirmer, 'Present Past: Culture and Memory in Berlin and Germany', *German Politics & Society*, Vol. 27, No. 4 (2009) p. 93.

67 Bill Niven, *Facing the Nazi Past: United Germany and the Legacy of the Third Reich* (New York: Routledge, 2002) p. 63.

68 David Clay Large, '"A Beacon in the German Darkness": The Anti-Nazi Resistance Legacy in West German Politics', *Journal of Modern History*, Vol. 64 (1992) p. 174.

69 Niven, *Facing the Nazi Past*, p. 74 ff.

70 Martyn Housden, *Resistance and Conformity in the Third Reich* (London: Routledge, 1997), Document 5.8, p. 100.

71 Hughes, '"Through No Fault of Our Own"', p. 210.

72 Ibid., p. 211.

Chapter 3

1 Richard Weizsäcker, 'Speech in the Bundestag on 8 May 1985 during the Ceremony Commemorating the 40th Anniversary of the End of War in Europe and of National-Socialist Tyranny'. Full text available at *Landesmedienzentrum Media Culture Online*, http://www.mediacultureonline.de/medienbildung/medienpraxis/sprechen-praesentieren/politische-reden-gegenwart.html

2 Ibid.

3 Jürgen Habermas, 'Defusing the Past: A Politico-Cultural Tract', G.H. Hartman (ed.), *Bitburg in Moral and Political Perspective* (Bloomington, Indiana: Indiana University Press, 1986) p. 49.

4 Saul Friedländer, 'Some German Struggles with Memory', Hartman, *Bitburg in Moral and Political Perspective*, p. 33.

5 Mary Fulbrook, *German National Identity after the Holocaust* (Cambridge: Polity Press, 1999) p. 99.

6 Andrew H. Beattie, 'The Victims of Totalitarianism and the Centrality of Nazi Genocide: Continuity and Change in German Commemorative Politics', Bill Niven (ed.), *Germans as Victims* (Basingstoke: Palgrave Macmillan, 2006) pp. 154–155. For further praise of Weizsäcker's speech, see Harold Marcuse, *Legacies of Dachau: The Uses and Abuses of a Concentration Camp, 1933–2001* (Cambridge: Cambridge University Press, 2001) p. 365.

7 Nicolas Berg, *Der Holocaust und die westdeutschen Historiker. Erforschung und Erinnerung* (Göttingen: Wallstein Verlag, 2003). On the reception of this book, see Irmtrud Wojak, 'Nicolas Berg and the West German Historians: A Response to His "Handbook" on the Historiography of the Holocaust', *German History*, Vol. 22, No. 1 (2004) pp. 101–118.

8 Cited in Thomas C. Fox, *Stated Memory: East Germany and the Holocaust* (Rochester, New York: Camden House, 1999) p. 21.

9 Kurt Pätzold, 'Persecution and the Holocaust: A Provisional Review of GDR Historiography', *Leo Baeck Institute Yearbook*, Vol. 40, No. 1 (1995) p. 302.

10 Fox, *Stated Memory*, pp. 21–30.

11 Konrad Jarausch, 'The Failure of East German Antifascism: Some Ironies of History as Politics', *German Studies Review*, Vol. 14, No. 1 (1991) p. 85.

12 Fox, *Stated Memory*, p. 22; Jeffrey Herf, 'East German Communists and the Jewish Question: The Case of Paul Merker', *Journal of Contemporary History*, Vol. 29, No. 4 (1994) pp. 627–661; Jeffrey Herf, *Divided Memory: The Nazi Past in the Two Germanys* (Cambridge, Massachusetts: Harvard University Press, 1997) pp. 106–161.

13 Fox, *Stated Memory*, p. 21; Pätzold, 'Persecution and the Holocaust', p. 295. The works in question are Siegbert Kahn, *Antisemitismus und Rassenhetze: Eine Übersicht über ihre Entwirklung in Deutschland* (Berlin: Dietz Verlag, 1948); Stefan Heymann, *Marxismus und Rassenfrage* (Berlin: Deitz Verlag, 1948).

14 For an overview of early Holocaust historiography in West Germany, see Wojak, 'Nicolas Berg and the West German Historians', pp. 103–104; Marina Cattaruzza, 'The Historiography of the Shoah: An Attempt at a Bibliographical Synthesis', *Totalitarismus und Demokratie*, Vol. 3 (2006) pp. 285–321.

15 Ibid., p. 107.

16 Dan Stone (ed.), *The Historiography of the Holocaust* (Basingstoke: Palgrave Macmillan, 2004) p. 2.

17 Cattaruzza, 'The Historiography of the Shoah', p. 292; Gavriel D. Rosenfeld, 'The Reception of William L. Shirer's The Rise and Fall of the Third Reich in the United States and West Germany, 1960–62', *Journal of Contemporary History*, Vol. 29, No. 1 (1994) pp. 95–128.

18 For more on this theme, see Peter Novick, *The Holocaust in Collective Memory The American Experience* (London: Bloomsbury, 2001); Caroline Sharples & Olaf Jensen (eds.), *Britain and the Holocaust: Remembering and Representing War and Genocide* (Basingstoke: Palgrave Macmillan, 2013); Andy Pearce, *Holocaust Consciousness in Contemporary Britain* (London: Routledge, 2014).

19 Fox, *Stated Memory*, p. 23.

20 Ibid.

21 Ibid., pp. 24–26.

22 Pätzold, 'Persecution and the Holocaust', p. 300.

23 Ibid., p. 294.

24 Jeremy Noakes, 'Hitler and the Third Reich', Dan Stone (ed.), *The Historiography of the Holocaust*, p. 41.

25 Christopher R. Browning, 'The Decision-Making Process', Stone, *The Historiography of the Holocaust*, p. 179.

26 Summarized in Cattaruzza, 'The Historiography of the Shoah', pp. 305–306. The works in question are Ulrich Herbert, *Fremdarbeiter: Politik und Praxis des 'Auslander-Einsatzes' in der Kriegswirtschaft des Dritten Reiches* (Berlin: JHW Dietz, 1985); Michael Zimmermann, *Verfolgt, vertrieben, vernichtet: die nationalsozialistische Vernichtungspolitik gegen Sinti und Roma* (Essen: Klartext, 1989); Burkhard Jellonek, *Homosexuelle unter dem Hakenkreuz:*

die Verfolgung der Homosexuellen im Dritten Reich (Paderborn: Schöningh, 1990); Rainer Hoffschildt, *Die Verfolgung der Homosexuellen in der NS-Zeit: Zahlen und Schicksale aus Norddeustchland* (Berlin: Rosa Winkel, 1999); Detlef Garbe, *Zwischen Widerstand und Martyrium: die Zeugen Jehovas im 'Dritten Reich'* (Munich: Oldenbourg, 1994).

27 For details on this event, see Hartman, *Bitburg in Moral and Political Perspective, passim*.

28 Cited in Marcuse, *Legacies of Dachau*, p. 363.

29 On this theme, see Andrei S. Markovits, 'Introduction to the Broszat-Friedländer Exchange', *New German Critique*, Vol. 44 (1988) pp. 81–84.

30 For translations of the original Historikerstreit documents, see James Knowlton & Truett Cates (eds.), *Forever in the Shadow of Hitler? Original Documents of the Historikerstreit, the Controversy Surrounding the Singularity of the Holocaust* (Atlantic Highlands, New Jersey: Humanities Press, 1993).

31 Ernst Nolte, 'The Past That Will Not Pass: A Speech That Could Be Written But Not Delivered'. Reproduced in ibid., pp. 18–23.

32 In 1986, Andreas Hillgruber published *Zweierlei Untergang* (Two Types of Downfall), which compared the expulsion of 'ethnic Germans' from the east with the victims of the Holocaust.

33 Geoff Eley, 'Nazism, Politics and the Image of the Past: Thoughts on the West German Historikerstreit, 1986-1987', *Past & Present*, No. 121 (1988) p. 177.

34 Norbert Frei, 'Forum: The *Historikerstreit* Twenty Years On', *German History*, Vol. 24, No. 4 (2006) p. 590.

35 Michael Geyer, 'Forum: The *Historikerstreit* Twenty Years On', *German History*, Vol. 24, No. 4 (2006) p. 595.

36 M. Lane Brunner, 'Strategies of Remembrance in Pre-Unification West Germany', *Quarterly Journal of Speech*, Vol. 86, No. 1 (2000) pp. 86–107.

37 Ibid.

38 See Margarete Myers Feinstein, *Holocaust Survivors in Postwar Germany, 1945–1957* (Cambridge: Cambridge University Press, 2010).

39 Regula Ludi, 'The Vectors of Postwar Victim Reparations: Relief, Redress and Memory Politics', *Journal of Contemporary History*, Vol. 41, No. 3 (2006) pp. 436–437.

40 Ibid., p. 439.

41 Herf, 'East German Communists and the Jewish Question', p. 628.

42 Ibid., p. 629.

43 Fox, *Stated Memory*, p. 11.

44 Paul Merker to the Chairman of the Socialist Unity Party of Germany, Wilhelm Pieck, 'Compensation Law in the Soviet Occupation Zone', 4 May 1948. Reproduced in *German History in Documents and Images*, '"Making Good"?: *Wiedergutmachung* in Occupied and Cold War Germany', http://germanhistorydocs.ghi-dc.org/sub_document.cfm?document_id=4478

45 Herf, *Divided Memory*, p. 632.

46 Ibid., p. 639.

47 Jacob Tovy, 'All Quiet on the Eastern Front: Israel and the Issue of Reparations from East Germany, 1951-1956', *Israel Studies*, Vol. 18, No. 1 (2013) p. 81.

48 'Decree on the Creation of a New Ordinance to Secure the Rights of Recognized Victims of Nazi Persecution', Ministry of Labour, 1953. Reproduced in *German History in Documents and Images*, '"Making Good"?: *Wiedergutmachung* in Occupied and Cold War Germany', http://germanhistorydocs.ghi-dc.org/sub_document.cfm?document_id=4506

49 Ibid.

50 Geoffrey J. Giles, 'Review of A. Pretzel & G. Roßbach eds, *Wegen der zu erwartenden hohen Strafe: Homosexuellenverfolgung in Berlin 1933–1945* and J. Müller & A. Sternwieler, *Homosexuelle Männer im KZ Sachsenhausen*', *Holocaust and Genocide Studies*, Vol. 17, No. 1 (2003) p. 200.

51 Gerald Hacke, *Zeugen Jehovas in der DDR. Verfolgung und Verhalten einer religiösen Minderheit* (Dresden: Hannah-Arendt-Institut für Totalitarismusforschung, 2000).

52 Erik N. Jensen, 'The Pink Triangle and Political Consciousness: Gays, Lesbians and the Memory of Nazi Persecution', *Journal of the History of Sexuality*, Vol. 11, Nos. 1–2 (2002) p. 324; *Der Spiegel*, 'Paragraph 175: Das Gesetz fallt? Bleibt die Achtung?', 12 May 1969, pp. 55–76.

53 *New York Times*, 'Germany Pardons En Masse Thousands Persecuted by Nazis', 29 May 1998.

54 Cited in Herf, *Divided Memory*, p. 282.

55 Ibid., p. 283.

56 Ibid., p. 288.

57 Susanna Schrafstetter, 'The Diplomacy of Wiedergutmachung: Memory, the Cold War and the Western European Victims of Nazism, 1956-1964', *Holocaust and Genocide Studies*, Vol. 17, No. 3 (2003), pp. 459–479.

58 Andrew Woolford & Stefan Wolejszo, 'Collecting on Moral Debts: Reparations for the Holocaust and Pořajmos', *Law and Society Review*, Vol. 40, No. 4 (2006) pp. 872–873.

59 Cited in Julia von dem Knesebeck, *The Roma Struggle for Compensation in Post-War Germany* (Hatfield: University of Hertfordshire Press, 2011) p. 79.

60 Cited in ibid., p. 168. Author's emphasis.

61 Cited in ibid., p. 81

62 Ibid., p. 82.

63 Ernst Heller, 'Restitution for National Socialist Injustice', *Die Neue Zeitung*, 19 March 1949. Full text reproduced at *German History in Documents and Images*, http://germanhistorydocs.ghi-dc.org/sub_document.cfm?document_id=4499.

64 Knesebeck, *The Roma Struggle for Compensation*, pp. 79–80.

65 Schrafstetter, 'The Diplomacy of Wiedergutmachung', p. 459.

66 Woolford & Wolejszo, 'Collecting on Moral Debts', pp. 879–880.

67 Ibid.

68 Ibid., p. 888.

69 Fox, *Stated Memory*, p. 10.

70 Cited in Siobhan Kattago, *Ambiguous Memory: The Nazi Past and German National Identity* (Westport, Connecticut: Praeger, 2001) p. 104.

71 Y. Michal Bodemann, 'Reconstructions of History: From Jewish Memory to Nationalized Commemoration of Kristallnacht in Germany', Y. Michal Bodemann (ed.), *Jews, Germans, Memory: Reconstructions of Jewish Life in Germany* (Ann Arbor Michigan: University of Michigan Press, 1996) pp. 184–185.

72 Kattago, *Ambiguous Memory*, p. 108.

73 Ibid.

74 Marcuse, *Legacies of Dachau*, p. 344; Janet Jacobs, 'Memorializing the Sacred: Kristallnacht in German National Memory', *Journal for the Scientific Study of Religion*, Vol. 47, No. 3 (2008) p. 485.

75 Cited in Marcuse, *Legacies of Dachau*, p. 357.

76 Jacobs, 'Memorializing the Sacred', p. 485.

77 'Stamp Commemorating Kristallnacht', *German History in Documents and Images*, http://germanhistorydocs.ghi-dc.org/sub_image.cfm?image_id=2510.

78 Marcuse, *Legacies of Dachau*, p. 367.

79 Elisabeth Domanksy, 'Kristallnacht, the Holocaust and German Unity: The Meaning of 9 November as an Anniversary in Germany', *History and Memory*, Vol. 4, No. 1 (1992) p. 64.

80 Kevin Costelloe, 'Jewish Leader Says Children Will Keep Memory Alive', *Associated Press*, 9 November 1988, AP News Archive, http://www.apnewsarchive.com/1988/Jewish-Leader-Says-Children-Will-Keep-Memory-Alive/id-3ed14922042081991107d6c7555dc82b

81 Cited in Domanksy, '"Kristallnacht", the Holocaust and German Unity', p. 66.

82 For more on Jenninger, see ibid., pp. 65–67; Fulbrook, *German National Identity*, pp. 100–2; Bruner, 'Strategies of Remembrance', pp. 96–102.

83 *Der Spiegel*, '75 Years Later: How the World Shrugged Off Kristallnacht', 5 November 2013.

84 *Der Spiegel*, 'Kristalnacht: Germany Remembers a Grim Anniversary', 6 November 2013. See also: *Die Zeit*, 'Knobloch wirbt für "aufgeklärten Patriotismus"', 9 November 2013.

85 Bodemann, 'Reconstructions of History', p. 209.

86 For a summary of historians' interpretations of Kristallnacht memorialization, see Jacobs, 'Memorializing the Sacred', p. 494.

87 Ibid., p. 494.

88 Knesebeck, *The Roma Struggle for Compensation*, p. 228

Chapter 4

1 See, for example, Donald Bloxham, 'British War Crimes Policy in Germany, 1945-1957: Implementation and Collapse', *Journal of British Studies*, Vol. 42, No. 1 (2003) pp. 91–118 and 'From the International Military Tribunal to the Subsequent Nuremberg Proceedings: The American Confrontation with Nazi Criminality Revisited', *History*, Vol. 98, No. 332 (2013) pp. 567–591; Tomaz Jardim, *Mauthausen Trial: American Military Justice in Germany* (Cambridge, Massachusetts: Harvard University Press, 2012); Fern Overbey Hilton, *The Dachau Defendants: Life Stories from Testimony and Documents of the War Crimes Proceedings* (Jefferson, North Carolina: McFarland, 2004); Kim Christian Priemel, 'Consigning Justice to History: Transitional Trials after the Second World War', *Historical Journal*, Vol. 56, No. 2 (2013) pp. 553–581; AP.V. Rogers, 'War Crimes Trials under the Royal Warrant: British Practice 1945-1949', *International and Comparative Law Quarterly*, Vol. 39, No. 4 (1990) pp. 780–800; Mark E. Spicka, 'The Devil's Chemists on Trial: The American Prosecution of IG Farben at Nuremberg', *Historian*, Vol. 61, No. 4 (1999) pp. 865–882; Paul Weindling, 'From International to Zonal Trials: The Origins of the Nuremberg Medical Trial', *Holocaust and Genocide Studies*, Vol. 14, No. 3 (2000) pp. 367–289.

2 Deborah E. Lipstadt, *The Eichmann Trial* (New York: Schocken and Nextbook, 2011); Leora Bilsky, Donald Bloxham, Lawrence Douglas, Annette Weinke & Devin Pendas, 'Forum: The Eichmann Trial Fifty Years On', *German History*, Vol. 29, No. 2 (2011) pp. 265–282; Devin O. Pendas, *The Frankfurt Auschwitz Trial, 1963-1965: Genocide, History and the Limits of the Law* (Cambridge: Cambridge University Press, 2006); Rebecca Wittmann, *Beyond Justice: The Auschwitz Trial* (Cambridge, Massachusetts: Harvard University Press, 2005).

3 Mark A. Wolfgram, 'Didactic War Crimes Trials and External Legal Culture: The Cases of the Nuremberg, Frankfurt Auschwitz, and Majdanek Trials in West Germany', *Global Change, Peace & Security*, Vol. 26, No. 3 (2014) pp. 281–297; Ulrike Weckel & Edgar Wolfrum (eds), *'Bestien' und 'Befehlsempfänger': Frauen und Männer in NS-Prozessen nach 1945* (Göttingen: Vandenhoeck & Ruprecht, 2003).

4 Key works in this field are Wendy Lower, 'Male and Female Holocaust Perpetrators and the East German Approach to Justice, 1949-1963', *Holocaust and Genocide Studies*, Vol. 24, No. 1 (2010) pp. 56–84; Annette Weinke, *Die Verfolgung von NS-Tätern im geteilten Deutschland: Vergangenheitsbewältigungen, 1949-1969, oder Eine deutsch-deutsche Beziehungsgeschichte im Kalten Krieg* (Munich: Ferdinand Schöningh Verlag, 2002).

5 See: Donald Bloxham, *Genocide on Trial: War Crimes Trials and the Formation of Holocaust History and Memory* (Oxford: Oxford University Press, 2001); Caroline Sharples, *West Germans and the Nazi Legacy* (New York: Routledge, 2012); Marouf Arif Hasian, *Rhetorical Vectors of Memory in National and International Holocaust Trials* (East Lansing, Michigan: Michigan State University Press, 2006); Lawrence Douglas, *The Memory of*

Judgement: Making Law and History in the Trials of the Holocaust (New Haven, Connecticut: Yale University Press, 2001).

6 Patricia Heberer & Jürgen Matthäus, *Atrocities on Trial: Historical Perspectives on the Politics of Prosecuting War Crimes* (Lincoln, Nebraska: University of Nebraska Press, 2008) p. XX.

7 C.M. Clark, 'West Germany Confronts the Nazi Past: Some Recent Debates on the Early Post-War Era, 1945-1960', *European Legacy*, Vol. 4, No. 1 (1999) p. 122.

8 Christiaan F. Rüter & Dick W. de Mildt (eds), *Justiz und NS-Verbrechen: Sammlung deutscher Strafurteile wegen nationalsozialistischer Tötungsverbrechen, 1945-1966. Register zu den Bänden I-XXII* (Amsterdam: APA – Holland University Press, 1998).

9 Ibid.

10 On the amnesty campaigns, see Norbert Frei, *Adenauer's Germany and the Nazi Past: The Politics of Amnesty and Integration*, translated by Joel Golb (New York: Columbia University Press, 2002).

11 Konrad Adenauer, 'Policy Statement of the German Federal Government', Bundestag, 20 September 1949. Full text available at *The History Collection*, http://digicoll.library.wisc.edu/cgi-bin/History/History-idx?type=div&did=HISTORY.GPARLIAMENT.ADENAUERK1&isize=text

12 Ibid., p. 177.

13 Ibid., pp. 177–178.

14 Elizabeth Noelle-Neumann & Erich Peter Neumann (eds), *Jahrbuch der offentlichen Meinung, 1947–1955* (Allensbach am Bodensee: Verlag für Demoskopie, 1955) p. 202.

15 Frei, *Adenauer's Germany*, p. 218.

16 Ibid., p. 217.

17 Katharina von Kellenbach, 'God's Love and Women's Love: Prison Chaplains Counsel the Wives of Nazi Perpetrators', *Journal of Feminist Studies in Religion*, Vol. 20, No. 2 (2004) p. 12.

18 Lower, 'Male and Female Holocaust Perpetrators', p. 57.

19 Jonathan Friedman, 'The Sachsenhausen Trials: War Crimes Prosecution in the Soviet Occupation Zone and in West and East Germany', Heberer & Matthäus (eds), *Atrocities on Trial*, p. 175.

20 Cited in Ibid., p. 161.

21 National Council of the National Front of Democratic Germany, *The Brown Book: War and Nazi Criminals in West Germany – State, Economy, Administration, Army, Justice, Science* (Dresden: Zeit im Bild, 1965).

22 Friedman, 'The Sachsenhausen Trials', p. 176.

23 Ibid., p. 175.

24 Ibid., p. 176.

25 Ibid.

26 Lower, 'Male and Female Holocaust Perpetrators', p. 59.

27 Ibid., pp. 60, 64.

28 Ibid., p. 74.

29 Cited in ibid., p. 65.

30 Ibid., p. 65.

31 Ibid., 73.

32 On the impact of the Ulm trial, see Jean-Paul Bier, 'The Holocaust, West Germany and Strategies of Oblivion, 1947-1979', Anson Rabinbach & Jack Zipes (eds), *Germans and Jews since the Holocaust: The Ongoing Situation in West Germany* (New York: Holmes & Meier, 1986) p. 189; Dick de Mildt, *In the Name of the People: Perpetrators of Genocide in the Reflection of their Post-War Prosecution in West Germany. The 'Euthanasia' and 'Aktion Reinhard' Trial Cases* (The Hague: Martinus Nijhoff, 1996) p. 27; Ulrich Brochhagen, *Nach Nürnberg: Vergangenheitsbewältigung und Westintegration in der Ära Adenauer* (Berlin: Ullstein, 1999) p. 292; Sharples, *West Germans and the Nazi Legacy*, pp. 30–50.

33 For details on these arrests, see Adalbert Rückerl, *The Investigation of Nazi Crimes, 1945-1978: A Documentation*, translated by D. Rutter (Karlsruhe: C.F. Müller, 1979) p. 48.

34 *Neue Presse*, 'Lieber Leser', 13 June 1958.

35 TNA, FO371/137596: War Crimes 1958; WG1661/16: Reports on the Trial at Ulm – Dispatch from the British Embassy, Bonn to the Western Department of the Foreign Office (5 September 1958).

36 *Frankfurter Rundschau*, 'Betrunken aus dem "Einsatz" zurück', 19 June 1958.

37 *Süddeutsche Zeitung*, 'Himmlers Henker hören den Staatsanwalt', 4 August 1958.

38 *Trierischer Volksfreund*, 'Zentrale Ermittlungsbehörde?', 15 September 1958. See also *Stuttgarter Zeitung*, 'Zentrale Ermittlungsbehörde muß klarheit uber NS-Verbrechen schaffen', 3 September 1958; *Freie Presse*, 'Nicht zögern', 12 September 1958; *Frankfurter Neue Presse*, 'Justiz und Konkurmasse', 3 October 1958; *Frankfurter Allgemeine Zeitung*,'Aufräumen' and 'Die Vergangenheit laßtet', 6 and 13 October 1958.

39 de Mildt, *In the Name of the People*, p. 27.

40 Peter Steinbach, 'Zur Auseinandersetzung mit nationalsozialistichen Gewaltverbrechen in der Bundesrepublik Deutschland', *Geschichte in Wissenschaft und Unterricht*, Vol. 35, No. 2 (1984) p. 68.

41 Survey of 2,000 people reported in Elizabeth Noelle and Erich Peter Neumann (eds), *Jahrbuch der öffentlichen Meinung, 1958-1964* (Allensbach & Bonn: Institut füür Demoskopie Allensbach, 1965) p. 211.

42 See, for example, *Müncher Merkur*, 'Stimmen zu den Urteilen im Ulmer Prozeß', 13 September 1958. For more on the reception afforded to the Central Investigating Agency, see Kurt Schrimm & Joachim Riedel, '50 Jahre Zentrale Stelle in Ludwigsburg', Vierteljahrshefte für *Zeitgeschichte*, Vol. 56, No. 4 (2008) pp. 525–555; Rüdiger Fleiter, 'Die Ludwigsburg Zentrale Stelle und ihr politisches und gesellschaftliches Umfeld', *Geschichte in Wissenschaft und Unterricht*, Vol. 53, No. 1 (2002) pp. 32–50.

43 For details on the newspaper coverage of these trials, see Akiba Cohen, T. Zemach-Marom, J. Wilke & B. Schenk (eds), *The Holocaust and the Press: Nazi War Crimes Trials in Germany and Israel* (Cresskill, New Jersey: Hampton Press, 2000) pp. 75–76; H. Lamm, *Der Eichmann Prozeß in der deutschen öffentlichen Meinung* (Frankfurt am Main: Ner-Tamid Verlag, 1961).

44 *Frankfurter Allgemeine Zeitung*, 'Ein Berg von Kinderleichen', 7 March 1964 and '25000 Ermordete in 24 Stunden', 9 October 1964.

45 Wittmann, *Beyond Justice*, p. 176.

46 Reported in the *Jewish Chronicle*, 'Adenauer is Worried', 17 March 1961, p. 19. See also *The Times*, 'Dr. Adenauer's Misgivings over Eichmann Trial', 11 March 1961, p. 7; 'Eichmann Reviving a Past Still Hard to Face', 7 April 1961, p. 11.

47 Reported in the *Jewish Chronicle*, 'Berlin Mayor Appeals to World Jewry', 24 March 1961, p. 20.

48 Cited in the *Jewish Chronicle*, 'German Reputation', 7 April 1961, p. 36.

49 *New York Times*, 'Eichmann: Impact on Germany', 16 April 1961, p. E4.

50 Noelle & Peter Neumann (eds), *Jahrbuch der Öffentlichen Meinung, 1958-1964*.

51 *Süddeutsche Zeitung*, 'Blick in eine düstere Vergangenheit', 20 February 1961.

52 Cornelia Brink, *'Auschwitz in der Paulskirche': Erinnerungspolitik in Fotoausstellungen der sechziger Jahre* (Marburg: Jonas Verlag, 2000) p. 25.

53 Konrad X. Schilling (ed.), *Monumenta Judaica: 2,000 Jahre Geschichte und Kultur der Juden am Rhein. Handbuch & Katalog* (Cologne: J. Melzer Verlag, 1963).

54 *AJR Information*, 'Monumenta Judaica in Cologne', vol. xix/3 (1964) p. 5.

55 Peter Weiss, *The Investigation: Oratorio in Eleven Cantos*, translated by A. Gross (London: Calder & Boyous, 1966). For further works relating to this play, see Robert Cohen, 'The Political Aesthetics of Holocaust Literature: Peter Weiss's "The Investigation" and Its Critics', *History and Memory*, Vol. 10 (1998) pp. 43–67; Christoph Weiss, *Auschwitz in der geteilten Welt: Peter Weiss und 'Die Ermittlung' im kalten Krieg* (St. Ingbert: Röhrig, 2000); *Der Spiegel*, 'Weiss: Gesang vor der Schaukel', Vol. 43 (1965); Michael Patterson, '"Bewältigung der Vergangenheit" or "überwältigung der Befangenheit": Nazism and the War in Post-War German Theatre', *Modern Drama*, Vol. 33, No. 1 (1990) pp. 125–126.

56 Hermann Langbein, *Der Auschwitz-Prozess: Eine Dokumentation* (Vienna: Europa Verlag, 1965).

57 *Kölnische Rundschau*, 'Schallplattenmusik übertönte Schüsse von Sachsenhausen', 16 October 1964.

58 Sharples, *West Germans and the Nazi Legacy*, pp. 51–72.

59 Marcuse, *Legacies of Dachau*, pp. 214–215.

60 Elisabeth Noelle & Erich Peter Neumann (eds), *Jahrbuch der öffentlichen Meinung, 1965-1967* (Allensbach: Institut für Demoskopie, 1967), p. 165.

61 Institut für Demoskopie, 'Verjährung von NS-Verbrechen' (Allensbach, 5 May 1965).

62 Helge Grabitz, 'Problems of Nazi Trials in the Federal Republic of Germany', *Holocaust and Genocide Studies*, Vol. 3, No. 2 (1988), p. 209.

63 Cited in TNA FO371/183153: Germany: Letter from A.W. Rhodes, British Embassy, Bonn to R.G. Sheridan, Western Department, Foreign Office, London, 23 January 1965. Bucher and the FDP remained opposed to altering the Statute throughout the debates.

64 Rüter & de Mildt, *Justiz und NS-Verbrechen Register zu den Bänden I-XXII and Vorläufiges Verfahrensregister zu den Banden XXIIIff.*

65 For further details, see Institute of Jewish Affairs, *Statute of Limitations and the Prosecution of Nazi Crimes in the Federal German Republic. Background Paper No. 14* (London: Institute of Jewish Affairs, 1969); Pendas, *The Frankfurt Auschwitz Trial*, pp. 556–571.

66 Robert A. Monson, 'The West German Statute of Limitations on Murder: A Political, Legal and Historical Exposition', *American Journal of Comparative Law*, Vol. 30, No. 4 (1982) p. 605.

67 See: EMNID, 'Verjährung für NS-Verbrechen', *EMNID-Informationen*, Vol. 11 (1978); Sample, 'Sollen NS-Verbrechen verjähren?', *Umfrage* (November 1978); EMNID, 'Verjährung für NS-Verbrechen', *EMNID-Informationen*, Vol. 2 (1979); Sample, 'Verjährung von NS-Verbrechen: Nach Holocaust ist jeder zweite dagegen', *Umfrage* (February 1979).

68 De Mildt, *In the Name of the People*, p. 30. The headline in the Swiss newspaper, *Tages-Anzeiger*, 'Verjährung seit Holocaust weniger popular', 30 March 1979, summed up the change in public mood. For further analysis on the impact of *Holocaust*, see Jeffrey Herf, 'The "Holocaust" Reception in West Germany: Right, Center and Left', *New German Critique*, Vol. 19, No. 1 (1980) pp. 30–52; Andreas Huyssen, 'The Politics of Identification: "Holocaust" and West German Drama', *New German Critique*, Vol. 19, No. 1 (1980) pp. 117–136; Wolf Kansteiner, 'Nazis, Viewers and Statistics: Television History, Television Audience Research and Collective Memory in West Germany', *Journal of Contemporary History*, Vol. 30, No. 4 (2004) pp. 575–598.

69 *Guardian*, 'John Demjanjuk, The "Littlest of Little Fish" Convicted for Nazi Atrocities', 12 May 2011.

70 *Der Spiegel*, 'Das Gespenst von Bad Feilnbach', 17 June 2011.

71 See, for example, *Der Spiegel*, 'Fahndung nach Nazi-Verbrechern: Ermittler sind 50 KZ-Aufsehern auf der Spur', 6 April 2013.

72 *Simon Wiesenthal Centre*, 'Under the Slogan "Late But Not Too Late," the Wiesenthal Center Launches a Publicity Campaign in Germany for Operation Last Chance II', 21 July 2013, http://www.wiesenthal.com/site/apps/nlnet/content2.aspx?c=lsKWLbPJLnF&b=4441467&ct=13224167 (accessed 29 May 2014).

Chapter 5

1 See, for example, Omer Bartov, *Hitler's Army: Soldiers, Nazis, and War in the Third Reich* (Oxford: Oxford University Press, 1992); Harold James, *Deutsche Bank and the Nazi Economic War against the Jews: The Expropriation of Jewish-Owned Property* (Cambridge: Cambridge University Press, 2001); Neil Gregor, *Daimler-Benz in the Third Reich* (New Haven, Connecticut: Yale University Press, 1998).

2 Michael Phayer, *The Catholic Church and the Holocaust, 1930–1965* (Bloomington, Indiana: Indiana University Press, 2001); Hannah Holtschneider, *German Protestants Remember the Holocaust: Theology and the Construction of Collective Memory* (Münster: LIT, 2001); Matthew Hockenos, *A Church Divided: German Protestants Confront the Nazi Past* (Bloomington, Indiana: Indiana University Press, 2004).

3 The NSDAP Programme, February 1920, Jeremy Noakes & Geoffrey Pridham (eds), *Nazism: A Documentary Reader, 1919–1945. Volume 1: The Rise to Power 1919–1934* (Exeter: University of Exeter Press, 1998) pp. 14–16.

4 On Nazism and religion, see Rainer Bucher & Rebecca Pohl, *Hitler's Theology: A Study in Political Religion* (London: Continuum, 2011); Angela Astoria Kurtz, 'God, Not Caesar: Revisiting National Socialism as "Political Religion"', *History of European Ideas*, Vol. 35, No. 2 (2009) pp. 236–252; Stanley Stowers, 'The Concepts of "Religion", "Political Religion" and the Study of Nazism', *Journal of Contemporary History*, Vol. 42, No. 1 (2007), pp. 9–24.

5 Kevin Spicer, 'Father Wilhelm Senn and the Legacy of the Brown Priests', *Holocaust and Genocide Studies*, Vol. 22, No. 2 (2008) pp. 293–319.

6 On the history of the German Christians, see Doris L. Bergen, *Twisted Cross: The German Christian Movement in the Third Reich* (Chapel Hill, North Carolina: University of North Carolina Press, 1996) and '"Germany Is Our Mission – Christ Is Our Strength": The Wehrmacht Chaplaincy and the "German Christian" Movement', *Church History: Studies in Christianity and Culture*, Vol. 66, No. 3 (1997) pp. 522–536.

7 Christopher J. Probst, *Demonizing the Jews: Luther and the Protestant Church in Nazi Germany* (Bloomington, Indiana: Indiana University Press, 2012). See also: Doris L. Bergen, 'Catholics, Protestants and Christian Antisemitism in Nazi Germany', *Central European History*, Vol. 27, No. 3 (1994) pp. 329–348; Richard Gutteridge, *Open Thy Mouth for the Dumb: The German Evangelical Church and the Jews, 1879–1950* (Oxford: Blackwell, 1976).

8 Robert P. Ericksen & Susannah X. Heschel, 'The German Churches and the Holocaust', D. Stone (ed.), *The Historiography of the Holocaust* (Basingstoke: Palgrave Macmillan, 2004) p. 298.

9 On the history of the Confessing Church, see Wolfgang Gerlach, *And the Witnesses Were Silent: The Confessing Church and the Persecution of the Jews* (Lincoln, Nebraska: University of Nebraska Press, 1999); Victoria Barnett, *For the Soul of the People: Protestant Protest against Hitler* (Oxford: Oxford University Press, 1998); Shelley Baranowski, 'Consent and Dissent: The Confessing Church and Conservative Opposition to National Socialism',

Journal of Modern History, Vol. 59, No. 1 (1987) pp. 53–78; Franklin Hamlin Littell, 'From Barmen (1934) to Stuttgart (1945): The Path of the Confessing Church in Germany', *A Journal of Church and State*, Vol. 3, No. 1 (1961) pp. 41–52.

10 Frank M. Buscher & Michael Phayer, 'German Catholic Bishops and the Holocaust, 1940-1952', *German Studies Review*, Vol. 11, No. 3 (1988) pp. 464–467.

11 'Mit Brennender Sorge', Encyclical of Pope Pius XI on the Church and the German Reich, 14 March 1937, *The Vatican*, http://www.vatican.va/holy_father/pius_xi/encyclicals/documents/hf_p-xi_enc_14031937_mit-brennender-sorge_en.html

12 'District Police Report from Ebermannstadt, Northern Bavaria, 29 June 1939', Jeremy Noakes & Geoffrey Pridham (eds), *Nazism 1919-1945: A Documentary Reader. Vol. 2: State, Economy and Society, 1933–1939* (Exeter: University of Exeter Press, 1997) Document No. 456, p. 589.

13 Jeremy Noakes, 'The Oldenburg Crucifix Struggle of November 1936: A Case Study of Opposition in the Third Reich', P.D. Stachura (ed.), *The Shaping of the Nazi State* (London: Croom Helm, 1978) pp. 210–233.

14 Michael Burleigh & Wolfgang Wipperman, *The Racial State: Germany 1933–1945* (Cambridge: Cambridge University Press, 1991) pp. 152–153, 157–159; Beth Griech-Polelle, 'Image of a Churchman-Resister: Bishop von Galen, the Euthanasia Project and the Sermons of Summer 1941', *Journal of Contemporary History*, Vol. 36, No. 1 (2001) pp. 41–57.

15 'Minute from Walter Tiessler to Martin Bormann, 13 August 1941', Jeremy Noakes & Geoffrey Pridham (eds), *Nazism 1919-1945: A Documentary Reader. Vol. 3: Foreign Policy, War and Racial Extermination* (Exeter: University of Exeter Press, 1997), Document No. 759, p. 1039.

16 Buscher & Phayer, 'German Catholic Bishops and the Holocaust, p. 471.

17 'Message to the Congregations', Treysa Conference, August 1945. Reproduced in Hockenos, *A Church Divided*, p. 185.

18 Ibid.

19 Hockenos, *A Church Divided*, p. 64.

20 'Message to the Congregations', in Ibid., p. 185.

21 Pastoral Letter by the Conference of Catholic Bishops at Fulda, 23 August 1945. Reproduced at *German History in Documents and Images*, http://germanhistorydocs.ghi-dc.org/sub_document.cfm?document_id=4454.

22 Ibid.

23 Ibid.

24 Hockenos, *A Church Divided*, passim.

25 'Message to the Pastors', Brethren Council, August 1945. Reproduced in Hockenos, *A Church Divided*, p. 181.

26 Ibid.

27 Michael Phayer, 'The German Catholic Church after the Holocaust', *Holocaust and Genocide Studies*, Vol. 10, No. 2 (1996) p. 152.

28 Ibid., p. 161.

29 Evangelical Church of Germany Council, Stuttgart Declaration of Guilt, 18–19 October 1945. Full text reproduced in the appendix of John S. Conway, 'How Shall the Nations Repent? The Stuttgart Declaration of Guilt, October, 1945', *Journal of Ecclesiastical History*, Vol. 38, No. 4 (1987) pp. 621–622.

30 Hockenos, *A Church Divided*, p. 86.

31 Ibid., p. 88.

32 Cited in Barnett, *For the Soul of the People*, p. 211.

33 Hockenos, *A Church Divided*, p. 97.

34 Cited in Barnett, *For the Soul of the People*, p. 213.

35 Phayer, 'German Catholics after the Holocaust', p. 154. Preysing had established the welfare office in Berlin during the Third Reich to provide assistance to victims of Nazi persecution. He was, therefore, pursuing long-held interests and concerns during the postwar era.

36 Cited in Barnett, *For the Soul of the People*, p. 294. Author's emphasis.

37 'To the Christians in England', Bishop Theophil Wurm, 14 December 1945 full text reproduced in Hockenos, *A Church Divided*, p. 190.

38 Ibid.

39 Ericksen & Heschel, 'The German Churches and the Holocaust', p. 313 – original emphasis.

40 'Message Concerning the Jewish Question', Council of Brethren of the Evangelical Church, 8 April 1948. Full text reproduced in Hockenos, *A Church Divided*, pp. 195–197.

41 'Statement on the Jewish Question', Synod of the Evangelical Church in Germany, Berlin-Weissensee, 27 April 1950. Reproduced in Hockenos, *A Church Divided*, p. 198.

42 Hockenos, *A Church Divided*, p. 170

43 On the reception of Hochhuth's play, see: Eric Bentley, *The Storm over 'The Deputy'* (New York: Grove Press, 1964); Jan Berg, *Hochhuth's 'Stellvertreter' und die 'Stellvertreter'-Debatte: Vergangenheitsbewältigung in Theater und Presse der sechziger Jahre* (Kronberg im Taunus: Scriptor, 1977); Michael Patterson, '"Bewältigung der Vergangenheit" or "Überwältigung der Befangenheit": Nazism and the War in Post-War German Theatre', *Modern Drama*, Vol. 33, No. 1 (1990) pp. 125–126.

44 Randolph L. Braham, 'Remembering and Forgetting: The Vatican, the German Catholic Hierarchy and the Holocaust', *Holocaust and Genocide Studies*, Vol. 13, No. 2 (1999) p. 223.

45 Ibid., p. 241.

46 Ibid., p. 225.

47 Ibid.

48 Ibid., p. 228.

49 Holtschneider, *German Protestants Remember the Holocaust.*

50 Phayer, 'German Catholics after the Holocaust', p. 154.

51 Ibid., p. 155.

52 Ibid.

53 Steven M. Schroeder, *To Forget It All and Begin Anew: Reconciliation in Occupied Germany, 1944–1954* (Toronto: University of Toronto Press, 2013) p. 68.

54 Phayer, 'German Catholics after the Holocaust', p. 160.

55 Ericksen & Heschel, 'The German Churches and the Holocaust', p. 297.

56 'Black Becomes White, or Automatic Denazification', September 1946. Reproduced at *German History in Documents and Images*, http://germanhistorydocs.ghi-dc.org/sub_image.cfm?image_id=2523

57 Buscher & Phayer, 'German Catholic Bishops and the Holocaust', p. 473.

58 Ronald Webster, 'Opposing "Victors' Justice": German Protestant Churchmen and Convicted War Criminals in Western Europe after 1945', *Holocaust and Genocide Studies*, Vol. 15, No. 1 (2001) pp. 47–69.

59 Ibid., p. 50.

60 Ibid., p. 48.

61 Ibid., p. 54.

62 Ibid., p. 56.

63 Ibid., p. 60.

64 Jerome S. Legge, 'Resisting a War Crimes Trial: The Malmédy Massacre, the German Churches and the US Army Counterintelligence Corps', *Holocaust and Genocide Studies*, Vol. 26, No. 2 (2012) p. 233.

65 Ibid., p. 238.

66 Ibid., pp. 239–240.

67 Buscher & Phayer, 'German Catholic Bishops and the Holocaust', p. 475.

68 Legge, 'Resisting a War Crimes Trial', p. 247.

69 Buscher & Phayer, 'German Catholic Bishops and the Holocaust', p. 478.

70 Ibid., p. 250.

71 Buscher & Phayer, 'German Catholic Bishops and the Holocaust', p. 481.

72 'Das Wort des Rates der EKD zu den NS-Vebrecher-Prozessen', *Kirchliches Jahrbuch* (1963) p. 79.

73 Ibid.

Chapter 6

1 Pierre Nora, 'Between History and Memory: Lieux de Mémoire', *Representations*, Vol. 26 (1989) pp. 7–24.

2 For a detailed overview of the range of memorial sites in Germany, see Bill Niven & Chloe Paver (eds), *Memorialization in Germany since 1945* (Basingstoke: Palgrave Macmillan, 2010).

3 James E. Young, *The Texture of Memory: Holocaust Memorials and Meaning* (New Haven, Connecticut: Yale University Press, 1993); Peter Carrier,

Holocaust Monuments and National Memory Cultures in France and Germany since 1989 (New York: Berghahn, 2005).

4 Harold Marcuse, 'Holocaust Memorials: The Emergence of a Genre', *American Historical Review*, Vol. 115, No. 1 (2010) pp. 53–89.

5 See, for example, James E. Young, 'Germany's Holocaust Memorial Problem – and Mine', *The Public Historian*, Vol. 24, No. 4 (2002) pp. 65–80; Henry W. Pickford, 'Conflict and Commemoration: Two Berlin Memorials', *Modernism/Modernity*, Vol. 12, No. 1 (2005) pp. 133–173; Caroline Gay, 'The Politics of Cultural Remembrance: The Holocaust Monument in Berlin', *International Journal of Cultural Policy*, Vol. 9, No. 2 (2003) pp. 153–166; Birgitte Sion, 'Affective Memory, Ineffective Functionality: Experiencing Berlin's Memorial to the Murdered Jews of Europe', Bill Niven & Chloe Paver (eds), *Memorialization in Germany since 1945* (Basingstoke: Palgrave Macmillan, 2010) and Niven & Paver, *Memorialization in Germany*, pp. 243–252.

6 Denkmal für die ermordeten Juden Europas und Ort der Information, *Informationen* (undated).

7 Speech by Lea Rosh, Director of the Association Memorial to the Murdered Jews of Europe, at the inauguration of the Memorial to the Murdered Jews of Europe, 5 May 2005. Reproduced at *Stiftung Denkmal für die ermordeten Juden Europas*, http://www.stiftung-denkmal.de/en/memorials/the-memorial-to-the-murdered-jews-of-europe/speeches-at-the-inaugiration-of-the-memorial-to-the-murdered-jews-of-europe.html

8 Young, *The Texture of Memory*, p. 2.

9 Speech by Wolfgang Thierse at the Inauguration of the Memorial to the Murdered Jews of Europe, 5 May 2005. Reproduced at *Stiftung Denkmal für die ermordeten Juden Europas* http://www.stiftung-denkmal.de/en/memorials/the-memorial-to-the-murdered-jews-of-europe/speeches-at-the-inaugiration-of-the-memorial-to-the-murdered-jews-of-europe.html

10 Young, *The Texture of Memory*, p. 5.

11 Irit Dekel, 'Ways of Looking: Observation and Transformation at the Holocaust Memorial, Berlin', *Memory Studies*, Vol. 2, No. 1 (2009) p. 72.

12 Speech by Dr Paul Spiegel, president of the Central Council of the Jews in Germany, at the inauguration of the Memorial to the Murdered Jews of Europe, 5 May 2005. Reproduced at *Stiftung Denkmal für die ermordeten Juden Europas*, http://www.stiftung-denkmal.de/en/memorials/the-memorial-to-the-murdered-jews-of-europe/speeches-at-the-inaugiration-of-the-memorial-to-the-murdered-jews-of-europe.html

13 Tim Cole, *Images of the Holocaust: The Myth of the 'Shoah Business'* (London: Duckworth, 1999).

14 Jenny Edkins, 'Authenticity and Memory at Dachau', *Cultural Values*, Vol. 5, No. 4 (2001) pp. 405–420.

15 Charles Hawley, 'Touring a Concentration Camp: A Day in Hell', *Der Spiegel International*, 27 January 2005, http://www.spiegel.de/international/touring-a-concentration-camp-a-day-in-hell-a-338820.html.

16 Cited in Dekel, 'Ways of Looking', p. 77.

17 Young, *The Texture of Memory*, p. 9.

18 For details on the various designs submitted for the memorial, see Young, 'Germany's Holocaust Memorial Problem – and Mine' and 'Berlin's Holocaust Memorial: A Report to the Bundestag Committee on Media and Culture', *German Politics and Society*, Vol. 17, No. 3 (1999) pp. 54–70; Carrier, *Holocaust Monuments and National Memory Cultures*.

19 Sion, 'Affective Memory', p. 246.

20 Young, 'Germany's Holocaust Memorial Problem – and Mine', pp. 75–76.

21 Bill Niven, *Facing the Nazi Past: United Germany and the Legacy of the Third Reich* (New York: Routledge, 2002) pp. 175–194.

22 Dekel, 'Ways of Looking', p. 76.

23 Young, *The Texture of Memory*, pp. 20–21. In specific response to the Berlin Holocaust memorial, Young commented 'better a thousand years of Holocaust memorial competitions and exhibitions in Germany than any single "final solution" to Germany's memorial problem' – 'Germany's Holocaust Memorial Problem – and Mine', p. 68.

24 Rafael Seligmann, 'Versiegelter Stein', *Welt am Sonntag*, 19 December 2004. Reproduced at German History in Documents and Images, http://germanhistorydocs.ghi-dc.org/docpage.cfm?docpage_id=4278

25 'Memorial to the Sinti and Roma of Europe Murdered under the National Socialist Regime', *Stiftung Denkmal für die ermordeten Juden Europas*, http://www.stiftung-denkmal.de/en/memorials/memorial-to-the-sinti-and-roma-murdered-unter-the-national-socialist-regime/dani-karavan.html

26 Overviews of each of the memorials can be found at *Stiftung Denkmal für die ermordeten Juden Europas*, http://www.stiftung-denkmal.de/en/home.html

27 Young, *The Texture of Memory*, p. 27.

28 For a discussion of the Harburg counter-monument, see Young, *Texture of Memory*, pp. 28–37; Corinna Tomberger, 'The Counter-Monument: Memory Shaped by Male Post-War Legacies', Bill Niven & Chloe Paver (eds), *Memorialization in Germany since 1945* (Basingstoke: Palgrave Macmillan, 2010); Niven & Paver, *Memorialization in Germany*, pp. 228–230; Noam Lupu, 'Memory Vanished, Absent and Confined: The Countermemorial Project in 1980s and 1990s Germany', *History and Memory*, Vol. 15, No. 2 (2003) pp. 130–164.

29 Tomberger, 'The Counter-Monument', p. 226.

30 Bill Niven notes that even when the US Military left Dachau in 1972, the Bavarian police sealed off the sections of the camp that they had been using – *Facing the Nazi Past*, p. 14.

31 Ibid.

32 Cited in Sarah Farmer, 'Symbols that Face Two Ways: Commemorating the Victims of Nazism and Stalinism at Buchenwald and Sachsenhausen', *Representations*, Vol. 49 (1995) pp. 109–110.

33 Ibid., p. 110.

34 Ibid.

35 Thomas C. Fox, *Stated Memory: East Germany and the Holocaust* (Rochester, New York: Camden House, 1999) p. 41.

36 Farmer, 'Symbols that Face Two Ways', p. 104.

37 Ibid., p. 100.

38 Insa Eschebach, 'Soil, Ashes, Commemoration: Processes of Sacralization at the Ravensbrück Former Concentration Camp', *History and Memory*, Vol. 23, No. 1 (2011) p. 143.

39 Reproduced from Fox, *Stated Memory*, p. 41.

40 Eschebach, 'Soil, Ashes, Commemoration', p. 133.

41 Robin Ostow, 'Reimaging Ravensbrück', *Journal of European Area Studies*, Vol. 9, No. 1 (2001) p. 115.

42 Eschebach, 'Soil, Ashes, Commemoration', pp. 145–147.

43 Ibid., p. 117.

44 Fox, *Stated Memory*, p. 43.

45 Ostow, 'Reimaging Ravensbrück', pp. 111–112, 117.

46 Eschebach, 'Soil, Ashes, Commemoration', p. 148.

47 Cited in ibid., pp. 141–142.

48 Niven, *Facing the Nazi Past*, pp. 15–16.

49 Harold Marcuse, 'Memorialising Persecuted Jews in Dachau and Other West German Concentration Camp Memorial Sites', Bill Niven & Chloe Paver (eds), *Memorialization in Germany since 1945* (Basingstoke: Palgrave Macmillan, 2010); Niven & Paver, *Memorialization in Germany*, p. 193.

50 Niven, *Facing the Nazi Past*, p. 16.

51 Ibid., p. 194.

52 Marcuse, 'Memorialising Persecuted Jews in Dachau', p. 197.

53 Cited in ibid., p. 194.

54 Cited in ibid., p. 197.

55 Ibid., p. 202.

56 Visitor statistics for Dachau after *Holocaust* can be found in Marcuse, *Legacies of Dachau: The Uses and Abuses of a Concentration Camp, 1933–2001* (Cambridge: Cambridge University Press, 2001) pp. 351–352.

57 Niven, *Facing the Nazi Past*, p. 25.

58 Deutsche Bundestag, *Unterrichtung durch den Beauftragten der Bundesregierung für Kultur und Medien: Fortschreibung der Gedenkstättenkonzeption des Bundes*, 19 June 2008.

59 Pickford, 'Conflict and Commemoration', p. 143. See also Karen E. Till, 'Staging the Past: Landscape Designs, Cultural Identity and Erinngerungspolitik at Berlin's Neue Wache', *Cultural Geographies*, Vol. 6, No. 3 (1999) pp. 251–283.

60 Eschebach, 'Soil, Ashes, Commemoration', p. 139.

61 Till, 'Staging the Past', p. 265.

62 Text of the Neue Wache memorial reproduced in Till, 'Staging the Past', p. 273.

63 See: Michael Imort, 'Stumbling Blocks: A Decentralized Memorial to Holocaust Victims', Bill Niven & Chloe Paver (eds), *Memorialization in Germany since 1945* (Basingstoke: Palgrave Macmillan, 2010); Niven & Paver, *Memorialization in Germany*, pp. 233–242; Kirsten Harjes, 'Stumbling Stones: Holocaust Memorials, National Identity and Democratic Inclusion in Berlin', *German Politics and Society*, Vol. 23, No. 1 (2005) pp. 138–151; Mary Rachel Gould and Rachel E. Silverman, 'Stumbling upon History: Collective Memory and the Urban Landscape', *GeoJournal*, Vol. 78, No. 5 (2013) pp. 791–801.

64 Imort, 'Stumbling Blocks', p. 235.

65 Ibid.

66 Ibid., p. 237.

67 Cited in ibid., p. 238.

68 'Stumbling Blocks Holocaust Memorial App Launched in Munich', *JTA*, 28 October 2013.

Chapter 7

1 Jean-Paul Bier, 'The Holocaust, West Germany and Strategies of Oblivion, 1947-1979', A. Rabinbach & J. Zipes (eds), *Germans and Jews since the Holocaust: The Ongoing Situation in West Germany* (New York: Holmes & Meier, 1986) p. 190.

2 See Theodor Adorno, *Can One live after Auschwitz: A Philosophical Reader*, ed. Rolf Tiedemann (Stanford, California: Stanford University Press, 2003) p. xvi. For a critical discussion on how Adorno's argument have been used by scholars, see: Klaus Hofmann, 'Poetry after Auschwitz – Adorno's Dictum', *German Life and Letters*, Vol. 58, No. 2 (2005) pp. 182–194. On the problems of Holocaust representation, see also: Francesa Haig, 'Holocaust Representations since 1975', *Modernism/Modernity*, Vol. 20, No. 1 (2013) pp. 1–13; Saul Friedländer (ed.), *Probing the Limits of Representation: Nazism and the 'Final Solution'* (Cambridge, Massachusetts: Harvard University Press, 1992); Dominick Lacapra, *Representing the Holocaust: History, Theory, Trauma* (Ithaca, New York: Cornell University Press, 1994); Berel Lang, *Holocaust Representation: Art within the Limits of History and Ethics* (Baltimore, Maryland: John Hopkins University Press, 2000).

3 Cited in Christine Haase, 'Ready for His Close-up? Representing Hitler in *Der Untergang* (*Downfall*, 2004)', *Studies in European Cinema*, Vol. 3, No. 3 (2006) p. 189.

4 Primo Levi, *The Drowned and the Saved* (London: Abacus, 1986) pp. 63–4

5 Lawrence Baron, 'Holocaust and Genocide Cinema: Crossing Disciplinary, Genre, and Geographical Borders', *Shofar: An Interdisciplinary Journal of Jewish Studies*, Vol. 20, No. 4 (2010) p. 4.

6 Wulf Kansteiner, 'Entertaining Catastrophe: The Reinvention of the Holocaust in the Television of the Federal Republic of Germany', *New German Critique*, Vol. 90 (2003) p. 146.

7 For more on the issue of trivialization, see Judith E. Doneson, 'Holocaust Revisited: A Catalyst for Memory or Trivialization?', *Annals of the American Academy of Political and Social Science*, Vol. 548 (1996) pp. 70–77.

8 Lang, *Holocaust Representation*, p. 50.

9 Wulf Kansteiner, 'Nazis, Viewers and Statistics: Television History, Television Audience Research and Collective Memory in West Germany', *Journal of Contemporary History*, Vol. 39, No. 4 (2004) p. 576.

10 Robert C. Reimer & Carol J. Reimer, *Nazi-retro Film: How German Narrative Cinema Remembers the Past* (New York: Maxwell Macmillan, 1992) p. 132.

11 Christine Haase, 'Theodor Kotulla's *Excerpts from a German Life* (*Aus einem deutschen Leben*, 1977) or The Inability to Speak: Cinematic Holocaust Representation in Germany', *Film and History*, Vol. 32, No. 2 (2002) p. 49; David Bathrick, 'Holocaust Film before the *Holocaust*: DEFA, Antifascism and the Camps', *Cinemas: Journal of Film Studies*, Vol. 18, No. 1 (2007) pp. 109–134.

12 Daniela Berghahn, 'Post-1990 German Screen Memories: How East and West German Cinema Remembers the Third Reich and the Holocaust', *German Life and Letters*, Vol. 59, No. 2 (2006) p. 297.

13 Thomas C. Fox, *Stated Memory: East Germany and the Holocaust* (Rochester, New York: Camden House, 1999) pp. 110–111.

14 Ibid., p. 111.

15 Anke Pinkert, *Film and Memory in East Germany* (Bloomington, Indiana: Indiana University Press, 2008) p. 7.

16 Fox, *Stated Memory*, p. 111.

17 Ursula von Keitz, 'Between Dramatization and Epicization: The Portrayal of Nazi Cries in Exemplary German Films from the Late 1940s to the 1970s', *New German Critique*, Vol. 102 (2007) p. 49.

18 Mark A. Wolfgram, 'The Holocaust through the Prism of East German Television: Collective Memory and Audience Perceptions', *Holocaust & Genocide Studies*, Vol. 20, No. 1 (2006), p. 65.

19 Fox, *Stated Memory*, p. 106.

20 Ibid., pp. 107, 105–106.

21 Wolfgram, 'The Holocaust through the Prism of East German Television', p. 66.

22 Fox, *Stated Memory*, p. 109.

23 Ibid., p. 138.

24 Mark. A. Wolfgram, 'West German and Unified German Cinema's Difficult Encounter with the Holocaust', *Film & History: An Interdisciplinary Journal of Film & Television Studies*, Vol. 32, No. 2 (2002), p. 25.

25 Ibid., p. 24.

26 Ibid., p. 29.

27 Haase, 'Theodor Kotulla's *Excerpts from a German Life*', pp. 56–57.

28 Wolfgram, 'West German and Unified German Cinema's Difficult Encounter', p. 30.

29 Andrei S. Markovits, '"Holocaust" Before and After the Event: Reactions in West Germany and Austria', *New German Critique*, Vol. 19, No. 1 (1980) p. 54.

30 Harold Marcuse, *Legacies of Dachau: The Uses and Abuses of a Concentration Camp, 1933–2001* (Cambridge: Cambridge University Press, 2001) p. 202.

31 Sabine Reichel, *What Did You Do in the War, Daddy? Growing Up German* (New York: Hill & Wang, 1989.)

32 Ibid.

33 Ibid.

34 Ibid.

35 Kansteiner, 'Entertaining Catastrophe', p. 138.

36 Figures compiled by Kansteiner, 'Nazis, Viewers and Statistics', p. 580.

37 Ibid., p. 581.

38 Ibid., p. 582.

39 Ibid., pp. 583–584.

40 Kansteiner, 'Entertaining Catastrophe', p. 143.

41 Ibid., pp. 139–141.

42 Ibid., pp. 141–142.

43 Kansteiner, 'Nazis, Viewers and Statistics', p. 585.

44 Ibid., p. 585.

45 Wolfgram, 'West German and Unified German Cinema's Difficult Encounter', p. 30.

46 Wolfgram, 'The Holocaust through the Prism of East German Television', p. 60.

47 On reactions in the US, see Jeffrey Shandler, *While America Watches: Televising the Holocaust* (Oxford: Oxford University Press, 1999), pp. 155–179.

48 Andreas Huyssen, 'The Politics of Identification: "Holocaust" and West German Drama', *New German Critique*, Vol. 19, No. 1 (1980) p. 118.

49 Jean-Paul Bier, 'The Holocaust and West Germany: Strategies of Oblivion, 1947-1979', *New German Critique*, Vol. 19, No. 1 (1980) p. 29.

50 *Der Spiegel*, '"Holocaust": Die Vergangenheit kommt zurück', 29 January 1979.

51 Werner Sollers, '*Holocaust* on West German Television: The (In)Ability to Mourn?', *The Massachusetts Review*, Vol. 20, No. 2 (1979) p. 377.

52 Markovits, '"Holocaust" Before and After the Event', p. 59.

53 Sollers, '*Holocaust* on West German Television', p. 378.

54 Cited in Jeffrey Herf, 'The "Holocaust" Reception in West Germany: Right, Center and Left', *New German Critique*, Vol. 19, No. 1 (1980) p. 36.

55 Elie Wiesel, 'Trivializing the Holocaust: Semi-Fact and Semi-Fiction', *New York Times*, 16 April 1978.

56 Cited in Herf, 'The "Holocaust" Reception', p. 38.

57 Julius H. Schoeps, 'The Emotional Impact of the Broadcast of "Holocaust", an American TV Miniseries, in the Federal Republic', 1979. Reproduced at German History in Documents and Images, http://germanhistorydocs.ghi-dc.org/sub_document.cfm?document_id=1155.

58 Sollers, '*Holocaust* on West German Television', p. 378.

59 Ibid.

60 Ibid., pp. 38–39.

61 Markovits, '"Holocaust" Before and After the Event', p. 64.

62 Lawrence Baron, 'The Germans' Reactions to NBC's *Holocaust*', *Sh'ma: A Journal of Jewish Ideas*, Vol. 9, No. 181 (1979) pp. 3–8.

63 Herf, 'The "Holocaust" Reception', p. 37.

64 Sollers, '*Holocaust* on West German Television', p. 380.

65 Huyssen, 'The Politics of Identification', p. 117.

66 Markovits, '"Holocaust" Before and After the Event', p. 58.

67 Schoeps, 'The Emotional Impact of the Broadcast of "Holocaust"'.

68 Cited in Siegfried Zielinski, 'History as Entertainment and Provocation: The TV Series "Holocaust" in West Germany', *New German Critique*, Vol. 19, No. 1 (1980) p. 91.

69 Cited in Marcuse, *Legacies of Dachau*, p. 346.

70 Markovits, '"Holocaust" Before and After the Event', p. 63.

71 Ibid.

72 Ibid.

73 Statistics cited in ibid., p. 65.

74 Sollers, '*Holocaust* on West German Television', p. 378. See also Bathrick, 'Holocaust Film before the *Holocaust*', p. 109.

75 Zielinski, 'History as Entertainment and Provocation', pp. 88–89.

76 Ibid., p. 93.

77 Sollers, '*Holocaust* on West German Television', p. 384.

78 Ibid., p. 379.

79 Markovits, '"Holocaust" Before and After the Event', p. 76.

80 Cited in Sollers, '*Holocaust* on West German Television', p. 382.

81 Cited in Huyssen, 'The Politics of Identification', p. 122.

82 Ibid., p. 134.

83 Herf, 'The "Holocaust" Reception', p. 32.

84 Ibid., p. 33.
85 Ibid., p. 34.
86 Ibid., p. 36.
87 Marcuse, *Legacies of Dachau*, p. 344.
88 Zielinski, 'History as Entertainment and Provocation', p. 87.
89 Herf, 'The "Holocaust" Reception', p. 37.
90 Ibid., p. 38.
91 Ibid.
92 Ibid., pp. 43–49.
93 Ibid., p. 50.
94 Marcuse, *Legacies of Dachau*, p. 345.
95 Ibid., p. 346.
96 Bill Niven, 'The Reception of Steven Spielberg's Schindler's List in the German Media', *Journal of European Studies*, Vol. 25, No. 2 (1995) pp. 165–166.
97 Ibid., p. 169.
98 *Guardian*, 'Schindler's List Taxes Germans', 2 March 1994.
99 Cited in Niven, 'The Reception of Steven Spielberg's Schindler's List', p. 168.
100 Cited in Ibid., p. 169.
101 Ibid., p. 171.
102 Ibid., pp. 171–172.
103 Ibid., p. 168.
104 Ibid., pp. 173–174.
105 Ibid., p. 175.
106 Ibid., pp. 176–177. Original emphasis.
107 Ibid., p. 177.
108 Ibid., p. 180.
109 Haase, 'Ready for His Close-up?', p. 191.
110 John Bendix, 'Facing Hitler: German Responses to "Downfall"', *German Politics and Society*, Vol. 25, No. 1 (2007) p. 72.
111 Ibid., p. 76.
112 Cited in ibid., p. 82
113 Ibid.
114 Haase, 'Ready for His Close-up?', p. 195.
115 Ibid., pp. 197–198.
116 Bendix, 'Facing Hitler', p. 78.
117 Ibid., p. 78.
118 Ibid.
119 Ibid., p. 79.
120 Cited in *Stern*, 'Das gespaltene Urteil der Historiker', 23 March 2013.

121 Ibid.

122 Ibid.

123 *Der Spiegel*, 'Our Mothers, Our Fathers: Next Generation WWII Atonement', 28 March 2013, http://www.spiegel.de/international/germany/zdf-tv-miniseries-reopens-german-wounds-of-wwii-past-a-891332.html.

Chapter 8

1 'What to Teach about the Holocaust', *International Holocaust Remembrance Alliance*, https://www.holocaustremembrance.com/node/318

2 See, for example, the work of the Centre for Holocaust Education at the Institute of Education in London, http://www.holocausteducation.org.uk/, and the Bundeszentrale für politische Bildung in Bonn, http://www.bpb.de/.

3 Lucy Dawidowicz, 'How They Teach the Holocaust', *Commentary*, Vol. 90, No. 6 (1990), pp. 25–31; Karen Shawn, 'Current Issues in Holocaust Education', *Dimensions: A Journal of Holocaust Studies*, Vol. 9, No. 2 (1995) pp. 15–18; Samuel Totten, *Holocaust Education: Issues and Approaches* (Boston, Massachusetts: Allyn & Bacon, 2002).

4 See, for example, Totten, *Holocaust Education*; Jeffrey Glanz, 'Ten Suggestions for Teaching the Holocaust', *The History Teacher*, Vol. 32, No. 4 (1999) pp. 547–565; William Benedict Russell III, 'Teaching About the Holocaust: A Resource Guide', *The Social Studies* (March-April 2005) pp. 93–96; Patricia Bromley & Susan Garnett Russell, 'The Holocaust as History and Human Rights: A Cross-National Analysis of Holocaust Education in Social Science Textbooks, 1970–2008', *Prospects*, Vol. 40 (2010) pp. 153–173.

5 Paula Cowan & Henry Maitles, 'Developing Positive Values: A Case Study of Holocaust Memorial Day in the Primary Schools of One Local Authority in Scotland', *Educational Review*, Vol. 54, No. 3 (2002) pp. 219–229; Vera Hanfland, *Holocaust: Ein Thema für die Grundschule? Eine empirische Untersuchung zum Geschichtsbewusstsein von Viertklässlern* (Münster: LIT, 2008); Jürgen Moysich & Matthias Heyl (eds), *Der Holocaust: Ein Thema für Kindergarten und Grundschule?* (Hamburg: Krämer, 1998).

6 See, for example, Paula Cowan & Henry Maitles, '"We Saw Inhumanity Close Up": What Is Gained by School Students from Scotland Visiting Auschwitz?', *Journal of Curriculum Studies*, Vol. 43, No. 2 (2011) pp. 163–184; Kathryn Hadley, 'Lessons from Auschwitz', *History Today*, Vol. 60, No. 9 (2010) pp. 4–5; Alon Lazar & Tal Litvak Hirsch, 'An Online Partner for Holocaust Remembrance Education: Students Approaching the Yahoo! Answers Community', *Educational Review*, Vol. 67, No. 1 (2013) pp. 1–14; Meghan McGlinn Manfra & Jeremy D. Stoddard, 'Powerful and Authentic Digital Media and Strategies for Teaching about Genocide and the Holocaust', *The Social Studies*, Vol. 99, No. 6 (2008) pp. 260–264; Michael Gray, *Contemporary Debates in Holocaust Education* (Basingstoke: Palgrave Macmillan, 2014) pp. 99–114.

7 Lucy Russell, *Teaching the Holocaust in School History: Teachers or Preachers?* (London: Continuum, 2006); Rachel N. Baum, '"What I Have

Learned to Feel": The Pedagogical Emotions of Holocaust Education', *College Literature*, Vol. 23, No. 3 (1996) pp. 44–57; Jane Clements, 'A Very Neutral Voice: Teaching about the Holocaust', *Educate*, Vol. 5, No. 1 (2005) pp. 39–49.

8 Margot Brown & Ian Davies, 'The Holocaust and Education for Citizenship: The Teaching of History, Religion and Human Rights in England', *Educational Review*, Vol. 50, No. 1 (1998) pp. 75–83; Arye Carmon, 'Teaching the Holocaust as a Means of Fostering Values', *Curriculum Inquiry*, Vol. 9, No. 3 (1979) pp. 209–228; Bruce Carrington & Geoffrey Short, 'Holocaust Education, Anti-Racism and Citizenship', *Educational Review*, Vol. 49, No. 3 (1997) pp. 271–282; Paula Cowan & Henry Maitles, 'Does Addressing Prejudice and Discrimination Through Holocaust Education Produce Better Citizens?', *Educational Review*, Vol. 59, No. 2 (2007) pp. 115–130; Nicolas Kinloch, 'Learning about the Holocaust: Moral or Historical Question?', *Teaching History*, Vol. 93 (1998) pp. 44–46.

9 Sekretariat der Ständigen Konferenz der Kultusminister der Länder in der Bundesrepublik Deutschland, *Zur Auseinandersetzung mit dem Holocaust in der Schule: Ein Beitrag zur Information von Länderseite* (1997) p. 11.

10 Ibid., 'Saarbrücker Erklärung der Kultusministerkonferenz zu Toleranz und Solidarität', 9 October 1992, p. 55.

11 Ieva Gundare & Pieter Batelaan, 'Learning about and from the Holocaust: The Development and Implementation of a Complex Instruction Unit in Latvia', *Intercultural Education*, Vol. 14, No. 2 (2003), p. 151.

12 Michal Frankl, 'Holocaust Education in the Czech Republic, 1989-2002', *Intercultural Education*, Vol. 14, No. 2 (2003) pp. 177–189; Michelle Kelso, '"And Roma Were Victims, Too": The Romani Genocide and Holocaust Education in Romania', *Intercultural Education*, Vol. 24, No. 1–2 (2013) pp. 61–78; Deborah L. Michaels, 'Holocaust Education in the "Black Hole of Europe": Slovakia's Identity Politics and History Textbooks Pre- and Post-1989', *Intercultural Education*, Vol. 24, No. 1–2 (2013) pp. 19–40; Boguslaw Milerski, 'Holocaust Education in Polish Public Schools: Between Remembrance and Civic Education', *Prospects*, Vol. 40, No. 1 (2010) pp. 115–132; E. Doyle Stevick, 'Education Policy as Normative Discourse and Negotiated Meanings: Engaging the Holocaust in Estonia', *Prospects*, Vol. 40, No. 2 (2010) pp. 239–256. For an overview of Holocaust education in Germany, see Stephen A. Pagaard, 'German Schools and the Holocaust: A Focus on the Secondary School System of Nordrhein-Westfalen', *The History Teacher*, Vol. 28, No. 4 (1995), pp. 541–554; Wolfgang Meseth & Matthias Proske, 'Mind the Gap: Holocaust Education in Germany between Pedgagogical Intentions and Classroom Interactions', *Prospects*, Vol. 40 (2010) pp. 201–222.

13 David Cesarani, 'Britain, the Holocaust and Its Legacy: The Theme for Holocaust Memorial Day 2002', *Holocaust Memorial Day Trust Theme Papers*, p. 3. http://hmd.org.uk/resources/theme-papers (accessed 4 February 2013).

14 For examples of Nazi teaching materials, see Jeremy Noakes & Geoffrey Pridham (eds), *Nazism 1919-1945: A Documentary Reader Vol. 2: State, Economy and Society, 1933–1939* (Exeter: University of Exeter Press, 1994);

Lisa Pine, *Education in Nazi Germany* (Oxford: Berg, 2010); Gilmer W. Blackburn, *Education in the Third Reich: A Study of Race and History in Nazi Textbooks* (Albany, New York: State University of New York Press, 1985).

15 On Allied re-education, see Hermann Rohrs, 'Education for Peace: A Neglected Aspect of Re-education in Germany', *Oxford Review of Education*, Vol. 15, No. 2 (1989) pp. 147–164; James F. Tent, 'Mission on the Rhine: American Educational Policy in Post-War Germany, 1945-1949', *History of Education Quarterly*, Vol. 22, No. 3 (1982) pp. 255–276; Benita Blessing, *The Antifascist Classroom: Denazification in Soviet Occupied Germany, 1945–1949* (Basingstoke: Palgrave Macmillan, 2006).

16 Michael Kater, 'Problems of Political Reeducation in West Germany, 1945-1960', *Simon Wiesenthal Annual*, Vol. 4, http://motlc.wiesenthal.com/site/pp.asp?c=gvKVLcMVIuG&b=395077

17 Ibid.

18 Bodo von Borries, 'The Third Reich in German History Textbooks since 1945', *Journal of Contemporary History*, Vol. 38, No. 1 (2003) p. 46.

19 Decision of the SED Executive Committee, 24 August 1949. Reproduced at *German History in Documents and Images*, http://germanhistorydocs.ghi-dc.org/sub_document.cfm?document_id=4485.

20 Borries, 'The Third Reich in German History Textbooks', p. 46.

21 Ibid., p. 48.

22 Cited in Thomas C. Fox, *Stated Memory: East Germany and the Holocaust* (Rochester, New York: Camden House, 1999) p. 32. Author's emphasis.

23 Borries, 'The Third Reich in German History Textbooks', p. 48.

24 Ibid., pp. 46–47.

25 Ibid., p. 47.

26 Cited in ibid., p. 48.

27 Fox, *Stated Memory*, p. 34.

28 Borries, 'The Third Reich in German History Textbooks', pp. 58–59.

29 Pagaard, 'German Schools and the Holocaust', p. 548.

30 Kater, 'Problems of Political Reeducation'.

31 Borries, 'The Third Reich in German History Textbooks', p. 50.

32 Ibid., p. 51.

33 Cited in ibid., p. 51.

34 Cited in ibid., p. 52.

35 Ibid., p. 53.

36 Statement by the Kirchentag: Conference of German Evangelical Churches held in Berlin 19–23 July 1961. Cited in *Common Ground*, Vol. 26, No. 1 (1962) pp. 19–20.

37 Harold Marcuse, *Legacies of Dachau: The Uses and Abuses of a Concentration Camp, 1933-2001* (Cambridge: Cambridge University Press, 2001), p. 201.

38 *Wiener Library Bulletin*, 'The Thorn in the Flesh', Vol. 10, No. 5–6 (1956) p. 38.

39 Heinz Keil (ed.), *Dokumentation über die Verfolgungen der Jüdischen Bürger von Ulm/Donau* (Hergestellt im Auftrage der Stadt Ulm, 1959) p. 303.

40 Ibid.

41 Wolfgang Koppel (ed.), *Ungesuhnte Nazijustiz: Hundert Urteile klagen ihre Richter an* (Karlsruhe: Organisationskomitees der Dokumentenausstellung 'Ungesühnte Nazijustiz', 1960).

42 Donald Mattheisen, 'History and Political Education in West Germany', *The History Teacher*, Vol. 1, No. 3 (1968) p. 42.

43 Pagaard, 'German Schools and the Holocaust', p. 544.

44 Mattheisen, 'History and Political Education', p. 42.

45 Reinhold Boschki, Bettina Reichmann & Wilhelm Schwendemann, 'Education after and about Auschwitz in Germany: Towards a Theory of Remembrance in the European Context', *Prospects*, Vol. 40 (2010) p. 135.

46 Ibid., p. 135.

47 Adorno, cited in ibid., p. 134. See also Friedrich Schweitzer, 'Education after Auschwitz: Perspectives from Germany', *Journal of Intercultural Education*, Vol. 95, No. 4 (2000) pp. 359–372; Matthias Heyl, 'Education after Auschwitz: Teaching the Holocaust in Germany', R.L. Millen (ed.), *New Perspectives on the Holocaust: A Guide for Teachers and Scholars* (New York: New York University Press, 1996) pp. 275–286.

48 Caroline Sharples, *West Germans and the Nazi Legacy* (New York: Routledge, 2012).

49 Emmi Bonhoeffer, *Auschwitz Trials: Letters from an Eyewitness*, translated by U. Stechow (Richmond, Virginia: John Knox Press, 1967) pp. 15, 20.

50 Gita Sereny, *The German Trauma: Experiences and Reflections, 1938–2001* (London: Penguin, 2000) p. 73.

51 *Westdeutsche Allgemeine Zeitung*, 'Überlebende gingen in die Schule', 12 February 1965.

52 *Der Spiegel*, 'Hitler kam von ganz alleine an die Macht', 15 August 1977.

53 Ibid.

54 Ibid.

55 Ibid.

56 Ibid.

57 *Der Spiegel*, 'Jeder dritte: "Ich weiss wenig"', 15 August 1977.

58 'Treatment of National Socialism in Teaching', Resolution of the KMK, 20 April 1978. Reproduced in Sekretariat der Ständigen Konferenz der Kultusminister der Länder in der Bundesrepublik Deutschland, *Zur Auseinandersetzung mit dem Holocaust in der Schule*, p. 51

59 Cited in Sekretariat der Ständigen Konferenz der Kultusminister der Länder in der Bundesrepublik Deutschland, *Zur Auseinandersetzung mit dem Holocaust in der Schule*, p. 23.

60 Borries, 'The Third Reich in German History Textbooks', p. 54.

61 Marcuse, *Legacies of Dachau*, p. 350.

62 'Empfehlung zur Behandlung des Widerstandes in der NS-Zeit im Unterricht', Beschluß der Kultusministerkonferenz, 4 December 1980. Reproduced in Sekretariat der Ständigen Konferenz der Kultusminister der Länder in der Bundesrepublik Deutschland, *Zur Auseinandersetzung mit dem Holocaust in der Schule*, p. 53

63 Ibid.

64 Borries, 'The Third Reich in German History Textbooks', pp. 56–57.

65 'Holocaust Education in Task Force Member Countries: Germany', Education Reports, *International Holocaust Remembrance Alliance*, https://www.holocaustremembrance.com/educate/education-reports.

66 Ibid.

67 Sekretariat der Ständigen Konferenz der Kultusminister der Länder in der Bundesrepublik Deutschland, *Zur Auseinandersetzung mit dem Holocaust in der Schule*, p. 6.

68 Pagaard, 'German Schools and the Holocaust', pp. 545–546.

69 Ibid., p. 546.

70 Sekretariat der Ständigen Konferenz der Kultusminister der Länder in der Bundesrepublik Deutschland, *Zur Auseinandersetzung mit dem Holocaust in der Schule*, pp. 11–16.

71 Pagaard, 'German Schools and the Holocaust', pp. 547–548.

72 Sekretariat der Ständigen Konferenz der Kultusminister der Länder in der Bundesrepublik Deutschland, *Zur Auseinandersetzung mit dem Holocaust in der Schule*, pp. 18–19.

73 IHRA, 'Holocaust Education in Task Force Member Countries: Germany'.

74 Stephan Marks, 'Teaching about National Socialism and the Holocaust: Narrative Approaches to Holocaust Education', *Interchange*, Vol. 38, No. 3 (2007) p. 273.

75 Ibid., p. 274.

76 Boschki, 'Education after and about Auschwitz', p. 137.

77 Ibid.

78 IHRA, 'Holocaust Education in Task Force Member Countries: Germany'.

79 Boschki, 'Education after and about Auschwitz', p. 142

80 Ibid.

81 Marks, 'Teaching about National Socialism', pp. 268–271.

82 Bodo von Borries, 'Research on the Attitudes of Pupils and Teachers towards the Shoah in Germany', *Intercultural Education*, Vol. 14, No. 2 (2003) pp. 204–212.

83 Ibid., pp. 203–204. See also Boschki, 'Education after and about Auschwitz', p. 140; Meseth & Proske, 'Mind the Gap', p. 203.

84 Marks, 'Teaching about National Socialism', pp. 263, 265.

85 Cited in ibid., p. 265.

86 Harald Welzer, 'Collateral Damage of History Education: National Socialism and the Holocaust in German Family Memory', *Social Research: An International Quarterly*, Vol. 75, No. 1 (2008) p. 297.

Conclusion

1 Speech by Federal Chancellor Angela Merkel to the Knesset, 18 March 2008. Full text translation available from *Bundesregierung*, http://www.bundesregierung.de/nn_6566/Content/EN/Reden/2008/03/2008-03-18-rede-knesset.html.

2 Ibid.

BIBLIOGRAPHY

Online sources

Avalon Project: Documents in Law, History and Diplomacy, http://avalon.law.yale.edu/imt/count.asp
German History in Documents and Images, http://germanhistorydocs.ghi-dc.org
International Holocaust Remembrance Alliance, https://www.holocaustremembrance.com/about-us/stockholm-declaration.
Stiftung für die ermordeten Juden Europas, http://www.stiftung-denkmal.de
Stiftung Topographie des Terrors, http://www.topographie.de/.
The Holocaust and the United Nations Outreach Programme, http://www.un.org/en/holocaustremembrance/docs/res607.shtml.
United States Holocaust Memorial Museum, http://www.ushmm.org

Archival sources

The National Archives, London:
FO371/137596: War Crimes 1958
FO371/183153: Germany
FO 946/43: German Reaction to Nuremberg Sentences
FO 1050/356: German Opinions on Denazification Measures.
FO 1056/166: Control Commission for Germany, Information Services Control Branch Publicity Material.
FO 1056/93: Control Commission for Germany, Information Services Control Branch.

Published primary sources

Document collections

Jeremy Noakes & Geoffrey Pridham (eds.), *Nazism: A Documentary Reader, 1919–1945*
Vol. 1 The Rise to Power 1919–1934 (Exeter: University of Exeter Press, 1998).
Vol. 2 State, Economy and Society, 1933–1939 (Exeter: University of Exeter Press, 1997).
Vol. 3 Foreign Policy, War and Racial Extermination (Exeter: University of Exeter Press, 1997).

C.F. Rüter & D.W. de Mildt (eds.), *Justiz und NS-Verbrechen: Sammlung deutscher Strafurteile wegen nationalsozialistischer Tötungsverbrechen 1945–1966. Register zu den Bänden I-XXII* (Amsterdam: APA - Holland University Press, 1998).

Government reports

Deutsche Bundestag, *Unterrichtung durch den Beauftragten der Bundesregierung für Kultur und Medien: Fortschreibung der Gedenkstättenkonzeption des Bundes*, 19 June 2008.

Sekretariat der Ständigen Konferenz der Kultusminister der Länder in der Bundesrepublik Deutschland, *Unterricht über Nationalsozialismus und Holocaust* (2005).

Sekretariat der Ständigen Konferenz der Kultusminister der Länder in der Bundesrepublik Deutschland, *Zur Auseinandersetzung mit dem Holocaust in der Schule* (1997).

Federal Ministry of Justice, *The Prosecution since 1945 of National Socialist Crimes by Public Prosecutors and Courts in the Territory of the Federal Republic of Germany* (Düsseldorf: Oskar Leiner-Druck KG, 1962).

Speeches and statements

Konrad Adenauer, 'Policy Statement of the German Federal Government', Bundestag, 20 September 1949. Full text available at *The History Collection*, http://digicoll.library.wisc.edu/cgi-bin/History/History-idx?type=div&did=HISTORY.GPARLIAMENT.ADENAUERK1&isize=text

Kirchliches Jahrbuch, 'Das Wort des Rates der EKD zu den NS-Verbrecher-Prozessen' (1963) pp. 75–89.

Protokoll der Verhandlungen der Landessynode, 'Wort des Rates der Evangelischen Kirche in Deutschland' (1963) pp. 21–22.

Richard Weizsäcker, 'Speech in the Bundestag on 8 May 1985 during the Ceremony Commemorating the 40th Anniversary of the End of War in Europe and of National-Socialist Tyranny'. *Landesmedienzentrum Media Culture Online*, http://www.mediacultureonline.de/medienbildung/medienpraxis/sprechen-praesentieren/politische-reden-gegenwart.html

Newspapers

Der Spiegel
Die Zeit
Frankfurter Allgemeine Zeitung
Frankfurter Rundschau
Freie Presse
Jewish Chronicle
Manchester Guardian
Milwaukee Journal
Müncher Merkur
Neue Presse

Neues Deutschland
New York Herald Tribune
New York Times
Stern
Stuttgarter Zeitung
Süddeutsche Zeitung
The Times
Time Magazine
Toronto Daily Star
Trierischer Volksfreund

Miscellaneous printed primary sources

E. Bonhoeffer, *Auschwitz Trials: Letters from an Eyewitness*, translated by U. Stechow (Richmond, Virginia: John Knox Press, 1967).

Joel Carmichael, 'The Eichmann Case: Reactions in West Germany', *Midstream*, Vol. 7, No. 3 (1961) pp. 13–27.

Institute of Jewish Affairs, *Statute of Limitations and the Prosecution of Nazi Crimes in the Federal German Republic. Background Paper No. 14* (London: Institute of Jewish Affairs, 1969).

H. Keil (ed.), *Dokumentation über die Verfolgungen der Jüdischen Bürger von Ulm/Donau* (Hergestellt im Auftrage der Stadt Ulm, 1960).

E. Kogon, *Der SS-Staat: Das System der deutschen Konzentrationslager* (Frankfurt am Main: Europäische Verlagsanstalt, 1946).

W. Koppel, *Ungesühnte Nazijustiz: Hundert Urteile Klagen ihre Richter an* (Karlsruhe: Organisationskomitees der Dokumentenausstellung 'Ungesühnte Nazijustiz', 1960).

H. Lamm, *Der Eichmann Prozeß in der deutschen öffentlichen Meinung* (Frankfurt am Main: Ner-Tamid-Verlag, 1961).

H. Langbein, *Der Auschwitz-Prozess: Eine Dokumentation* (Vienna: Europa Verlag, 1965).

Manfred Overesch (ed.), *Buchenwald und die DDR oder die Suche nach Selbstlegitimation* (Göttingen: Vandenhoeck & Ruprecht, 1995).

Sabine Reichel, *What Did You Do in the War, Daddy? Growing Up German* (New York: Hill & Wang, 1989).

Konrad Schilling (ed.), *Monumenta Judaica: 2,000 Jahre Geschichte und Kultur der Juden am Rhein. Handbuch & Katalog* (Cologne: J. Melzer Verlag, 1963).

Peter Weiss, *The Investigation: Oratorio in Eleven Cantos*, translated by A. Gross (London: Calder & Boyous, 1966).

Rebecca West, *A Train of Powder* (London: Virago, 1984).

Contemporary reports and opinion polls

Institut für Demoskopie Allensbach am Bodensee, *Die Stimmung im Bundesgebiet*:
- 'Die KZ-Prozesse' (27 October 1958);
- 'Der Fall Eichmann' (12 August 1960);
- 'Verjährung von NS-Vebrechen' (5 May 1965);
- 'Verjährung der Nazi-Verbrechen?' (13 February 1969).

Elizabeth Noelle & Erich Peter Neumann (eds.), *Jahrbuch der öffentlichen Meinung, 1947–1955* (Allensbach am Bodensee: Verlag für Demoskopie, 1956).
Elizabeth Noelle & Erich Peter Neumann (eds.), *Jahrbuch der öffentlichen Meinung, 1958–1964* (Allensbach & Bonn: Institut füür Demoskopie Allensbach, 1965).
Elizabeth Noelle & Erich Peter Neumann (eds.), *Jahrbuch der öffentlichen Meinung, 1965–1967* (Allensbach & Bonn: Institut fur Demoskopie Allensbach, 1967).
EMNID, 'Verjährung für NS-Verbrechen', *EMNID-Informationen*, No. 11 (1978).
EMNID, 'Verjährung für NS-Verbrechen', *EMNID-Informationen*, No. 2 (1979).
Morris Janowitz, 'German Reactions to Nazi Atrocities', *American Journal of Psychology*, Vol. 52, No. 2 (1946) pp. 141–146.
Anna J. Merritt & Richard L. Merritt (eds.), *Public Opinion in Occupied Germany: The OMGUS Surveys, 1945–1949* (Urbana, Illinois: University of Illinois Press, 1970).
Sample, 'Sollen NS-Verbrechen verjähren?', *Umfrage* (November, 1978).
Sample, 'Verjährung von NS-Verbrechen: Nach Holocaust ist jeder zweite dagegen', *Umfrage* (February 1979).

Secondary sources

Germans, Nazism and the Holocaust, 1933–1945

Omer Bartov, *Hitler's Army: Soldiers, Nazis, and War in the Third Reich* (Oxford: Oxford University Press, 1992).
Michael Burleigh & Wolfgang Wipperman, *The Racial State: Germany 1933–1945* (Cambridge: Cambridge University Press, 1991).
Robert Gellately, *Backing Hitler: Consent and Coercion in Nazi Germany* (Oxford: Oxford University Press, 2002).
Robert Gellately & Natan Stoltzfus (eds.), *Social Outsiders in Nazi Germany* (Princeton, New Jersey: Princeton University Press, 2001).
Martyn Housden, *Resistance and Conformity in the Third Reich* (London: Routledge, 1997).
Jeremy Noakes, 'The Oldenburg Crucifix Struggle of November 1936: A Case Study of Opposition in the Third Reich,' P.D. Stachura (ed.), *The Shaping of the Nazi State* (London: Croom Helm, 1978) pp. 210–233.
Nikolaus Wachsmann & Jane Caplan (eds.), *Concentration Camps in Nazi Germany: The New Histories* (London: Routledge, 2010).
Nikolaus Wachsmann & Christian Goeschel (eds.), 'Before the Holocaust: New Approaches to the Nazi Concentration Camps, 1933–1939', special issue of *Journal of Contemporary History*, Vol. 45, No. 3 (2010) pp. 515–698.

Postwar politics

Mike Dennis, *The Rise and Fall of the German Democratic Republic, 1945–1990* (London: Longman, 2000).
Harold James, 'The Prehistory of the Federal Republic', *Journal of Modern History*,

Vol. 63, No. 1 (1991) pp. 99–115.

Robert G. Moeller (ed.), *West Germany under Construction: Politics, Society and Culture in the Adenauer Era* (Ann Arbor, Michigan: University of Michigan Press, 1997).

David Reynolds, 'The Origins of the Cold War: The European Dimension, 1944-1951', *Historical Journal*, Vol. 28, No. 2 (1985) pp. 497–515.

Tony Sharp, *The Wartime Alliance and the Zonal Division of Germany* (Oxford: Oxford University Press, 1975).

Rolf Steiniger, 'Germany after 1945: Divided and Integrated or United and Neutral?', *German History*, Vol. 7, No. 1 (1989) pp. 5–18.

General works on Vergangenheitsbewältigung, memory and German national identity after 1945

Wolfgang Benz, 'Nachkriegsgesellschaft und Nationalsozialismus. Erinnerung, Amnesie, Abwehr', *Dachauer Hefte*, Vol. 6 (1990) pp. 12–24.

Nicolas Berg, *Der Holocaust und die westdeutschen Historiker. Erforschung und Erinnerung* (Göttingen: Wallstein Verlag, 2003).

Stefan Berger, 'A Return to the National Paradigm? National History Writing in Germany, Italy, France and Britain from 1945 to the Present', *Journal of Modern History*, Vol. 77, No. 3 (2005) pp. 629–678.

Werner Bergmann, 'Die Reaktion auf den Holocaust in Westdeutschland von 1945 bis 1989', *Geschichte in Wissenschaft und Unterricht*, Vol. 43 (1992) pp. 327–350.

Ulrich Brochhagen, *Nach Nürnberg: Vergangensheitsbewältigung und Westintegration in der Ära Adenauer* (Berlin: Ullstein, 1999).

Ian Buruma, *The Wages of Guilt: Memories of War in Germany and Japan* (London: Vintage, 1995).

Marina Cattaruzza, 'The Historiography of the Shoah: An Attempt at a Bibliographical Synthesis', *Totalitarismus und Demokratie*, Vol. 3 (2006) pp. 285–321.

C.M. Clark, 'West Germany Confronts the Nazi Past: Some Recent Debates on the Early Post-war Era, 1945-1960', *European Legacy*, Vol. 4, No. 1 (1999) pp. 113–130.

Alon Confino, *Germany as a Culture of Remembrance: Promises and Limits of Writing History* (Chapel Hill, North Carolina: University of North Carolina Press, 2006).

Sebastian Conrad, 'Entangled Memories: Versions of the Past in Germany and Japan, 1945-2001', *Journal of Contemporary History*, Vol. 38, No. 1 (2003) pp. 85–99.

A. Dirk Moses, 'The Non-German German and the German German: Dilemmas of Identity after the Holocaust', *New German Critique*, Vol. 101 (2007) pp. 45–94.

H. Dubiel, *Niemand ist frei von der Geschichte: Die nationalsozialistische Herrschaft in den Debatten des Deutschen Bundestages* (Munich: Carl Hanser Verlag, 1999).

Geoff Eley (ed.), *The Goldhagen Effect. History, Memory, Nazism- Facing the German Past* (Ann Arbor, Michigan: University of Michigan Press, 2000).

Thomas C. Fox, *Stated Memory: East Germany and the Holocaust* (Rochester,

New York: Camden House, 1999).

Mary Fulbrook, *German National Identity after the Holocaust* (Cambridge: Polity Press, 1999).

Ralph Giordano, *Die Zweite Schuld oder von der Last ein Deutscher zu sein* (Hamburg: Rasch und Rohring, 1987).

Jeffrey Herf, *Divided Memory: The Nazi Past in the Two Germanys* (Cambridge, Massachusetts: Harvard University Press, 1997).

C. Hoffmann, *Stunden Null? Vergangenheitsbewaltigung in Deutschland, 1945 und 1989* (Bonn: Bouvier Verlag, 1992).

Konrad H. Jarausch, '1945 and the Continuities of German History: Reflections on Memory, Historiography and Politics', G. Giles (ed.), *Stunde Null: The End and the Beginning Fifty Years Ago* (Washington, District of Columbia: German Historical Institute, Occasional Paper No. 20, 1997) pp. 9–24.

Konrad H. Jarausch, 'The Failure of East German Antifascism: Some Ironies of History as Politics', *German Studies Review*, Vol. 14, No. 1 (1991) pp. 85–102.

Siobhan Kattago, *Ambigous Memory: The Nazi Past and German National Identity* (Westport, Connecticut: Praeger, 2001).

V. Knigge & N. Frei (eds.), *Verbrechen erinnern: Die Auseinandersetzung mit Holocaust und Völkermord* (Munich: Beck, 2002).

M. Lane Bruner, 'Strategies of Remembrance in Pre-Unification West Germany', *Quarterly Journal of Speech*, Vol. 86, No. 1 (2000) pp. 86–107.

Eric Langenbacher, 'The Mastered Past? Collective Memory Trends in Germany since Unification', *German Politics & Society*, Vol. 28, No. 1 (2010) pp. 42–68.

Hermann Lübbe, 'Der Nationalsozialismus im Deutschen Nachkriegsbewusstsein', *Historische Zeitschrift*, Vol. 236 (1983) pp. 585–587.

Alf Ludtke, '"Coming to Terms with the Past": Illusions of Remembering, Ways of Forgetting Nazism in West Germany', *Journal of Modern History*, Vol. 65 (1993) pp. 542–572.

Charles Maier, *The Unmasterable Past: Holocaust and German National Identity* (Cambridge, Massachusetts: Harvard University Press, 1988).

Judith Miller, *One by One by One: Facing the Holocaust* (New York: Simon & Schuster, 1990).

Robert Moeller, *War Stories: The Search for a Usable Past in the Federal Republic of Germany* (Berkeley, California: University of California Press, 2001).

Klaus Neumann, *Shifting Memories: The Nazi Past in the New Germany* (Ann Arbor, Michigan: University of Michigan Press, 2000).

Bill Niven, *Facing the Nazi Past: United Germany and the Legacy of the Third Reich* (New York; Routledge, 2002).

Jeffrey K. Olick & Daniel Levy, 'Collective Memory and Cultural Constraint: Holocaust Myth and Rationality in German Politics', *American Sociological Review*, Vol. 62, No. 6 (1997) pp. 921–936.

Kurt Pätzold, 'Persecution and the Holocaust: A Provisional Review of GDR Historiography', *Leo Baeck Institute Yearbook*, Vol. 40, No. 1 (1995) pp. 291–312.

Jeffrey M. Peck, 'East Germany', D.S. Wyman (ed.), *The World Reacts to the Holocaust* (Baltimore, Maryland and London: John Hopkins University Press, 1996) pp. 447–474.

David Robb, 'Playing with the 'Erbe': Songs of the 1848 Revolution in the GDR', *German Life & Letters*, Vol. 63, No. 3 (2010) pp. 295–310.

Robert Sackett, 'Memory by Way of Anne Frank: Enlightenment and Denial among West Germans circa 1960', *Holocaust and Genocide Studies*, Vol. 16, No. 2 (2002) pp. 243–265.
Robert A. Shandley (ed.), *Unwilling Germans? The Goldhagen Debate* (Minneapolis, Minnesota: University of Minnesota Press, 1998).
Alan E. Steinweiss, 'The Auschwitz Analogy: Holocaust Memory and American Debates over Intervention in Bosnia and Kosovo in the 1990s', *Holocaust and Genocide Studies*, Vol. 19, No. 2 (2005) pp. 276–289.
Dan Stone, 'Beyond the "Auschwitz Syndrome": Holocaust Historiography after the Cold War', *Patterns of Prejudice*, Vol. 44, No. 5 (2010) p. 454–468.

Regional studies

Celia Applegate, *A Nation of Provincials: The German Idea of Heimat* (Berkeley, California: University of California Press, 1990).
Alon Confino, *The Nation as a Local Metaphor: Wurttemberg, Imperial Germany and National Memory, 1871–1918* (Chapel Hill, North Carolina: University of North Carolina Press, 1997).
Alon Confino & Ajay Skaria, 'The Local Life of Nationhood', *National Identities*, Vol. 4, No. 1 (2002) pp. 7–24.
Neil Gregor, *Haunted City: Nuremberg and the Nazi Past* (New Haven, Connecticut: Yale University Press, 2008).
Neil Gregor, '"The Illusion of Remembrance": The Karl Diehl Affair and the Memory of National Socialism in Nuremberg, 1945-1999', *Journal of Modern History*, Vol. 75, No. 3 (2003) pp. 590–633..
Jason James, 'Retrieving a Redemptive Past: Protecting Heritage and Heimat in East German Cities', *German Politics & Society*, Vol. 27, No. 3 (2009) pp. 1–27.
Sven Keller, *Gunzburg und der Fall Josef Mengele: Die Heimatstadt und die Jagd nach dem NS-Verbrecher* (Munich: Oldenbourg, 2003).
Harold Marcuse, *Legacies of Dachau: The Uses and Abuses of a Concentration Camp, 1933–2001* (Cambridge: Cambridge University Press, 2001).
Peter Reichel, *Das Gedachtnis der Stadt: Hamburg im Umgang mit seiner nationalsozialistischen Vergangenheit* (Hamburg: Döllig & Galitz Verlag, 1997).
Gavriel D. Rosenfeld, *Munich and Memory: Architecture, Monuments and the Legacy of the Third Reich* (Berkeley, California: University of California Press, 2000).
Gavriel D. Rosenfeld & Paul B. Jaskot (eds.), *Beyond Berlin: Twelve German Cities Confront the Nazi Past* (Ann Arbor, Michigan: University of Michigan Press, 2007).

German victimhood

Dagmar Barnouw, *The War in the Empty Air: Victims, Perpetrators and Post-war Germans* (Bloomington, Indiana: Indiana University Press, 2003).
Frank Biess, '"Pioneers of a New Germany": Returning POWs from the Soviet Union and the Making of East German Citizens, 1945-1950', *Central European History*, Vol. 32, No. 2 (1999) pp. 143–180.
Frank Biess, 'Survivors of Totalitarianism: Returning POWs and the Reconstruction

of Masculine Citizenship in West Germany, 1945-1955', H. Schissler (ed.), *The Miracle Years: A Cultural History of West Germany, 1949–1968* (Princeton, New Jersey: Princeton University Press, 2001) pp. 57–82.

Elizabeth Corwin, 'The Dresden Bombing as Portrayed in German Accounts, East and West', *UCLA Historical Journal*, Vol. 8 (1987) pp. 71–96.

Neil Gregor, '"Is he still alive, or long since dead?": Loss, Absence and Remembrance in Nuremberg, 1945-1956', *German History*, Vol. 21, No. 2 (2003) pp. 183–203.

Atina Grossmann, 'Grams, Calories and Food: Languages of Victimization, Entitlement and Human Rights in Occupied Germany, 1945-1949', *Central European History*, Vol. 44 (2011) pp. 118–148.

Elizabeth Heinemann, 'The Hour of the Woman: Memories of Germany's Crisis Years and West German National Identity', *American Historical Review*, Vol. 101, No. 2 (1996) pp. 354–395.

Michael L. Hughes, '"Through No Fault of Our Own": West Germans Remember Their War Losses', *German History*, Vol. 18, No. 2 (2000) pp. 193–213.

Hans Kundnani, 'Perpetrators and Victim: Germany's 1968 Generation and Collective Memory', *German Life and Letters*, Vol. 64, No. 2 (2011) pp. 272–282.

Daniel Levy & Natan Sznaider, 'Memories of Universal Victimhood: The Case of Ethnic German Expellees', *German Politics & Society*, Vol. 23, No. 2 (2005) pp. 1–27.

Gilad Margalit, 'Dresden and Hamburg: Official Memory and Commemoration of the Victims of Allied Air Raids in the Two Germanies', H. Schmitz (ed.), *A Nation of Victims? Representations of German Wartime Suffering from 1945 to the Present* (Amsterdam: Rodopi, 2007) pp. 125–140.

Brenda Melendy, 'Expellees on Strike: Competing Victimization Discourses and the Dachau Refugee Camp Protest Movement, 1948-1949', *German Studies Review*, Vol. 28, No. 1 (2005) pp. 107–125.

Robert G. Moeller, 'Germans as Victims? Thoughts on a Post-Cold War History of World War II's Legacies', *History & Memory*, Vol. 17, No. 1–2 (2005) pp. 147–194.

Peter Monteath, 'Organizing Antifascism: The Obscure History of the VVN', *European History Quarterly*, Vol. 29, No. 2 (1999) pp. 289–303.

Peter Monteath, 'A Day to Remember: East Germany's Day of Remembrance for the Victims of Fascism', *German History*, Vol. 26, No. 2 (2008) pp. 195–218.

Klaus Neumann, 'When History Isn't Made but Happens: Memories of Victimhood in Halberstadt (Germany)', *Memory Studies*, Vol. 2, No. 2 (2009) pp. 171–194.

Bill Niven (ed.), *Germans as Victims* (Basingstoke: Palgrave Macmillan, 2006).

Alfred-Maurice De Zayas, *The German Expellees: Victims in War and Peace* (New York: St. Martin's Press, 1993).

Recalling victims of Nazi persecution after 1945

Omer Bartov, 'Defining Enemies, Making Victims: Germans, Jews and the Holocaust', *American Historical Review*, Vol. 103, No. 3 (1998) pp. 771–816.

C. Goschler, "The Attitude towards Jews in Bavaria after the Second World War", *Leo Baeck Yearbook*, Vol. 36 (1991) pp. 443–458.

C. Goschler, *Wiedergutmachung: Westdeutschland und die Verfolgten des*

Nationalsozialismus, 1945–1954 (Munich: Oldenbourg, 1992).
L. Herbst, *Wiedergutmachung in der Bundesrepublik Deutschland* (Munich: Oldenbourg, 1989).
Jeffrey Herf, 'East German Communists and the Jewish Question: The Case of Paul Merker', *Journal of Contemporary History*, Vol. 29, No. 4 (1994) pp. 627–661.
H.G. Hocketers, "Wiedergutmachung in Deutschland: Eine historische Bilanz, 1945-2000", *Vierteljahrshefte für Zeitgeschichte*, Vol. 49 (2001) pp. 167–214.
Erik N. Jensen, 'The Pink Triangle and Political Consequences: Gays, Lesbians and the Memory of Nazi Persecution', *Journal of the History of Sexuality*, Vol. 11, No. 1–2 (2002) pp. 319–349.
Regula Ludi, 'The Vectors of Postwar Victim Reparations: Relief, Redress and Memory Politics', *Journal of Contemporary History*, Vol. 41, No. 3 (2006) pp. 436–7.
Margarete Myers Feinstein, *Holocaust Survivors in Postwar Germany, 1945–1957* (Cambridge: Cambridge University Press, 2010).
Y. Michal Bodemann (ed.), *Jews, Germans, Memory: Reconstructions of Jewish Life in Germany* (Ann Arbor Michigan: University of Michigan Press, 1996).
Peter Monteath, 'Review Article: The German Democratic Republic and the Jews', *German History*, Vol. 22, No. 3 (2004) pp. 448–468.
A. Rabinbach & J. Zipes (eds.), *Germans and Jews since the Holocaust: The Ongoing Situation in West Germany* (New York: Holmes & Meier, 1986).
Susanna Schrafstetter, 'The Diplomacy of Widergutmachung: Memory, the Cold War and the Western European Victims of Nazism, 1956-1964', *Holocaust and Genocide Studies*, Vol. 17, No. 3 (2003) pp. 459–479.
Jacob Tovy, 'All Quiet on the Eastern Front: Israel and the Issue of Reparations from East Germany, 1951-1956', *Israel Studies*, Vol. 18, No. 1 (2013) pp. 77–100.
Julia von dem Knesebeck, *The Roma Struggle for Compensation in Post-War Germany* (Hatfield: University of Hertfordshire Press, 2011).
Andrew Woolford & Stefam Wolejszo, 'Collecting on Moral Debts: Reparations for the Holocaust and Pořajmos', *Law & Society Review*, Vol. 40, No. 4 (2006) pp. 871–901.

The *Historikerstreit*

Martin Broszat & Saul Friedländer, 'A Controversy about the Historicization of National Socialism', *New German Critique*, Vol. 44 (1988) pp. 85–126.
Jane Caplan, Norbert Frei, Michael Geyer, Mary Nolan & Nick Stargardt, 'Forum: The *Historikerstreit* Twenty Years On', *German History*, Vol. 24, No. 4 (2006) pp. 587–607.
Geoff Eley, 'Nazism, Politics and the Image of the Past: Thoughts on the West German Historikerstreit, 1986-1987', *Past and Present*, Vol. 121 (1988) pp. 171–208.
Richard S. Evans, *In Hitler's Shadow: West German Historians and the Attempt to Escape from the Nazi Past* (London: Pantheon, 1989).
Richard J. Evans, 'The New Nationalism and the Old History: Perspectives on the West German Historikerstreit', *Journal of Modern History*, Vol. 59 No. 4 (1987) pp. 761–797.
Geoffrey H. Hartman (ed.), *Bitburg in Moral and Political Perspective*

(Bloomington, Indiana: Indiana University Press, 1986).
James Knowlton & Truett Cates (eds.), *Forever in the Shadow of Hitler? Original Documents of the Historikerstreit, the Controversy Surrounding the Singularity of the Holocaust* (Atlantic Highlands, New Jersey: Humanities Press, 1993).

War criminals

S.S. Alderman, 'Negotiating the Nuremberg Trial Agreements, 1945', Raymond Dennett & Joseph E. Johnson (eds.), *Negotiating with the Russians* (Boston, Massachusetts: World Peace Foundation, 1951) pp. 49–100.
Shlomo Aronson, 'Preparations for the Nuremberg Trial: The OSS, Charles Dwork and the Holocaust', *Holocaust and Genocide Studies*, Vol. 12 (1998) pp. 257–281.
Jürgen Baumann, *Der Aufstand des schlechten Gewissens: ein Diskussionsbeitrag zur Verjährung der NS-Gewaltverbrechen* (Bielefeld: Gieseking, 1965).
Leora Bilsky, Donald Bloxham, Lawrence Douglas, Annette Weinke & Devin Pendas, 'Forum: The Eichmann Trial Fifty Years On', *German History*, Vol. 29, No. 2 (2011) pp. 265–282.
Donald Bloxham, 'British War Crimes Policy in Germany, 1945-1957: Implementation and Collapse', *Journal of British Studies*, Vol. 42, No. 1 (2003) pp. 91–118.
Donald Bloxham, 'From the International Military Tribunal to the Subsequent Nuremberg Proceedings: The American Confrontation with Nazi Criminality Revisited', *History*, Vol. 98, No. 332 (2013) pp. 567–591.
Donald Bloxham, *Genocide on Trial: War Crimes Trials and the Formation of Holocaust History and Memory* (Oxford: Oxford University Press, 2001).
Donald Bloxham, 'The Missing Camps of Aktion Reinhard: The Judicial Displacement of a Mass Murder', P. Gray & K. Oliver (eds.), *The Memory of Catastrophe* (Manchester: Manchester University Press, 2004) pp. 118–134.
M. Broszat, "Siegerjustiz oder Strafrechtliche 'Selbstreinigung': Aspekte der Vergangenheitsbewältigung der deutschen Justiz während der Besatzungszeit, 1945-1949", *Vierteljahreshefte für Zeitgeschichte*, Vol. 4 (1981) pp. 477–544.
Christoph Burchard, 'The Nuremberg Trial and its Impact on Germany', *Journal of International Criminal Justice*, Vol. 4 (2006) pp.800–829.
Akiba Cohen, T. Zemach-Marom, J. Wilke & B. Schenk (eds.), *The Holocaust and the Press: Nazi War Crimes Trials in Germany and Israel* (Cresskill, New Jersey: Hampton Press, 2000).
John Cramer, *Belsen Trial 1945: der Lüneburger Prozess gegen Wachpersonal der Konzentrationslager Auschwitz und Bergen-Belsen* (Göttingen: Wallstein Verlag, 2011).
Lawrence Douglas, "Film as Witness: Screening Nazi Concentration Camps before the Nuremberg Tribunal", *The Yale Law Journal*, Vol. 105, No. 2 (1995) pp. 449–481.
Lawrence Douglas, *The Memory of Judgement: Making Law and History in the Trials of the Holocaust* (New Haven, Connecticut: Yale University Press, 2001).
R. Fleiter, "Die Ludwigsburg Zentrale Stelle und ihr politisches und gesellschaftliches Umfeld", *Geschichte in Wissenschaft und Unterricht*, Vol. 53, No. 1 (2002) pp. 32–50.
John Fox, 'The Jewish Factor in British War Crimes Policy in 1942', *English*

Historical Review, Vol. 92, No. 362 (1977) pp. 82–106.

Norbert Frei, *Adenauer's Germany and the Nazi Past: The Politics of Amnesty and Integration*, translated by J. Golb (New York: Columbia University Press, 2002).

Jörg Friedrich, *Die kalte Amnestie. NS-Täter in der Bundesrepublik* (Frankfurt am Main: Fischer Taschenbuch, 1984).

Fritz Bauer Institut (ed.), 'Auschwitz: Geschichte, Rezeption und Wirkung', *Jahrbuch zur Geschichte und Wirkung des Holocaust* (Frankfurt am Main: Campus, 1996).

Fritz Bauer Institut (ed.), '"Gerichtstag haben über uns selbst…" Geschichte und Wirkungsgeschichte des ersten Frankfurter Auschwitz-Prozesses', *Jahrbuch zur Geschichte und Wirkung des Holocaust* (Frankfurt am Main: Campus, 2001).

George Ginsburgs, *Moscow's Road to Nuremberg: The Soviet Background to the Trial* (The Hague: Martinus Nijhoff, 1996).

George Ginsburgs, *The Nuremberg Trial and International Law* (Dordrecht: Nijhoff Publishers, 1990).

Helge Grabitz, 'Problems of Nazi Trials in the Federal Republic of Germany', *Holocaust and Genocide Studies*, Vol. 3, No. 2 (1988) pp. 209–222.

Joshua M. Greene, *Justice at Dachau: The Trials of an American Prosecutor* (New York: Broadway, 2003).

Erich Haberer, 'History and Justice: Paradigms of the Prosecution of Nazi Crimes', *Holocaust and Genocide Studies*, Vol. 19, No. 3 (2005) pp. 487–519, 493.

Marouf Arif Hasian, *Rhetorical Vectors of Memory in National and International Holocaust Trials* (East Lansing, Michigan: Michigan State University Press, 2006).

Patricia Heberer & Jürgen Matthäus, *Atrocities on Trial: Historical Perspectives on the Politics of Prosecuting War Crimes* (Lincoln, Nebraska: University of Nebraska Press, 2008).

Tomasz Jardim, *The Mauthausen Trial: American Military Justice in Germany* (Cambridge, Massachusetts: Harvard University Press, 2012).

Arieh J. Kochavi, 'The British Foreign Office versus the United Nations War Crimes Commission during the Second World War', *Holocaust and Genocide Studies*, Vol. 8, No. 1 (1994) pp. 28–49.

Wendy Lower, 'Male and Female Holocaust Perpetrators and the East German Approach to Justice, 1949-1963', *Holocaust and Genocide Studies*, Vol. 24, No. 1 (2010) pp. 56–84.

Michael Marrus, 'The Holocaust at Nuremberg', *Yad Vashem Studies*, Vol. 26 (1998) pp. 5–41.

Christian Meyer-Seltz, 'NS-Prozesse in der SBZ', *Tribüne*, Vol. 39, No. 155 (2000) pp. 132–137.

Dick de Mildt, *In the Name of the People: Perpetrators of Genocide in the Reflection of their Post-war Prosecution in West Germany. The 'Euthanasia' and 'Aktion Reinhard' Trial Cases* (The Hague: Martinus Nijhoff, 1996).

Christina Morina, 'Instructed Silence, Constructed Memory: The SED and the Return of German Prisoners of War as "War Criminals" from the Soviet Union to East Germany, 1950-1956', *Contemporary European History*, Vol. 13, No. 3 (2004) pp. 323–343.

Fern Overbey-Hilton, *The Dachau Defendants: Life Stories from Testimony and Documents of the War Crimes Prosecutions* (Jefferson, North Carolina: McFarland, 2004).

Devin O. Pendas, 'Retroactive Law and Proactive Justice: Debating Crimes against Humanity in Germany, 1945-1950', *Central European History*, Vol. 43, No. 1 (2010) pp. 428–463.

Devin O. Pendas, *The Frankfurt Auschwitz Trial, 1963-1965: Genocide, History and the Limits of the Law* (Cambridge: Cambridge University Press, 2006).

Kim Christian Priemal, 'Consigning Justice to History: Transitional Trials after the Second World War', *Historical Journal*, Vol. 56, No. 2 (2013) pp. 553–581.

Alexandra Przyrembel, 'Transfixed by an Image: Ilse Koch, the "Kommandeuse of Buchenwald"', *German History*, Vol. 19, No. 3 (2001) pp. 369–399.

A.P.V. Rogers, 'War Crimes Trials under the Royal Warrant: British Practice 1945-1949', *International and Comparative Law Quarterly*, Vol. 39, No. 4 (1990) pp. 780–800.

Adalbert Rückerl, *The Investigation of Nazi Crimes, 1945-1978: A Documentation*, translated by D. Rutter (Karlsruhe: C.F. Müller, 1979).

Kurt Schrimm & Joachim Riedel, '50 Jahre Zentrale Stelle in Ludwigsburg', *Vierteljahrshefte für Zeitgeschichte*, Vol. 56, No. 4 (2008) pp. 525–555.

Alaric Searle, 'The Tolsdorff Trials in Traunstein: Public and Judicial Attitudes to the *Wehrmacht* in the Federal Republic, 1954-60', *German History*, Vol. 23, No. 1 (2005) pp. 50–78.

Alaric Searle, *Wehrmacht Generals, West German Society and the Rearmament Debate, 1949–1959* (Westport, Connecticut: Praeger, 2003).

Caroline Sharples, *West Germans and the Nazi Legacy* (New York: Routledge, 2012).

Bradley F. Smith, *The Road to Nuremberg* (London: Deutsch, 1981).

Mark E. Spicka, 'The Devil's Chemists on Trial: The American Prosecution of IG Farben at Nuremberg', *Historian*, Vol. 61, No. 4 (1999) pp. 865–882.

P. Steinbach, 'Zur Auseinandersetzung mit nationalsozialistischen Gewaltverbrechen in der Bundesrepublik Deutschland', *Geschichte in Wissenschaft und Unterricht*, Vol. 35, No. 2 (1984) pp. 65–85.

Nathan Stoltzfus & Henry Friedlander (eds.), *Nazi Crimes and the Law* (Cambridge: Cambridge University Press, 2009).

Susan Twist, 'Evidence of Atrocities or Atrocious Use of Evidence: The Controversial Use of Atrocity Film at Nuremberg', *Liverpool Law Review*, Vol. 26, No. 3 (2005) pp. 267–302.

Katharina von Kellenbach, 'God's Love and Women's Love: Prison Chaplains Counsel the Wives of Nazi Perpetrators', *Journal of Feminist Studies in Religion*, Vol. 20, No. 2 (2004) pp. 7–24.

M. von Miquel, *Ahnden oder Amnestieren? Westdeutsche Justiz und Vergangenheitspolitik in den sechziger Jahre* (Göttingen: Wallstein Verlag, 2004).

Paul Weindling, 'From International to Zonal Trials: The Origins of the Nuremberg Medical Trial', *Holocaust and Genocide Studies*, Vol. 14, No. 3 (2000) pp. 367–289.

Ulrike Weckel & Edgar Wolfrum (eds.), *'Bestien' und 'Befehlsempfänger': Frauen und Männer in NS-Prozessen nach 1945* (Göttingen: Vandenhoeck & Ruprecht, 2003).

Annette Weinke, *Die Verfolgung von NS-Tätern im geteilten Deutschland: Vergangenheitsbewältigungen, 1949–1969, oder Eine deutsch-deutsche Beziehungsgeschichte im Kalten Krieg* (Munich: Ferdinand Schöningh Verlag 2002).

Rebecca Wittmann, *Beyond Justice? The Auschwitz Trial* (Cambridge, Massachusetts: Harvard University Press, 2005).

Jürgen Wilke, Birgit Schenk, Akiba A. Cohen & Tamar Zemach, *Holocaust und NS-Prozesse* (Cologne: Bohlau Verlag, 1995).

Robert Wolfe, 'Flaws in the Nuremberg Legacy: An Impediment to International War Crimes Tribunals' Prosecution of Crimes against Humanity', *Holocaust and Genocide Studies*, Vol. 12, No. 3 (1998) pp. 434–453.

Mark A. Wolfgram, 'Didactic War Crimes Trials and External Legal Culture: The Cases of the Nuremberg, Frankfurt Auschwitz and Majdanek Trials in West Germany', *Global Change, Peace & Security*, Vol. 26, No. 3 (2014) pp. 281–297.

Denazification and re-education

Michael Balfour & John Mair, *Four Power Control in Germany and Austria, 1945–1946* (Oxford: Oxford University Press, 1956).

Heinrich Best & Axel Salheiser, 'Shadows of the Past: National Socialist Backgrounds of the GDR's Functional Elites', *German Studies Review*, Vol. 29, No. 3 (2006) pp. 589–602.

Perry Biddiscombe, *The Denazification of Germany: A History, 1945–1950* (Stroud: Tempus, 2007).

Donald Bloxham, 'The Genocidal Past in Western Germany and the Experience of Occupation, 1945-6', *European History Quarterly*, Vol. 34, No. 3 (2004) pp. 305–335.

Susan L. Carruthers, 'Compulsory Viewing: Concentration Camp Film and German Re-education', *Millennium: Journal of International Studies*, Vol. 30 (2001) pp. 733–755.

Constantine Fitzgibbon, *Denazification* (New York: W.W. Norton, 1969).

Wolfgang Friedmann, *The Allied Military Government of Germany* (London: Stevens & Sons, 1947).

John Gimbel, *The American Occupation of Germany: Politics and the Military, 1945–1949* (Stanford, California: Stanford University Press, 1968).

Robert Knight, 'Denazification and Reintegration in the Austrian Province of Carinthia', *Journal of Modern History*, Vol. 79, No. 3 (2007) pp. 572–573.

Barbara Marshall, 'German Attitudes to British Military Government, 1945-7', *Journal of Contemporary History*, Vol. 15, No. 4 (1980) pp. 655–684.

Norman Naimark, *The Russians in Germany: A History of the Soviet Zone of Occupation, 1945–1949* (Cambridge, Massachusetts: Harvard University Press, 1995).

Lutz Niethammer, *Entnazifizierung in Bayern: Säuberung und Rehabilitierung unter amerikanischer Besatzung* (Frankfurt: Fischer Verlag, 1972).

James Tent, *Mission on the Rhine: Re-education and Denazification in American Occupied Germany* (Chicago, Illinois: University of Chicago Press, 1982).

Ian Turner (ed.), *Reconstruction in Post-war Germany: British Occupation Policy and the Western Zones, 1945–1955* (Oxford: Oxford University Press, 1989).

Timothy Vogt, *Denazification in Soviet-Occupied Germany: Brandenburg, 1945–1948* (Cambridge, Massachusetts: Harvard University Press, 2000).

German churches and the Holocaust

Shelley Baranowski, 'Consent and Dissent: The Confessing Church and Conservative Opposition to National Socialism', *Journal of Modern History*, Vol. 59, No. 1 (1987) pp. 53–78.

Victoria Barnett, *For the Soul of the People: Protestant Protest against Hitler* (Oxford: Oxford University Press, 1998).

Doris L. Bergen, 'Catholics, Protestants and Christian Antisemitism in Nazi Germany', *Central European History*, Vol. 27, No. 3 (1994) pp. 329–348.

Doris L. Bergen, '"Germany is our Mission - Christ is our Strength": The Wehrmacht Chaplaincy and the "German Christian" Movement', *Church History: Studies in Christianity and Culture*, Vol. 66, No. 3 (1997) pp. 522–536.

Doris L. Bergen, *Twisted Cross: The German Christian Movement in the Third Reich* (Chapel Hill, North Carolina: University of North Carolina Press, 1996).

Randolph L. Braham, 'Remembering and Forgetting: the Vatican, the German Catholic Hierarchy and the Holocaust', *Holocaust and Genocide Studies*, Vol. 13, No. 2 (1999) pp. 222–251.

Susan Brown-Fleming, '"The Worst Enemies of a Better Germany": Post-war Antisemitism among Catholic Clergy and US Occupation Forces', *Holocaust and Genocide Studies*, Vol. 18, No. 3 (2004) pp. 379–401.

Rainer Bucher & Rebecca Pohl, *Hitler's Theology: A Study in Political Religion* (London: Continuum, 2011).

Frank M. Buscher & Michael Phayer, 'German Catholic Bishops and the Holocaust, 1940-1952', *German Studies Review*, Vol. 11, No. 3 (1988) pp. 463–485.

John S. Conway, 'How Shall the Nations Repent? The Stuttgart Declaration of Guilt, October, 1945', *Journal of Ecclesiastical History*, Vol. 38, No. 4 (1987) pp. 596–622.

Robert P. Ericksen & Susannah Heschel, 'The German Churches and the Holocaust', D. Stone (ed.), *The Historiography of the Holocaust* (Basingstoke: Palgrave Macmillan, 2004) pp. 296–318.

Luke Fenwick, 'The Protestant Churches in Saxony-Anhalt in the Shadow of the German Christian Movement and National Socialism, 1945-1949', *Church History*, Vol. 82, No. 4 (2013) pp. 877–903.

Wolfgang Gerlach, *And the Witnesses were Silent: The Confessing Church and the Persecution of the Jews* (Lincoln, Nebraska: University of Nebraska Press, 1999).

Beth Griech-Polelle, 'Image of a Churchman-Resister: Bishop von Galen, the Euthanasia Project and the Sermons of Summer 1941', *Journal of Contemporary History*, Vol. 36, No. 1 (2001) pp. 41–57.

Richard Gutteridge, *Open Thy Mouth for the Dumb: The German Evangelical Church and the Jews, 1879–1950* (Oxford: Blackwell, 1976).

Franklin Hamlin Littell, 'From Barmen (1934) to Stuttgart (1945): The Path of the Confessing Church in Germany', *A Journal of Church and State*, Vol. 3, No. 1 (1961) pp. 41–52.

Hannah Holtschneider, *German Protestants Remember the Holocaust: Theology and the Construction of Collective Memory* (Münster: LIT, 2001).

Matthew Hockenos, *A Church Divided: German Protestants Confront the Nazi Past* (Bloomington, Indiana: Indiana University Press, 2004).

Heinz Kremers, 'The First German Church Faces the Challenge of the Holocaust: A Report', *Annals of the American Academy of Political and Social Science*, Vol. 450 (1980) pp. 190–201.

Angela Astoria Kurtz, 'God, not Caesar: Revisiting National Socialism as "Political Religion"', *History of European Ideas*, Vol. 35, No. 2 (2009) pp. 236–252.

Jerome S. Legge, 'Resisting a War Crimes Trial: The Malmédy Massacre, the German Churches and the US Army Counterintelligence Corps', *Holocaust and Genocide Studies*, Vol. 26, No. 2 (2012) pp. 229–260.

Michael Phayer, *The Catholic Church and the Holocaust, 1930–1965* (Bloomington, Indiana: Indiana University Press, 2001).

Michael Phayer, 'The German Catholic Church after the Holocaust', *Holocaust & Genocide Studies*, Vol. 10, No. 2 (1996) pp. 151–167.

Christopher J. Probst, *Demonizing the Jews: Luther and the Protestant Church in Nazi Germany* (Bloomington, Indiana: Indiana University Press, 2012).

Kevin Spicer, 'Father Wilhelm Senn and the Legacy of the Brown Priests', *Holocaust & Genocide Studies*, Vol. 22, No. 2 (2008) pp. 293–319.

Stanley Stowers, 'The Concepts of "Religion", "Political Religion" and the Study of Nazism', *Journal of Contemporary History*, Vol. 42, No. 1 (2007), pp. 9–24.

Ronald Webster, 'Opposing "Victors' Justice": German Protestant Churchmen and Convicted War Criminals in Western Europe after 1945', *Holocaust & Genocide Studies*, Vol. 15, No. 1 (2001) pp. 47–69.

Paul Weindling, '"For the Love of Christ": Strategies of International Catholic Relief and the Allied Occupation of Germany, 1945-1948', *Journal of Contemporary History*, Vol. 43, No. 3 (2008) pp. 477–492.

Cultural representations of the Holocaust

Theodor Adorno, *Can One live After Auschwitz: A Philosophical Reader*, edited by Rolf Tiedemann (Stanford, California: Stanford University Press, 2003).

Lawrence Baron, 'The Germans' Reaction to NBC's', *Holocaust*', *Sh'ma: A Journal of Jewish Ideas*, Vol. 9, No. 181 (1979) pp. 3–8.

Lawrence Baron, 'Holocaust and Genocide Cinema: Crossing Disciplinary, Genre, and Geographical Borders', *Shofar: An Interdisciplinary Journal of Jewish Studies*, Vol. 20, No. 4 (2010) pp. 1–9.

David Bathrick, 'Holocaust Film before the *Holocaust*: DEFA, Antifascism and the Camps', *Cinémas: Journal of Film Studies*, Vol. 18, No. 1 (2007) pp. 109–143.

John Bendix, 'Facing Hitler: German Responses to "Downfall"', *German Politics & Society*, Vol. 25, No. 1 (2007) pp. 70–89.

Eric Bentley, *The Storm over 'The Deputy'* (New York: Grove Press, 1964).

Jan Berg, *Hochhuth's 'Stellvertreter' und die 'Stellvertreter'-Debatte: Vergangenheitsbewältigung in Theater und Presse der sechziger Jahre* (Kronberg im Taunus: Scriptor, 1977).

Daniela Berghahn, 'Post-1990 Screen Memories: How East and West German Cinema Remembers the Third Reich and the Holocaust', *German Life & Letters*, Vol. 59, No. 2 (2006) pp. 294–308.

Ursula Bessen, *Trümmer und Träume: Nachkriegszeit und fünfziger Jahre auf Zelluloid. Deutsche Spielfilme als zeugnisse ihrer Zeit* (Bochum: Brockmeyer, 1989).

David Brenner, 'Working through the Holocaust Blockbuster: Schindler's List and Hitler's Willing Executioners, Globally and Locally', *The Germanic Review: Literature, Culture, Theory*, Vol. 75, No. 4 (2000) pp. 296–316.

Christoph Classen, *Bilder der Vergangenheit: Die Zeit des Nationalsozialismus im Fernsehen der Bundesrepublik Deutschland, 1955–1965* (Cologne: Böhlau Verlag, 1999).

Robert Cohen, 'The Political Aesthetics of Holocaust Literature: Peter Weiss's The Investigation and its Critics', *History & Memory*, Vol. 10, No. 2 (1998) pp. 43–67.

Tim Cole, *Images of the Holocaust: The Myth of the 'Shoah Business'* (London: Duckworth, 1999).

William C. Donahue, 'Pretty Boys and Nasty Girls: The Holocaust Figured in Two German Films of the 1990s', *New England Review*, Vol. 21, No. 4 (2000) pp. 108–124.

Judith E. Doneson, 'Holocaust Revisited: A Catalyst for Memory or Trivialization?', *Annals of the American Academy of Political and Social Science*, Vol. 548 (1996) pp. 70–77.

Thomas Elsaesser, 'Absence as Presence, Presence as Parapraxis: On Some Problems of Representing "Jews" in the New German Cinema', *Framework: The Journal of Cinema & Media*, Vol. 49, No. 1 (2008) pp. 106–120.

Saul Friedländer (ed.), *Probing the Limits of Representation: Nazism and the 'Final Solution'* (Cambridge, Massachusetts: Harvard University Press, 1992).

Christine Haase, 'Theodor Kotulla's Excerpts from a German Life (Aus einem deutschen Leben, 1977): or The Inability to Speak: Cinematic Holocaust Representation in Germany', *Film & History: An Interdisciplinary Journal of Film & Television Studies*, Vol. 32, No. 2 (2002) pp. 48–61.

Christine Haase, 'Ready for his Close-up? Representing Hitler in Der Untergang (Downfall, 1994)', *Studies in European Cinema*, Vol. 3, No. 3 (2007) pp. 189–199.

Francesa Haig, 'Holocaust Representations since 1975', *Modernism/Modernity*, Vol. 20, No. 1 (2013) pp. 1–13.

Jeffrey Herf, 'The "Holocaust" Reception in West Germany: Right, Center and Left', *New German Critique*, Vol. 19, No. 1 (1980) pp. 30–52.

Klaus Hofmann, 'Poetry after Auschwitz - Adorno's Dictum', *German Life and Letters*, Vol. 58, No. 2 (2005) pp. 182–194.

Andreas Huyssen, 'The Politics of Identification: "Holocaust" and West German Drama', *New German Critique*, Vol. 19, No. 1 (1980) pp. 117–136.

Wolf Kansteiner, 'Entertaining Catastrophe: The Reinvention of the Holocaust in the Television of the Federal Republic of Germany', *New German Critique*, Vol. 90 (2003) pp. 135–162.

Wolf Kansteiner, 'Nazis, Viewers and Statistics: Television History, Television Audience Research and Collective Memory in West Germany', *Journal of Contemporary History*, Vol. 30, No. 4 (2004) pp. 575–598.

Lutz Koepnick, 'Reframing the Past: Heritage Cinema and Holocaust in the 1990s', *New German Critique*, Vol. 87 (2002) pp. 47–82.

Dominick LaCapra, *Representing the Holocaust: History, Theory, Trauma* (Ithaca, New York: Cornell University Press, 1994).

Berel Lang, *Holocaust Representation: Art within the Limits of History and Ethics* (Baltimore, Maryland: John Hopkins University Press, 2000).

Andrei S. Markovits, '"Holocaust" Before and After the Event: Reactions in West Germany and Austria', *New German* Critique, Vol. 19, No. 1 (1980) pp. 53–80.

Inge Marszolek, '"Join In, Go Ahead and Don't Remain Silent": The National Socialist Past and Reconstruction in Post-war German Broadcasting', *New German Critique*, Vol. 95 (2005) pp. 122–138.

Bill Niven, 'The Reception of Steven Spielberg's Schindler's List in the German Media', *Journal of European Studies*, Vol. 25 (1995) pp. 165–189.

Michael Patterson, '"Bewältigung der Vergangenheit" or "Überwältigung der Befangenheit": Nazism and the War in Post-war German Theatre', *Modern Drama*, Vol. 33, No. 1 (1990) pp. 120–128.

Anke Pinkert, *Film and Memory in East Germany* (Bloomington, Indiana: Indiana University Press, 2008).

Moishe Postone, 'Antisemitism and National Socialism: Notes on the German Reaction to "Holocaust"', *New German Critique*, Vol. 19, No. 1 (1980) pp. 97–115.

Robert C. Reimer and Carol J. Reimer, *Nazi-retro Film: How German Narrative Cinema Remembers the Past* (New York: Maxwell Macmillan, 1992).

Lars Rensmann, 'Holocaust Memory and Mass Media in Contemporary Germany: Reflections on the Goldhagen Debate', *Patterns of Prejudice*, Vol. 33, No. 1 (1999) pp. 59–76.

Robert Sackett, 'Pictures of Atrocity: Public Discussions of *Der gelbe Stern* in Early 1960s West Germany', *German History*, Vol. 24, No. 1 (2006) pp. 526–561.

Jeffrey Shandler, *While America Watches: Televising the Holocaust* (Oxford: Oxford University Press, 1999).

Werner Sollers, '*Holocaust* on West German Television: The (In)Ability to Mourn?', *The Massachusetts Review*, Vol. 20, No. 2 (1979) pp. 377–386.

Ursual von Keitz, 'Between Dramatization and Epicization: The Portrayal of Nazi Crimes in Exemplary German Films from the Late 1940s to the 1970s', *New German Critique*, Vol. 102 (2007) pp. 45–60.

René Wolf, 'Mass Deception without Deceivers? The Holocaust on East and West German Radio in the 1960s', *Journal of Contemporary History*, Vol. 41, No. 4 (2006) pp. 741–755.

Mark A. Wolfgram, 'West German and Unified German Cinema's Difficult Encounter with the Holocaust', *Film & History: An Interdisciplinary Journal of Film & Television Studies*, Vol. 32, No. 2 (2002) pp. 24–37.

Mark A. Wolfgram, 'The Holocaust through the Prism of East German Television: Collective Memory and Audience Perceptions', *Holocaust & Genocide Studies*, Vol. 20, No. 1 (2006) pp. 57–79.

Siegfried Zielinksi, 'History as Entertainment and Provocation: The TV Series "Holocaust" in West Germany', *New German Critique*, Vol. 19, No. 1 (1980) pp. 81–96.

Representations of the Holocaust within public exhibitions

Esra Akcan, 'Apology and Triumph: Memory Transference, Erasure and a Rereading of the Berlin Jewish Museum', *New German Critique*, Vol. 37, No. 2 (2010) pp. 153–179.

Cornelia Brink, *'Auschwitz in der Paulskirche': Erinnerungspolitik in Fotoausstellungen der sechziger Jahre* (Marburg: Jonas Verlag, 2000).

Hannes Heer & Jane Caplan, 'The Difficulty of Ending a War: Reactions to the Exhibition "War of Extermination: Crimes of the Wehrmacht 1941 to 1944"', *History Workshop Journal*, Vol. 46 (1998) pp. 187–203.

Christine R. Nugent, 'The Voice of the Visitor: Popular Reactions to the Exhibition *Vernichtungskrieg: Verbrechen der Wehrmacht, 1941-1944*', *Journal of European Studies*, Vol. 44, No. 3 (2014) pp. 249–262.

Chloe Paver, 'Exhibiting the Nazi Past: An Overview of Recent German Exhibitions', *Journal of European Studies*, Vol. 29, No. 2 (2009) pp. 225–249.

Eve Rosenhaft, 'Facing up to the Past – Again? "Crimes of the Wehrmacht"', *Debatte*, Vol. 5, No. 1(1997) pp. 105–118.

James E. Young, 'Daniel Libeskind's Jewish Museum in Berlin: The Uncanny Arts of Memorial Architecture', *Jewish Social Studies*, Vol. 6, No. 2 (2000) pp. 1–23.

Holocaust education

Reinhold Boschki, Bettina Reichmann & Wilhelm Schwendemann, 'Education After and About Auschwitz in Germany: Towards a Theory of Remembrance in the European Context', *Prospects*, Vol. 40 (2010) pp. 133–152.

Zehavit Gross, 'Teaching about the Holocaust: Major Educational Predicaments, Proposals for Reform and Change - An International Perspective', *International Journal of Educational Reform*, Vol. 22, No. 2 (2013) pp. 137–151.

Stephan Marks, 'Teaching about National Socialism and the Holocaust: Narrative Approaches to Holocaust Education', *Interchange*, Vol. 38, No. 3 (2007) pp. 263–284.

Donald Mattheisen, 'History and Political Education in West Germany', *The History Teacher*, Vol. 1, No. 3 (1968) pp. 41–47.

Wolfgang Meseth & Matthias Proske, 'Mind the Gap: Holocaust Education in Germany between Pedagogical Intentions and Classroom Interactions', *Prospects*, Vol. 40 (2010) pp. 201–222.

Stephen A. Pagaard, 'German Schools and the Holocaust: A Focus on the Secondary School System of Nordrhein-Westfalen', *The History Teacher*, Vol. 28, No. 4 (1995) pp. 541–554.

Friedrich Schweitzer, '"Education after Auschwitz": Perspectives from Germany' *Religious Education*, Vol. 95, No. 4 (2000) pp. 359–372.

Bodo von Borries, 'Research on the Attitudes of Pupils and Teachers towards the Shoah in Germany', *Intercultural Education*, Vol. 14, No. 2 (2003) pp. 201–214.

Bodo von Borries, 'The Third Reich in German History Textbooks since 1945', *Journal of Contemporary History*, Vol. 31, No. 1 (2003) pp. 45–62.

Harald Welzer, 'Collateral Damage of History Education: National Socialism and the Holocaust in German Family Memory', *Social Research: An Intercultural Quarterly*, Vol. 75, No. 1 (2008) pp. 287–314.

Memorials, sites of memory and commemorations

Maoz Azaryahu, 'RePlacing Memory: The Reorientation of Buchenwald', *Cultural Geographies*, Vol. 10, No. 1 (2003) pp. 1–20.

Peter Carrier, *Holocaust Monuments and National Memory Cultures in France and Germany since 1989* (New York: Berghahn, 2005).

Irit Dekel, 'Ways of Looking: Observation and Transformation at the Holocaust Memorial, Berlin', *Memory Studies*, Vol. 2, No. 1 (2009) pp. 71–86.

Elisabeth Domanksy, '"Kristallnacht", the Holocaust and German Unity: The Meaning of November 9 as an Anniversary in Germany', *History & Memory*, Vol. 4, No. 1 (1992) pp. 60–94.

Jenny Edkins, 'Authenticity and Memory at Dachau', *Cultural Values*, Vol. 5, No. 4 (2001) pp. 405–420.

Insa Eschebach, 'Soil, Ashes, Commemoration: Processes of Sacralization at the Ravensbrück Former Concentration Camp', *History and Memory*, Vol. 23, No. 1 (2011) pp. 131–156.

Sarah Farmer, 'Symbols that Face Two Ways: Commemorating the Victims of Nazism and Stalinism at Buchenwald and Sachsenhausen', *Representations*, Vol. 49 (1995) pp. 97–119.

Caroline Gay, 'The Politics of Cultural Remembrance: The Holocaust Monument in Berlin', *International Journal of Cultural Policy*, Vol. 9, No. 2 (2003) pp. 153–166.

Mary Rachel Gould & Rachel E. Silverman, 'Stumbling upon History: Collective Memory and the Urban Landscape', *GeoJournal*, Vol. 78 (2013) pp. 791–801.

Elke Grenzer, 'The Topographies of Memory in Berlin: The Neue Wache and the Memorial for the Murdered Jews of Europe', *Canadian Journal of Urban Research*, Vol. 11, No. 1 (2002) pp. 93–110.

Kirsten Harjes, 'Stumbling Stones: Holocaust Memorials, National Identity and Democratic Inclusion in Berlin', *German Politics & Society*, Vol. 23, No. 1 (2005) pp. 138–151.

Janet Jacobs, 'Memorializing the Sacred: Kristallnacht in German National Memory', *Journal for the Scientific Study of Religion*, Vol. 47, No. 3 (2008) pp. 485–498.

Alexandra Kaiser, 'Performing the New German Past: The People's Day of Mourning and 27 January as Postunification Commemorations', *German Politics & Society*, Vol. 26, No. 4 (2008) pp. 28–49.

Noam Lupu, Memory Vanished, Absent and Confused: The Countermemorial Project in 1980s and 1990s Germany', *History & Memory*, Vol. 15, No. 2 (2003) pp. 130–164.

Harold Marcuse, 'Holocaust Memorials: The Emergence of a Genre', *American Historical Review*, Vol. 115, No. 1 (2010) pp. 53–89.

Michael Meng, 'East Germany's Jewish Question: The Return and Preservation of Jewish Sites in East Berlin and Potsdam, 1945-1989', *Central European History*, Vol. 38, No. 4 (2005) pp. 606–636.

Bill Niven & Chloe Paver (eds.), *Memorialization in Germany since 1945* (Basingstoke: Palgrave Macmillan, 2010).

Pierre Nora, 'Between History and Memory: Lieux de Mémoire', *Representations*, Vol. 26 (1989) pp. 7–24.

Robin Ostow, 'Reimaging Ravensbrück', *Journal of European Area Studies*, Vol. 9, No. 1 (2001) pp. 107–123.

Henry W. Pickford, 'Conflict and Commemoration: Two Berlin Memorials', *Modernism/Modernity*, Vol. 12, No. 1 (2005) pp. 133–173.

Karen E. Till, 'Staging the Past: Landscape Designs, Cultural Identity and

Erinnerungspolitik at Berlin's Neue Wache', *Cultural Geographies*, Vol. 6, No. 3 (1999) pp. 251–283.

James E. Young, 'Berlin's Holocaust Memorial: A Report to the Bundestag Committee on Media and Culture, 3 March 1999', *German Politics & Society*, Vol. 17, No. 3 (1999) pp. 54–70.

James E. Young, 'Germany's Holocaust Memorial Problem - and Mine', *The Public Historian*, Vol. 24, No. 4 (2002) pp. 65–80.

James E. Young, *The Texture of Memory: Holocaust Memorials and Meaning* (New Haven, Connecticut: Yale University Press, 1993).

Generational conflict

Rob Burns, *Protest and Democracy in West Germany: Extra-Parliamentary Opposition and the Democratic Agenda* (Basingstoke: Palgrave Macmillan, 1988).

Carole Fink, Philipp Gassert & Detlef Junker (eds.), *1968: The World Transformed* (Cambridge: Cambridge University Press, 1998).

Philipp Gassert & Alan E. Steinweiss (eds.), *Coping with the Nazi Past: West German Debates on Nazism and Generational Conflict, 1955–1975* (New York: Berghahn, 2007).

Detlev Siegfried, '"Don't Trust Anyone Older Than 30?" Voices of Conflict and Consensus between Generations in 1960s West Germany', *Journal of Contemporary History*, Vol. 40, No. 4 (2005) pp. 727–744.

Dorothee Wierling, 'Generations and Generational Conflicts in East and West Germany', C. Klessmann (ed.), *The Divided Past: Rewriting Postwar German History* (Oxford: Berg, 2001) pp. 69–89.

International perspectives on the Holocaust

David Art, *The Politics of the Nazi Past in Germany and Austria* (Cambridge: Cambridge University Press, 2005).

Lawrence Baron, 'The Holocaust and the American Public Memory, 1945-1960', *Holocaust and Genocide Studies*, Vol. 17, No. 1 (2003) pp. 62–88.

Günter Bischof, 'Victims? Perpetrators? "Punching Bags" of European Historical Memory? The Austrians and their World War II Legacies', *German Studies Review*, Vol. 27, No. 1 (2004) pp. 17–32.

Matti Bunzl, 'On the Politics and Semantics of Austrian Memory: Vienna's Monument against War and Fascism', *History and Memory*, Vol. 7, No. 2 (1995) pp. 7–40.

Hannah Caven, "Horror in our Time: Images of the Concentration Camps in the British Media, 1945", *Historical Journal of Film, Radio and Television*, Vol. 21, No. 3 (2001) pp. 205–253.

Robert S.C. Gordon, 'The Holocaust in Italian Collective Memory: *Il giorno della memoria*, 27 January 2001', *Modern Italy*, Vol. 11, No. 2 (2006) pp. 167–188.

Robert S.C. Gordon, 'Which Holocaust? Primo Levi and the Field of Holocaust Memory in Post-War Italy', *Italian Studies*, Vol. 61, No. 1 (2006) pp. 85–113.

Robert G. Knight 'Contours of Memory in Post-Nazi Austria', *Patterns of Prejudice*, Vol. 34, No. 4 (2000) pp. 5–11.

Tony Kushner, *The Holocaust and the Liberal Imagination: A Social and Cultural History* (Oxford: Blackwell, 1994).
Pieter Lagrou, 'Victims of Genocide and National Memory: Belgium, France and the Netherlands, 1945-1965', *Past and Present*, Vol. 154 (1997) pp. 181–222.
Andrea Mammone, 'A Daily Revision of the Past: Fascism, Anti-Fascism, and Memory in Contemporary Italy', *Modern Italy*, Vol. 11, No. 2 (2006) pp. 211–226.
Peter Novick, *The Holocaust in Collective Memory: The American Experience* (London: Bloomsbury, 2001).
Andy Pearce, *Holocaust Consciousness in Contemporary Britain* (London: Routledge, 2014).
Ljiljana Radonic, 'Croatia: Exhibiting Memory and History at the "Shores of Europe"', *Culture Unbound*, Vol. 3 (2011) pp. 355–367.
Joanne Reilly, *Belsen: The Liberation of a Concentration Camp* (London: Routledge, 1998).
Stefan Rohdewald, 'Post-Soviet Remembrance of the Holocaust and National Memories of the Second World War in Russia, Ukraine and Lithuania', *Forum for Modern Language Studies*, Vol. 44, No. 2 (2008) pp. 173–184.
Caroline Sharples & Olaf Jensen (eds.), *Britain and the Holocaust: Remembering and Representing War and Genocide* (Basingstoke: Palgrave Macmillan, 2013).
Heidemarie Uhl, 'Of Heroes and Victims: World War II in Austrian Memory', *Austrian History Yearbook*, Vol. 42 (2011) pp. 185–200.
Robert Ventresca, 'Mussolini's Ghost: Italy's Duce in History and Memory', *History and Memory*, Vol. 18, No. 1 (2006) pp. 86–119.
Hermann W. von der Dunk, 'The Netherlands and the Memory of the Second World War', *European Review*, Vol. 4 (1996) pp. 221–239.
Bella Zisere, 'The Memory of the Shoah in the Post-Soviet Latvia', *East European Jewish Affairs*, Vol. 35, No. 2 (2005) pp. 155–165.

INDEX